Microsoft Viva Engage

The Future of Workplace Communication

Kiet Huynh

Table of Contents

PART I
Introduction to Microsoft Viva Engage

1.1 What is Microsoft Viva Engage?

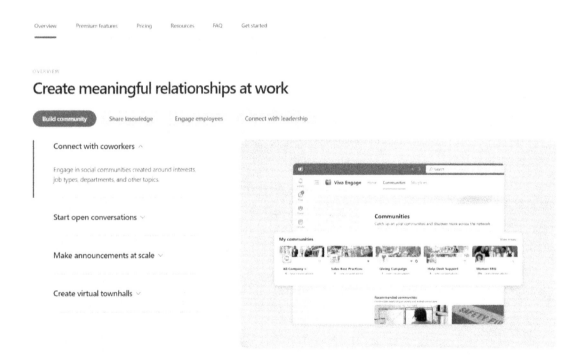

Introduction

In today's digital workplace, employee engagement and communication play a crucial role in fostering productivity, collaboration, and a positive work culture. As organizations embrace remote and hybrid work environments, the need for effective internal communication platforms has never been greater. Microsoft Viva Engage is a powerful tool designed to enhance workplace communication, collaboration, and knowledge-sharing across an organization.

Viva Engage is part of the Microsoft Viva suite, which integrates with Microsoft 365 to provide a seamless experience for employees to connect, communicate, and collaborate. Whether used by executives, team leads, or frontline workers, Viva Engage helps create a dynamic and inclusive digital workspace where employees can stay informed, participate in discussions, and share ideas in a social and engaging manner.

This section explores what Microsoft Viva Engage is, how it functions, and why it is an essential tool for modern businesses.

Understanding Microsoft Viva Engage

Microsoft Viva Engage is an enterprise social networking platform designed to facilitate employee engagement, knowledge sharing, and collaboration within organizations. It evolved from **Yammer**, which was Microsoft's long-standing workplace social networking tool. While Yammer focused on open communication within organizations, Viva Engage takes this experience a step further by integrating deeply with Microsoft 365 and the broader Viva ecosystem.

With Viva Engage, employees can:

- Share updates, ideas, and achievements

- Join discussions within communities and groups

- Collaborate with colleagues across different departments

- Access important company announcements and resources

- Engage in two-way communication with leadership

Unlike traditional messaging and email-based communication, Viva Engage provides an interactive platform where employees can participate in conversations, comment on posts, react with emojis, and use rich media like images, videos, and GIFs.

The Evolution from Yammer to Viva Engage

Microsoft has continuously refined its approach to enterprise communication. Originally launched in 2008, Yammer became one of the most popular enterprise social networks, allowing employees to connect and collaborate within a secure, private company network.

However, as Microsoft 365 evolved to include more integrated communication and collaboration tools like Microsoft Teams and SharePoint, Yammer needed a transformation to align better with the broader Microsoft ecosystem. Microsoft rebranded Yammer's core capabilities into **Viva Engage** in 2022, bringing a more modern and engaging user experience while maintaining the social networking capabilities that organizations had come to rely on.

Viva Engage now integrates directly into Microsoft Teams, making it easier for employees to engage without leaving their workflow. It also connects with other Viva modules, such as Viva Connections and Viva Insights, to provide a more holistic employee experience.

Key Components of Microsoft Viva Engage

Viva Engage is built around several core components that make it a powerful engagement and communication tool:

1. Communities and Groups

One of the primary features of Viva Engage is the ability to create and join **Communities** (previously called Groups in Yammer). These communities serve as collaborative spaces for employees who share common interests, projects, or job functions.

- **Public Communities:** Open to all employees, allowing anyone in the organization to join and participate in discussions.

- **Private Communities:** Restricted to selected members, ensuring confidentiality for sensitive discussions.

- **Company-wide Communities:** Created by administrators to broadcast company-wide messages and updates.

Communities help employees find information relevant to their work, share best practices, and build relationships across departments.

2. Conversations and Engagement Features

Viva Engage fosters interaction by providing tools for employees to:

- Post updates and announcements

- Share files, links, images, and videos

- React to posts using "like" and emoji reactions

- Comment and reply to discussions

- Mention colleagues using **@mentions**

- Use **hashtags** to categorize discussions

These features make workplace communication more dynamic and engaging, encouraging employees to participate in company-wide conversations.

3. Leadership Communication and Announcements

Viva Engage allows leadership teams to communicate directly with employees through structured announcements, live events, and Q&A sessions. Leaders can:

- Publish official announcements with high visibility

- Host **"Ask Me Anything" (AMA)** sessions to address employee concerns

- Use video updates to deliver key messages in an engaging format

This transparency fosters trust and improves overall employee morale.

4. Integration with Microsoft 365

Viva Engage seamlessly integrates with other Microsoft 365 apps, making it easy for employees to collaborate and access essential tools. Some key integrations include:

- **Microsoft Teams:** Employees can access Viva Engage conversations within Teams, eliminating the need to switch between apps.

- **SharePoint and OneDrive:** Users can share and access documents stored in SharePoint and OneDrive directly within Viva Engage.

- **Microsoft Outlook:** Employees receive notifications and updates about Viva Engage activities via email.

By integrating with Microsoft 365, Viva Engage becomes a part of employees' daily workflow, enhancing engagement without disrupting productivity.

5. Viva Engage Storylines and Stories

A relatively new feature, **Storylines** and **Stories** provide a way for employees to share updates in a more personal and engaging format, similar to social media platforms like LinkedIn or Instagram.

- **Storylines:** A personalized feed where employees can post updates, achievements, and insights.

- **Stories:** Short videos and images that appear in a carousel format, making updates more visual and interactive.

This feature encourages more informal sharing and helps employees connect beyond work-related topics.

Why Microsoft Viva Engage Matters

Microsoft Viva Engage addresses several critical challenges in today's workplace:

- **Improves Internal Communication:** It serves as a centralized platform for company updates, reducing reliance on long email threads.
- **Enhances Employee Engagement:** Employees feel more connected when they can share their thoughts, ask questions, and receive recognition.
- **Fosters a Sense of Community:** Virtual communities help employees network and collaborate across different locations and teams.
- **Encourages Knowledge Sharing:** Employees can document and share insights, ensuring valuable information is accessible to all.
- **Supports Remote and Hybrid Work:** With remote work becoming the norm, Viva Engage helps maintain a strong company culture even when employees are not physically in the office.

Conclusion

Microsoft Viva Engage is more than just a communication tool; it is a **strategic asset** for businesses looking to foster an engaged and connected workforce. Whether you're an executive looking to share updates, an HR professional seeking to improve internal communication, or an employee looking to collaborate with peers, Viva Engage offers a powerful and intuitive platform to enhance workplace interaction.

In the next section, we will explore the key features and benefits of Viva Engage in greater detail, helping you understand how to maximize its potential for your organization.

1.2 Key Features and Benefits

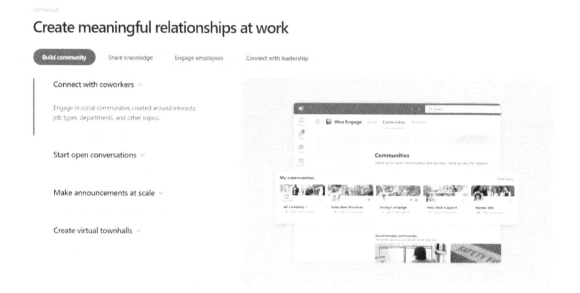

Introduction

In today's digital workplace, seamless communication and collaboration are essential for success. Microsoft Viva Engage, a part of the Microsoft Viva suite, is designed to enhance workplace communication, foster engagement, and strengthen team collaboration. Whether employees work in the office, remotely, or in a hybrid environment, Viva Engage provides a social networking experience tailored for businesses.

This section explores the key features and benefits of Microsoft Viva Engage, highlighting how it helps organizations create a connected, engaged, and productive workforce.

Key Features of Microsoft Viva Engage

Microsoft Viva Engage includes a variety of features designed to improve internal communication, encourage knowledge sharing, and build a strong company culture. Here are the core features:

1. Social Networking for the Workplace

Viva Engage provides an internal social networking experience similar to popular platforms like Facebook and LinkedIn. Employees can connect, share ideas, and engage in conversations through posts, comments, and reactions.

- **Newsfeed and Timeline** – Users can view the latest updates, announcements, and discussions happening within their organization.

- **Hashtags and Mentions** – Employees can use hashtags to categorize topics and @mentions to tag colleagues in posts, ensuring relevant discussions reach the right people.

- **Like, Comment, and Share** – Similar to social media, Viva Engage allows users to like, comment on, and share posts to keep discussions active.

2. Communities and Groups

Communities in Viva Engage enable employees to join or create groups based on departments, projects, interests, or company-wide initiatives.

- **Public and Private Communities** – Some communities are open for everyone, while others are private, allowing for secure discussions among specific teams.

- **Community Management Tools** – Admins can set roles, moderate discussions, and customize community settings to ensure smooth collaboration.

- **Pinned Posts and Announcements** – Important messages can be pinned to the top of the community feed to keep everyone informed.

3. Rich Media Support

Viva Engage supports various types of media content to make communication more engaging and effective.

- **Image and Video Uploads** – Users can share visual content to enhance storytelling and improve message clarity.

- **GIFs and Emojis** – To create a more expressive and engaging workplace culture, employees can use GIFs and emojis in their messages.

- **Live Events and Video Broadcasts** – Companies can host live Q&A sessions, training sessions, or leadership updates, making communication more interactive.

4. Integration with Microsoft 365

As part of the Microsoft ecosystem, Viva Engage seamlessly integrates with other Microsoft 365 applications.

- **Microsoft Teams Integration** – Users can access Viva Engage directly from Teams, enabling discussions without switching platforms.

- **SharePoint and OneDrive Connectivity** – Files and documents can be shared directly within Viva Engage, ensuring easy collaboration.

- **Outlook Integration** – Employees can receive Viva Engage notifications and updates within their Outlook inbox.

5. Employee Recognition and Engagement

Viva Engage includes features that promote a culture of appreciation and recognition.

- **Praise Feature** – Employees can recognize colleagues for their hard work by sending appreciation messages.

- **Surveys and Polls** – Organizations can collect feedback from employees on various topics, helping leaders make informed decisions.

- **Leadership Engagement** – Executives can use Viva Engage to communicate with employees directly, fostering transparency and alignment with company goals.

6. Mobile Accessibility

Viva Engage is available on desktop and mobile devices, allowing employees to stay connected on the go.

- **Mobile App** – Available for iOS and Android, ensuring accessibility anywhere.

- **Push Notifications** – Users receive instant updates on important messages and discussions.

7. Analytics and Insights

Viva Engage provides insights into engagement levels, helping companies measure the impact of their communication efforts.

- **Post Reach and Engagement Metrics** – Organizations can track the visibility and interaction rates of posts.

- **Community Growth Analytics** – Admins can monitor how communities grow over time and adjust strategies to enhance participation.

Key Benefits of Microsoft Viva Engage

Implementing Microsoft Viva Engage offers numerous benefits for organizations, particularly in improving communication, collaboration, and employee engagement.

1. Strengthens Workplace Communication

Effective communication is crucial for productivity and collaboration. Viva Engage ensures that important messages reach employees in an interactive and engaging way.

- Reduces reliance on long email threads by offering a more dynamic platform for discussions.

- Enables leadership to communicate directly with employees, enhancing transparency.

- Encourages open discussions, allowing employees to voice their ideas and concerns.

2. Fosters Employee Engagement and Connection

With remote and hybrid work environments becoming the norm, employee engagement is more important than ever. Viva Engage helps organizations build a connected workforce.

- Employees can interact with leadership through Q&A sessions and live events.

- Company culture is strengthened as employees share personal milestones and achievements.

- Teams feel more connected, leading to higher job satisfaction and retention.

3. Encourages Knowledge Sharing and Collaboration

Organizations benefit from employees sharing expertise and best practices. Viva Engage creates an environment where knowledge flows freely.

- Experts within the organization can share insights with employees, reducing the need for repetitive training.

- Employees can crowdsource solutions to challenges by engaging in discussions with colleagues.

- Teams working on projects can collaborate in dedicated groups, streamlining communication.

4. Enhances Productivity and Efficiency

By integrating with Microsoft 365, Viva Engage reduces the need for switching between applications.

- Employees spend less time searching for information as discussions and files are centralized.

- Collaboration is improved with real-time discussions and document sharing.

- Decisions are made faster as employees can quickly gather feedback from relevant stakeholders.

5. Supports a Culture of Recognition and Inclusion

A workplace that values its employees sees higher engagement and performance. Viva Engage promotes a positive work environment.

- Recognition tools help boost morale and motivation.

- Inclusive communication allows employees at all levels to participate in discussions.

- Diversity of thought is encouraged, as all employees can contribute ideas.

6. Provides Valuable Insights for Organizations

With built-in analytics, companies can measure engagement and refine their communication strategies.

- Leadership can identify what topics resonate most with employees.

- Data-driven decisions help optimize internal communication.

- Insights allow companies to track progress on cultural initiatives.

Conclusion

Microsoft Viva Engage is a powerful tool for modern workplaces, offering a range of features that enhance communication, engagement, and collaboration. By providing an interactive platform for employees to connect, share knowledge, and recognize each other's contributions, Viva Engage fosters a more connected and engaged workforce.

Organizations that adopt Viva Engage can expect improved teamwork, higher employee satisfaction, and a more transparent company culture. As businesses continue to navigate remote and hybrid work environments, tools like Viva Engage will play a critical role in shaping the future of workplace communication.

1.3 How Viva Engage Fits into Microsoft 365

Introduction

Microsoft Viva Engage is an integral part of the Microsoft 365 ecosystem, providing organizations with a social networking platform designed for internal communication, collaboration, and employee engagement. While many organizations already use Microsoft Teams, SharePoint, and Outlook for daily operations, Viva Engage adds a crucial layer by fostering open conversations, knowledge sharing, and community-building across departments.

In this section, we will explore how Microsoft Viva Engage integrates with Microsoft 365, how it complements other tools in the ecosystem, and how organizations can leverage it to create a connected and engaged workforce.

Understanding Microsoft Viva in the Microsoft 365 Ecosystem

Microsoft Viva is a broader employee experience platform within Microsoft 365 that includes several modules: Viva Connections, Viva Insights, Viva Learning, Viva Goals, and Viva Engage. Each of these modules plays a unique role in improving employee engagement and productivity. Viva Engage, in particular, focuses on **social communication, collaboration, and knowledge-sharing**.

Unlike Microsoft Teams, which is primarily designed for structured communication and collaboration within teams and departments, Viva Engage serves as an **organization-wide platform** where employees can interact more freely, participate in discussions, and access company-wide information in an informal yet professional setting.

Key aspects of Viva Engage within the Microsoft 365 environment include:

- **Seamless Integration with Microsoft Teams** – Viva Engage can be accessed directly within Teams, allowing employees to participate in discussions without leaving their workflow.

- **Connected to SharePoint and OneDrive** – Users can easily share and access files stored in SharePoint or OneDrive through Viva Engage posts.

- **Tied to Microsoft Entra ID (formerly Azure AD)** – Authentication and user management in Viva Engage are controlled through Entra ID, ensuring security and compliance.

- **Enhanced by Microsoft AI and Viva Insights** – AI-driven recommendations help personalize content and engagement, while Viva Insights provides analytics on participation and interactions.

Integration with Microsoft Teams

One of the most significant advantages of Viva Engage is its deep integration with **Microsoft Teams**, which is the hub for teamwork in Microsoft 365. This integration allows employees to stay connected with their communities and engage in company-wide discussions without switching between different applications.

Key Ways Viva Engage Works with Microsoft Teams

1. **Embedded Viva Engage App**

   - Organizations can add Viva Engage as an app inside Microsoft Teams, enabling users to access Viva Engage feeds, post updates, and interact with colleagues directly from the Teams interface.

   - This ensures that social interactions and company-wide discussions are easily accessible without disrupting workflow.

2. **Cross-Posting Between Teams and Viva Engage**

   o Users can share Teams messages directly into Viva Engage communities, ensuring that important discussions reach a broader audience.

   o This feature is especially useful for leadership communications, company-wide announcements, and knowledge-sharing.

3. **Viva Engage Notifications in Teams**

   o Viva Engage notifications appear in the Teams activity feed, making it easier for employees to stay updated on new posts, mentions, and conversations.

   o Employees can engage with these notifications without switching between different platforms.

4. **Live Events and Town Halls**

   o Organizations can host **live events and town halls** using Microsoft Teams and stream them to Viva Engage communities.

   o This feature enables leadership teams to engage with employees on a larger scale, fostering transparency and open communication.

Integration with SharePoint and OneDrive

Viva Engage is designed to **work seamlessly with SharePoint and OneDrive**, allowing users to **share and access files, documents, and multimedia content** without duplication or complex file transfers.

How Viva Engage Utilizes SharePoint and OneDrive

1. **Embedding Viva Engage in SharePoint**

   o Organizations can embed Viva Engage conversations directly within SharePoint pages, enabling employees to interact with discussions while browsing company news and updates.

   o This is particularly useful for creating **interactive intranet experiences** where employees can engage with content in real time.

2. **Sharing Files and Documents**

- o When users attach a file to a Viva Engage post, it is automatically stored in **SharePoint or OneDrive**, ensuring that all documents remain within the secure Microsoft 365 environment.

- o This integration helps avoid data silos and ensures that documents are easily searchable and accessible.

3. **Knowledge Management and Document Collaboration**

- o Employees can share knowledge, best practices, and company documents within Viva Engage communities.

- o Because these files are stored in SharePoint or OneDrive, they remain **version-controlled and accessible**, reducing redundancy and ensuring that employees always have the latest information.

Viva Engage and Microsoft Outlook

Viva Engage also integrates with **Microsoft Outlook**, allowing employees to interact with Viva Engage content directly from their email inbox.

Key Features of Viva Engage in Outlook

1. **Email Notifications and Digest Summaries**

- o Employees receive **email notifications** for new mentions, replies, and updates from their Viva Engage communities.

- o **Digest emails** summarize key discussions, ensuring employees stay informed even if they do not log into Viva Engage frequently.

2. **Replying to Conversations via Email**

- o Users can reply to Viva Engage posts directly from their email inbox, making it easier to engage without logging into the platform.

- o This feature is particularly useful for executives or employees who rely heavily on email communication.

3. **Embedding Viva Engage Conversations in Emails**

- o Organizations can embed Viva Engage discussions in internal newsletters or announcements, encouraging more employees to participate in important conversations.

Security, Compliance, and Governance in Microsoft 365

Since Viva Engage operates within **Microsoft 365**, it adheres to the **same security, compliance, and governance standards** that organizations expect from Microsoft products.

Key Security and Compliance Features

1. **Data Protection and Encryption**

   - o All data shared in Viva Engage is **encrypted in transit and at rest**, ensuring that company communications remain secure.

2. **Access Management with Microsoft Entra ID (Azure AD)**

   - o IT administrators can control user access and permissions using **Microsoft Entra ID**, ensuring that sensitive information is protected.

3. **Compliance with Industry Standards**

   - o Viva Engage meets compliance requirements for **GDPR, HIPAA, ISO 27001, and other industry regulations**, making it suitable for organizations with strict security needs.

4. **Content Moderation and Governance**

   - o Admins can **set up policies, monitor discussions, and enforce content guidelines** to ensure a safe and productive work environment.

Conclusion

Microsoft Viva Engage is a powerful tool that fits seamlessly into the Microsoft 365 ecosystem, providing organizations with a **centralized communication platform** that enhances collaboration, engagement, and knowledge-sharing. By integrating with **Microsoft Teams, SharePoint, OneDrive, Outlook, and Entra ID**, Viva Engage enables companies to **create a connected workplace** where employees feel heard, engaged, and empowered.

For organizations looking to **improve internal communication, boost employee engagement, and leverage the full potential of Microsoft 365**, Viva Engage is an essential component of the modern digital workplace.

1.4 Who Can Use Microsoft Viva Engage?

Microsoft Viva Engage is a powerful communication and collaboration tool designed to enhance workplace connectivity. It serves as a social networking platform for businesses, fostering engagement, knowledge sharing, and collaboration among employees. But who exactly can use Microsoft Viva Engage? The answer spans a wide range of individuals and organizations, from small businesses to large enterprises, as well as specific teams and departments within a company.

In this chapter, we will explore the various types of users who can benefit from Microsoft Viva Engage, including:

- Employees in different roles and departments

- Business leaders and managers

- Remote and hybrid workers

- HR and internal communications teams

- IT administrators and compliance officers

- Small and large organizations

By understanding how different users can leverage Viva Engage, businesses can maximize its potential to create a more connected and engaged workplace.

Employees in Different Roles and Departments

Enhancing Collaboration for Teams

One of the key benefits of Microsoft Viva Engage is its ability to connect teams across various functions. Employees from different departments can use the platform to collaborate on projects, share important updates, and communicate efficiently.

For instance, marketing teams can use Viva Engage to share campaign ideas, get feedback from colleagues, and collaborate with other departments such as sales or product development. Similarly, customer support teams can create groups to discuss common issues, share best practices, and provide quicker resolutions to customer problems.

Knowledge Sharing Across the Organization

Viva Engage provides a space where employees can ask questions and share insights, creating a culture of continuous learning. Instead of sending multiple emails or scheduling meetings, employees can post a question in a group, allowing colleagues from different time zones or departments to provide input at their convenience.

For example, a junior engineer might post a question about a technical issue, and a senior engineer from another location can provide a solution, benefiting not just the individual but also other employees who might face similar challenges in the future.

Breaking Down Organizational Silos

In large organizations, different departments often operate in silos, making it difficult to share information. Viva Engage breaks down these barriers by providing an open platform where employees can interact beyond their immediate teams. Whether it's finance, HR, sales, or operations, all employees can participate in discussions, stay informed about company-wide updates, and contribute to a more transparent workplace culture.

Business Leaders and Managers

Strengthening Leadership Communication

Business leaders and managers can use Microsoft Viva Engage to communicate directly with employees, share company vision, and provide updates in an engaging way. Unlike traditional emails, Viva Engage allows leaders to interact in real-time through discussions, announcements, and live events.

For example, a CEO might post a message outlining the company's goals for the upcoming quarter, and employees can comment, ask questions, and provide feedback. This two-way communication helps foster trust and transparency within the organization.

Recognizing Employee Achievements

One of the best ways to boost morale and motivation is through recognition. Managers can use Viva Engage to celebrate team successes, highlight employee achievements, and acknowledge outstanding contributions.

For instance, a manager might post about a team's successful project completion, tagging individual employees to give them public recognition. This kind of appreciation encourages engagement and reinforces a positive work culture.

Enhancing Decision-Making with Employee Input

Leaders can also use Viva Engage as a tool for gathering feedback from employees. Whether it's through polls, surveys, or open discussions, managers can gain insights from the workforce, helping them make more informed decisions.

For example, a company considering changes to its remote work policy could create a poll asking employees for their preferences. This not only ensures that employees feel heard but also helps leaders make decisions that align with the workforce's needs.

Remote and Hybrid Workers

Bridging the Gap Between Remote and In-Office Teams

With the rise of remote and hybrid work, many organizations face challenges in keeping employees connected. Viva Engage acts as a virtual watercooler, allowing remote employees to stay engaged with their colleagues, participate in discussions, and feel like a valued part of the company culture.

For example, a remote employee working in a different country can still participate in team discussions, celebrate company events, and engage with leadership updates, just like their in-office counterparts.

Supporting Asynchronous Communication

One of the biggest advantages of Viva Engage is that it allows employees to communicate asynchronously. Unlike real-time chat tools like Microsoft Teams, Viva Engage enables employees to post updates and reply to conversations at their convenience. This is especially beneficial for teams working across different time zones.

For instance, a project manager in the U.S. might post an update at the end of their workday, and team members in Europe or Asia can respond when they start their shifts, ensuring smooth communication without scheduling conflicts.

Encouraging Social Interaction and Well-Being

Remote workers often miss out on casual office conversations and social interactions. Viva Engage provides a way for employees to connect on a personal level by joining interest-based groups, participating in virtual events, and engaging in fun discussions.

For example, a company might have groups for hobbies like photography, fitness, or book clubs, where employees can interact beyond work-related topics, fostering a sense of community.

HR and Internal Communications Teams

Streamlining Internal Communications

HR and internal communications teams play a crucial role in employee engagement, and Viva Engage provides them with an effective platform to reach the entire organization.

For instance, HR teams can use Viva Engage to share company announcements, policy updates, and training resources. They can also create FAQ threads where employees can ask questions about benefits, leave policies, or professional development opportunities.

Onboarding and Training New Employees

Viva Engage is also a valuable tool for onboarding new hires. Instead of overwhelming them with emails and documents, HR teams can create onboarding groups where new employees can access important resources, ask questions, and connect with their peers.

For example, a new hire might join an "Employee Onboarding" group where they can find welcome messages, training schedules, and introductions to key team members.

Fostering Diversity, Equity, and Inclusion (DEI)

HR teams can also use Viva Engage to promote DEI initiatives by creating groups dedicated to employee resource networks, cultural celebrations, and inclusion efforts.

For instance, a company might have a "Women in Leadership" group where female employees can share experiences, mentor each other, and participate in leadership development discussions.

IT Administrators and Compliance Officers

Managing User Access and Security

IT administrators are responsible for ensuring that Viva Engage is used securely within the organization. They can manage user access, enforce security policies, and monitor activity to ensure compliance with company regulations.

For example, IT teams can set permissions on who can create groups, control external sharing, and ensure data security through Microsoft 365 compliance tools.

Ensuring Regulatory Compliance

For industries with strict compliance requirements, such as finance or healthcare, IT and compliance teams can use Viva Engage's governance features to ensure that all communication follows regulatory guidelines.

For instance, they can set up archiving rules, monitor sensitive content, and generate reports to meet compliance standards.

Conclusion

Microsoft Viva Engage is a versatile platform that benefits employees at all levels, from frontline workers to senior executives. Whether it's fostering collaboration, improving internal communication, or enhancing remote work engagement, Viva Engage helps organizations build a more connected, informed, and engaged workforce. By understanding who can use Viva Engage and how they can leverage its features, businesses can unlock the full potential of this powerful workplace communication tool.

PART II
Getting Started with Viva Engage

2.1 Accessing Viva Engage on the Web

2.1.1 Logging into Microsoft Viva Engage

Microsoft Viva Engage is a powerful communication and collaboration tool designed to help employees connect, share knowledge, and engage with their workplace community. Before users can fully utilize its features, they need to know how to access the platform and log in correctly. This section provides a step-by-step guide to logging into Microsoft Viva Engage on the web, troubleshooting login issues, and ensuring a secure and seamless experience.

1. Understanding Microsoft Viva Engage Access

Microsoft Viva Engage is part of the Microsoft 365 ecosystem, meaning users typically access it using their work or school accounts. Unlike standalone social networking platforms, Viva Engage is integrated with Microsoft services like Teams, SharePoint, and Outlook, ensuring seamless workplace collaboration.

To log in, users must have:

- A valid Microsoft 365 work or school account.

- A supported web browser such as Microsoft Edge, Google Chrome, Mozilla Firefox, or Safari.

- Internet access and the necessary permissions set by their organization's IT department.

If you are unsure whether you have access, check with your organization's IT administrator to confirm your account credentials and permissions.

2. Steps to Log into Microsoft Viva Engage

Step 1: Open Your Web Browser

To access Viva Engage, open a web browser on your computer or mobile device. Ensure your browser is updated to avoid compatibility issues.

Step 2: Navigate to the Microsoft Viva Engage Website

Type the following URL into the address bar and press **Enter**:

🔗 https://www.microsoft.com/en-gb/microsoft-viva/engage

Alternatively, you can access Viva Engage through the Microsoft 365 homepage:

1. Visit https://www.office.com.

2. Sign in with your Microsoft 365 credentials.

3. Click on the **Viva Engage** icon from the list of available Microsoft 365 apps.

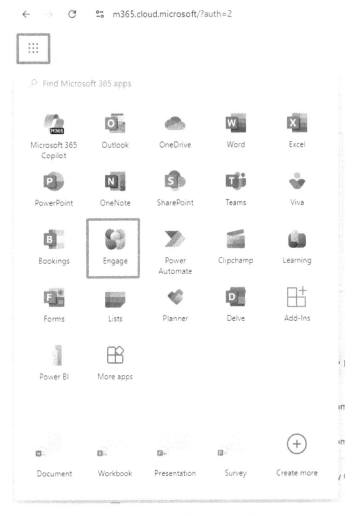

Step 3: Enter Your Microsoft 365 Credentials

Once on the Microsoft Viva Engage login page:

- Enter your **work or school email address** (e.g., yourname@company.com).

- Click **Next**.

- Enter your **password** and click **Sign in**.

📌 **Tip:** If you are using a shared or public computer, avoid selecting the **Keep me signed in** option for security reasons.

Step 4: Complete Multi-Factor Authentication (If Enabled)

Depending on your organization's security policies, you may need to complete a **multi-factor authentication (MFA)** process. This could involve:

- Entering a code sent to your mobile phone via SMS.

- Approving a notification on the **Microsoft Authenticator app**.

- Answering a security question.

Follow the instructions on the screen to complete the authentication process.

Step 5: Access Your Viva Engage Dashboard

Once logged in, you will be directed to the **Viva Engage homepage**, where you can view recent posts, notifications, and updates from your communities and colleagues.

3. Troubleshooting Login Issues

Forgotten Password or Username

If you cannot remember your password:

1. Click **"Forgot password?"** on the sign-in page.

2. Follow the instructions to reset your password via email or phone verification.

If you are unsure about your username, contact your IT department for assistance.

Account Locked or Disabled

Microsoft may temporarily lock your account due to multiple failed login attempts. If this happens:

- Wait for at least **15 minutes** before trying again.
- Reset your password if necessary.
- Contact your IT administrator to unlock your account.

Browser or Cache Issues

If you experience login issues, try these troubleshooting steps:

- **Clear your browser cache and cookies**:
  - In Chrome: **Settings > Privacy and security > Clear browsing data**.
  - In Edge: **Settings > Privacy, search, and services > Clear browsing data**.
- **Try a different browser** or switch to an incognito/private window.
- **Disable browser extensions** that might be interfering with the login page.
- **Check your internet connection** and ensure your network is stable.

Authentication Issues

If MFA is not working:

- Make sure your mobile device has a stable internet connection.
- Check if your Microsoft Authenticator app is up to date.
- If you changed your phone recently, reset your MFA settings through your Microsoft account.

Organizational Restrictions

Some organizations **restrict access to Viva Engage** outside of the company network. If you are unable to log in from home or a remote location, try:

- Connecting to your company's **VPN (Virtual Private Network)**.

- Checking with IT to see if external access is allowed.

4. Best Practices for a Secure Login

Use Strong Passwords

Your Microsoft 365 password should be:
✓ At least **12 characters** long.
✓ A mix of **uppercase and lowercase letters, numbers, and symbols**.
✓ Different from passwords used on other websites.

Enable Multi-Factor Authentication

Even if your organization does not require MFA, enabling it adds an extra layer of security to your account.

Avoid Logging in on Public Computers

If you must use a shared device:

- **Do not save your password** in the browser.

- **Use private browsing mode** (incognito).

- **Sign out completely** and clear browsing data when finished.

Regularly Update Your Credentials

Changing your password every **90 days** reduces the risk of unauthorized access.

5. Summary

Logging into **Microsoft Viva Engage** is a straightforward process, but ensuring a smooth and secure experience requires understanding best practices and troubleshooting common issues. By following the steps outlined in this section, users can confidently access Viva Engage and begin collaborating with their colleagues.

Key Takeaways:

✓ Use a **supported web browser** and ensure you have an **active Microsoft 365 account**.

✓ Follow the correct **login steps** and complete **multi-factor authentication** if required.

✓ If you experience login issues, check your **password, browser settings, and organizational policies**.

✓ Protect your account by using **strong passwords** and **enabling MFA**.

With successful login, users can now move on to **navigating the interface** and customizing their profiles, which will be covered in the next sections of this book.

2.1.2 Navigating the Interface

Microsoft Viva Engage offers an intuitive and user-friendly interface designed to facilitate workplace communication, collaboration, and engagement. Whether you're new to the platform or transitioning from another workplace communication tool, understanding the interface is essential to making the most out of Viva Engage.

This section will guide you through the main components of the Viva Engage web interface, providing a detailed breakdown of key navigation elements and their functionalities. By the end of this section, you will be able to confidently explore the platform, access different features, and customize your workspace for a seamless user experience.

1. The Home Page – Your Viva Engage Dashboard

When you log into Microsoft Viva Engage, you will land on the **Home Page**, which serves as the central hub for all interactions, updates, and activities. This page provides a quick overview of the latest discussions, announcements, and posts from your colleagues and groups.

Key Sections of the Home Page

1.1 Top Navigation Bar

At the top of the Viva Engage interface, you will find the **Top Navigation Bar**, which provides quick access to essential features and settings. It typically includes:

- **Home Button** – Returns you to the main feed at any time.

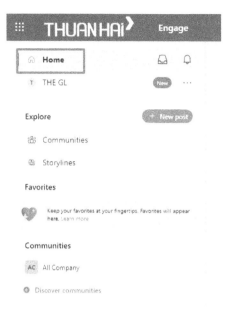

- **Search Bar** – Helps you find posts, people, and groups quickly.

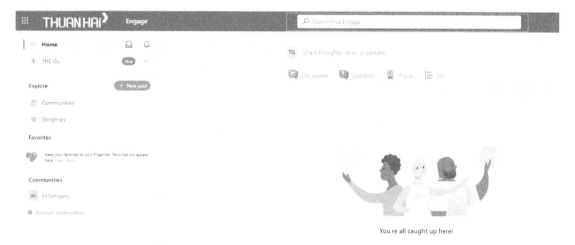

- **Create Post Button** – Allows you to share updates, post questions, or upload files.

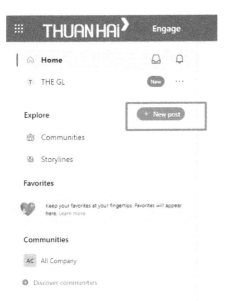

- **Notifications Icon** – Displays alerts for mentions, replies, and group activities.

- **Messages Icon** – Provides access to your private conversations.

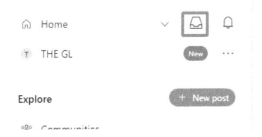

- **Profile Menu** – Enables you to access your account settings, profile, and sign-out options.

THUAN HAI   Sign out

View account
My Microsoft 365 profile

1.2 The Main Content Feed

The **Main Content Feed** (or Home Feed) is the central part of the Viva Engage interface, displaying posts from your groups, colleagues, and organizational updates.

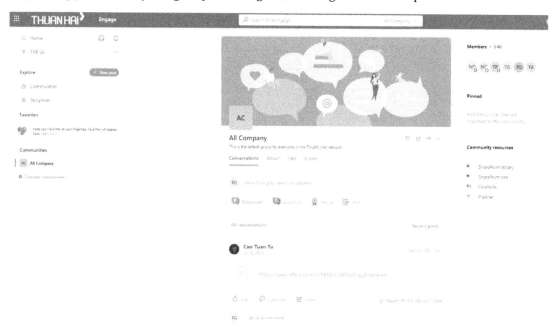

It typically consists of:

- **Trending Posts** – Highlights the most engaged-with discussions.

- **Recent Activity** – Displays new posts, replies, and announcements from your groups.

- **Pinned Posts** – Important or frequently accessed posts pinned by administrators.

- **Post Composer** – A text box where you can create and publish your posts.

1.3 Right-Side Panel – Quick Access Tools

The right-hand panel on the Home Page often includes:

- **Suggested Groups** – Recommendations for groups based on your interests.

- **Upcoming Events** – Notifications for upcoming meetings or company-wide announcements.

- **Popular Topics** – Trending hashtags and topics across the organization.

2. Exploring the Left-Side Navigation Panel

On the left-hand side of the interface, you'll find the **Navigation Panel**, which provides quick links to different sections of Viva Engage. This panel is crucial for accessing specific features and organizing your workflow efficiently.

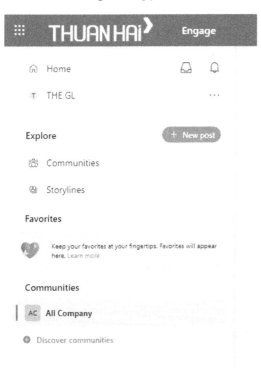

Key Sections of the Navigation Panel

- Home

This option returns you to the **Main Content Feed**, where you can view the latest discussions and updates from your network.

- Inbox (Messages & Notifications)

The **Inbox** contains:

- **Private Messages** – One-on-one and group chats.

- **Mentions & Replies** – Notifications when someone tags you in a conversation.

- **Followed Content** – Updates from posts and discussions you follow.

- Communities (Groups & Networks)

The **Communities Section** is where you manage and interact with different **groups** within Viva Engage.

- **Your Groups** – Displays the groups you are a part of.

- **Discover Groups** – Suggests new groups you might be interested in joining.

- **Create a New Group** – Allows you to form a new community.

- All Company (Organization-Wide Feed)

This section contains **announcements and company-wide updates**, often used by HR, leadership, or internal communications teams.

- Files & Documents

Microsoft Viva Engage integrates with **SharePoint and OneDrive**, allowing users to:

- Upload and share files.

- Access recently shared documents.

- Organize files within specific groups.

3. Understanding the Viva Engage Post Composer

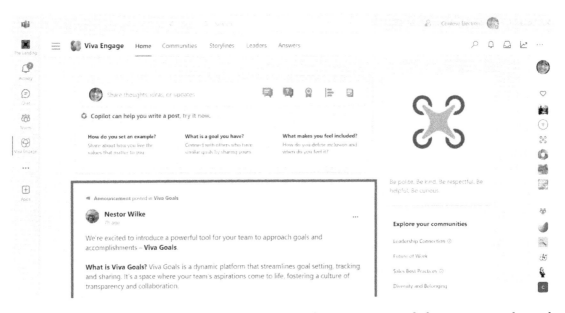

One of the core functions of Viva Engage is the ability to create and share content through posts. The **Post Composer**, located at the top of the Main Content Feed, allows users to engage with colleagues through different types of content.

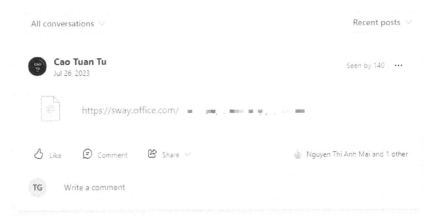

Components of the Post Composer

- Text Box

- Enter your message, announcement, or discussion topic.

- Use formatting options such as **bold, italics, bullet points, and links** to improve readability.

- **Attachments and Multimedia**

  - **Upload Files** – Attach documents, spreadsheets, or presentations.

  - **Add Images or GIFs** – Enhance engagement with visual content.

  - **Embed Videos** – Share recorded meetings or training materials.

- **Tagging and Hashtags**

  - **@Mentions** – Tag colleagues or groups to notify them.

  - **#Hashtags** – Categorize discussions for easy discovery.

- **Polls and Surveys**

  - Conduct quick polls to gather feedback from colleagues.

- **Post Visibility Options**

  - Choose whether to share your post with specific groups or company-wide.

4. Personalizing Your Viva Engage Experience

To enhance productivity and streamline your workflow, you can **customize your Viva Engage settings** to match your preferences.

Customizing Your Feed Preferences

- Prioritize posts from certain groups or people.

- Mute or unfollow irrelevant conversations.

Changing Language and Accessibility Settings

- Adjust Viva Engage's interface language.

- Enable screen reader support for better accessibility.

5. Quick Tips for Efficient Navigation

To maximize your efficiency while using Microsoft Viva Engage, keep these **quick tips** in mind:

1. **Use Keyboard Shortcuts** – Familiarize yourself with shortcuts for faster navigation.

2. **Bookmark Frequently Accessed Groups** – Pin important groups for easy access.

3. **Follow Important Conversations** – Use the "Follow" feature to stay updated.

4. **Use the Search Bar Effectively** – Filter results by posts, people, or documents.

5. **Experiment with Different Post Formats** – Mix text, images, and polls to engage your audience.

Conclusion

Mastering the Viva Engage interface is the first step toward fully utilizing the platform for workplace collaboration and engagement. By understanding the layout, key navigation elements, and available tools, you can communicate more efficiently, engage with colleagues effectively, and contribute to a more connected digital workplace.

2.1.3 Understanding the Dashboard

Introduction to the Microsoft Viva Engage Dashboard

Once you have successfully logged into **Microsoft Viva Engage** and familiarized yourself with basic navigation, the next crucial step is understanding its **dashboard**. The dashboard serves as the central hub for all your activities, including communication, collaboration, and engagement with colleagues. It is designed to be intuitive, making it easy for users to access different features and stay informed.

In this section, we will explore each component of the **Viva Engage dashboard**, detailing how to use its features effectively.

1. Overview of the Viva Engage Dashboard

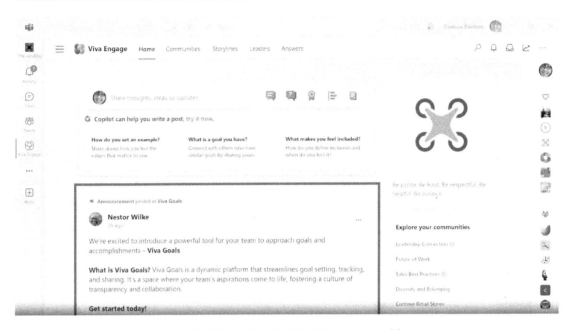

The **Microsoft Viva Engage dashboard** is divided into several key areas:

- **Top Navigation Bar** – Provides access to search, settings, and profile management.

- **Left Sidebar** – Contains shortcuts to key sections like Home, Communities, Inbox, and Notifications.

- **Main Content Area** – Displays your feed, discussions, announcements, and trending posts.

- **Right Sidebar (Optional)** – Features additional insights, recommendations, and trending topics.

Each of these sections plays a vital role in ensuring a smooth and engaging user experience. Let's break them down one by one.

2. Top Navigation Bar: Your Primary Controls

The **Top Navigation Bar** is always visible, no matter where you are in Viva Engage. It includes the following elements:

2.1 Search Bar

The **Search Bar** allows you to quickly find posts, groups, files, and people within your Viva Engage network. To use it effectively:

- Type a **keyword** or phrase related to what you're searching for.

- Use **filters** (such as posts, files, or people) to refine your search.

- Click on results to navigate directly to the relevant content.

💡 *Tip:* Use **hashtags (#)** in your posts so that others can find related discussions more easily.

2.2 Profile and Settings

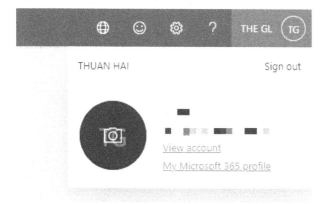

On the **top right corner**, you'll see your **profile picture**. Clicking on it allows you to:

- **Edit your profile** (change name, title, bio, etc.).

- **Manage account settings** (privacy, notifications, language preferences).

- **Sign out** from Viva Engage.

2.3 Notifications and Activity Alerts

Next to your profile icon, the **bell icon** 🔔 represents notifications. These include:

- Mentions (@yourname) in discussions.

- Replies to your comments.

- Important announcements from your organization.

Clicking the bell icon opens a dropdown list with **recent alerts**, allowing you to stay up to date.

3. Left Sidebar: Quick Access to Key Sections

The **Left Sidebar** is your navigation menu for moving between different sections of Viva Engage. Here's a breakdown of its key components:

Home (News Feed)

The **Home** button brings you to your personalized news feed, where you see:

- Posts from groups and people you follow.

- Trending topics and conversations.

- Recommended content based on your activity.

You can **interact with posts** by **liking, commenting, and sharing** to contribute to discussions.

3.2 Communities (Groups & Networks)

Clicking on **Communities** lets you:

- **Join or create groups** based on your interests or work teams.
- **Access private or public communities** depending on their privacy settings.
- **Discover new communities** suggested based on your role or interests.

💡 *Tip:* Use **pinned communities** to quickly access groups you frequently interact with.

3.3 Inbox (Messages & Conversations)

The **Inbox** in Viva Engage functions as your direct messaging hub. It allows you to:

- **Send and receive private messages** with colleagues.
- **View threaded conversations** for easy tracking.
- **Share attachments, images, and links** in messages.

Inbox is especially useful for quick, informal discussions that don't require an email.

3.4 Notifications

Similar to the **bell icon in the top bar**, this section provides an **expanded view** of all your recent notifications. Clicking on a notification takes you directly to the related conversation or post.

3.5 Files & Resources

This section gives you quick access to all files shared within Viva Engage, allowing you to:

- Search for **recently shared documents**.
- View **files organized by groups**.
- Open and edit **Microsoft 365 documents** without leaving Viva Engage.

4. Main Content Area: Your Personalized Feed

The **Main Content Area** is where most of the interaction happens. It is divided into the following sections:

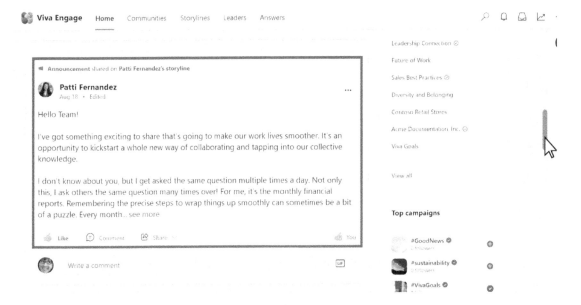

The News Feed

The **news feed** is similar to a social media timeline, displaying:

- **Recent posts** from groups you follow.

- **Company-wide announcements** from leadership.

- **Pinned and trending posts** that are important to your organization.

You can interact with posts by:

- **Liking** 👍 – To show appreciation.

- **Commenting** 💬 – To join the discussion.

- **Sharing** ⬜ – To repost content within your network.

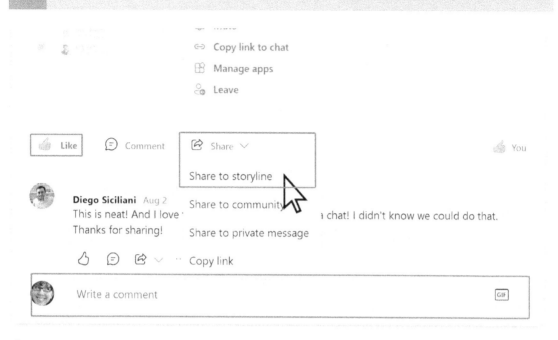

💡 *Tip:* To make your posts more engaging, include **images, videos, or polls**.

Trending Topics & Announcements

Viva Engage highlights **popular discussions** happening across the platform, helping you:

- Stay updated on **company news**.

- Engage in **industry-relevant conversations**.

- Find **useful knowledge-sharing posts** from colleagues.

5. Customizing Your Dashboard Experience

Viva Engage allows some **customization options** to make navigation more convenient:

Pinning Groups & Important Posts

- Click the **three-dot menu (...)** on a group or post.

- Select **"Pin to Top"** for quick access.

Adjusting Notification Preferences

- Go to **Settings → Notifications**.

- Choose which alerts you want to receive via **email or mobile notifications**.

Changing Layout & Theme (If Available)

- Some organizations allow switching to **dark mode or different layouts**.
- Check **Settings** → **Display Options** for customization.

Next Steps

Now that you are familiar with the **dashboard**, the next section will guide you on **setting up your profile**, ensuring you create a professional and engaging presence within Viva Engage.

2.2 Setting Up Your Profile

2.2.1 Updating Profile Information

Microsoft Viva Engage is designed to foster collaboration and communication within an organization. One of the key aspects of making the most out of Viva Engage is ensuring that your profile is complete and up to date. A well-structured profile enhances visibility, helps colleagues connect with you easily, and improves engagement within the platform.

In this section, we will walk you through updating your profile information in Viva Engage, covering each step in detail.

1. Why Updating Your Profile Information Matters

Before diving into the steps, let's explore why keeping your profile information up to date is important:

- **Improves Discoverability** – A complete profile makes it easier for colleagues to find you in Viva Engage, especially when searching by name, department, or expertise.

- **Enhances Professionalism** – Your profile serves as your digital identity within the organization. A well-maintained profile reflects professionalism and credibility.

- **Encourages Engagement** – People are more likely to connect and interact with you when they know who you are, your role, and your interests.

- **Facilitates Collaboration** – When colleagues can see your skills and background, they can reach out for advice, collaboration, or networking opportunities.

- **Aligns with Company Directories** – Many organizations integrate Viva Engage with Microsoft 365, meaning your profile information can be reflected in Outlook, Teams, and SharePoint.

Now that we understand its importance, let's proceed with updating your profile step by step.

2. Accessing Your Profile Settings

To update your profile information in Viva Engage, follow these steps:

Step 1: Log into Microsoft Viva Engage

1. Open your preferred web browser (Google Chrome, Microsoft Edge, Firefox, etc.).

2. Go to https://www.microsoft.com/en-gb/microsoft-viva/engage or access Viva Engage from the **Microsoft 365 App Launcher**.

3. Sign in with your work or school Microsoft account.

Step 2: Navigate to Your Profile

1. After logging in, click on your **profile picture or initials** in the top-right corner.

2. From the dropdown menu, select **"View Profile"** or **"Edit Profile"**.

3. You will be taken to your profile page, where you can see your basic details, contact information, and other sections.

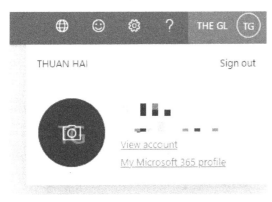

3. Updating Your Basic Information

3.1 Editing Your Name and Job Title

Your name and job title are essential for your colleagues to identify you correctly.

1. On the profile page, locate the **"Edit" button** near your name.

2. If allowed by your organization, update your **first name** and **last name**.

3. Update your **job title** to reflect your current role.

4. Click **"Save Changes"**.

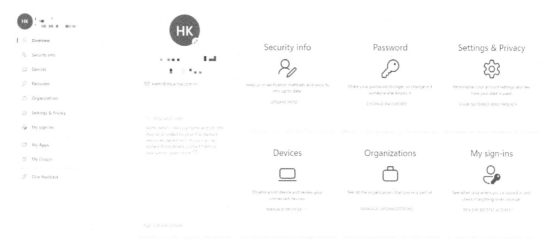

Note: Some organizations restrict name and job title changes as they sync directly from the company's HR system. If you cannot edit these fields, contact your IT or HR department.

3.2 Updating Contact Information

Keeping your contact details updated ensures that colleagues can easily reach you.

1. Navigate to the **"Contact Information"** section.

2. Update your **email address** (if editable).

3. Add or modify your **phone number** and **extension**.

4. Enter your **office location** to help team members find you in the office.

5. Click **"Save Changes"**.

3.3 Adding Your Department and Manager Information

Specifying your department and manager helps structure the organization's directory.

1. Scroll to the **"Organization"** section.

2. Select or update your **department** from the dropdown menu.

3. If applicable, add or modify your **manager's name**.

4. Save your changes.

4. Enhancing Your Profile with Additional Information

Beyond basic information, you can add more details to personalize your profile.

4.1 Writing a Professional Bio

A short bio helps introduce yourself to your colleagues.

1. Find the **"Bio" or "About Me"** section.

2. Click **"Edit"** and write a concise description, including:

    o   Your background and experience.

    o   Key responsibilities in your role.

    o   Areas of expertise.

    o   Fun facts or personal interests (if appropriate).

3. Keep it professional yet engaging.

4. Click **"Save Changes"**.

4.2 Adding Skills and Expertise

Listing your skills can help others recognize your strengths and seek your assistance.

1. Locate the **"Skills" or "Expertise"** section.

2. Click **"Add Skills"** and type in relevant skills (e.g., project management, data analysis, graphic design).

3. Select from suggested skills or enter new ones manually.

4. Save your changes.

4.3 Uploading a Professional Profile Picture

A clear and professional profile picture increases recognition and trust.

1. Click on your **profile picture** (or the placeholder icon).

2. Select **"Upload a New Photo"**.

3. Choose a professional and high-quality image from your device.

4. Adjust the cropping if necessary.

5. Click **"Save"**.

Tip: Use a high-resolution photo with a neutral background. Avoid casual selfies or group photos.

4.4 Updating Your Cover Photo

Your cover photo adds a personal touch to your profile.

1. Click the **"Edit Cover Photo"** button.

2. Upload a professional or company-branded background image.

3. Adjust the positioning if needed.

4. Click **"Save"**.

---

5. Managing Privacy and Visibility Settings

Some profile information may be visible to everyone in your organization, while other details can be restricted.

5.1 Adjusting Privacy Settings

1. Navigate to the **"Privacy Settings"** section.

2. Choose which information is visible to **everyone**, **colleagues only**, or **private**.

3. Restrict sensitive details, such as personal phone numbers, if necessary.

4. Save your preferences.

5.2 Controlling Notifications

1. Go to the **"Notification Settings"** tab.

2. Customize email and push notifications for profile updates, messages, and mentions.

3. Save your changes.

6. Troubleshooting Profile Issues

6.1 Profile Information Not Updating

- Ensure you are logged in with the correct Microsoft account.

- Some details are managed by your IT department and cannot be changed manually.

6.2 Profile Picture Not Uploading

- Check the file format (JPG, PNG) and size (under 5MB).

- Refresh the page and try again.

6.3 Missing Contact Information

- Your organization may restrict certain details from being displayed.

- Contact your IT administrator for assistance.

7. Final Tips for Optimizing Your Viva Engage Profile

- **Keep your profile updated** – Regularly check and update your information as needed.

- **Use a professional tone** – Ensure your bio and skills section reflect your expertise.

- **Engage with others** – A well-maintained profile encourages more interactions and networking.

- **Check privacy settings** – Adjust visibility settings to balance professionalism and security.

By following these steps, you will ensure that your Viva Engage profile is accurate, professional, and engaging, helping you make meaningful connections within your organization.

2.2.2 Adding a Profile Picture and Cover Photo

Your **Microsoft Viva Engage** profile is your digital identity within your organization's network. A well-maintained profile enhances visibility, helps colleagues recognize you, and fosters engagement. One of the simplest but most impactful ways to personalize your profile is by adding a **profile picture** and a **cover photo**.

This section will guide you through the process of uploading, updating, and optimizing your profile picture and cover photo in Microsoft Viva Engage on the web.

1. Why Add a Profile Picture and Cover Photo?

Before diving into the step-by-step process, let's explore why adding a profile picture and cover photo is important:

- **Enhances Recognition** – A profile picture helps colleagues and team members recognize you, making communication more personal.

- **Builds Credibility** – A professional image establishes trust and makes you more approachable.

- **Improves Engagement** – People are more likely to engage with someone who has a completed profile.

- **Personalizes Your Experience** – Your cover photo allows you to express your personality or highlight your professional interests.

2. How to Add or Update Your Profile Picture

Your **profile picture** is the small image next to your name that appears on posts, comments, and messages in **Viva Engage**. To upload or change your profile picture, follow these steps:

Step 1: Accessing Your Profile

1. Open a web browser and go to **Microsoft Viva Engage**.

2. Sign in with your **Microsoft 365 account**.

3. Click on your **profile picture** or initials in the top right corner.

4. Select **"View Profile"** from the dropdown menu.

Step 2: Uploading a Profile Picture

1. In your profile page, hover over your current profile picture (or default avatar).

2. Click on the **"Edit Profile Picture"** button.

3. Select **"Upload Photo"** to choose a picture from your device.

4. Pick an image that meets the following criteria:

   o **File Format**: PNG, JPG, or JPEG

   o **Recommended Size**: At least **400x400 pixels** for a clear, high-quality image

   o **File Size Limit**: Typically **less than 5MB**

Step 3: Adjusting and Saving Your Picture

1. After selecting an image, you may see options to **crop or adjust** the picture.

2. Ensure that your face is centered and clearly visible.

3. Click **"Save"** to apply the changes.

Your new profile picture is now set and will be visible across **Microsoft Viva Engage** and other integrated Microsoft 365 apps.

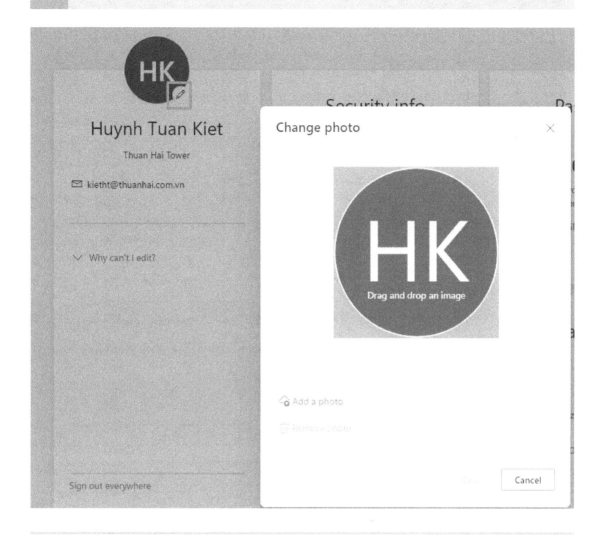

3. How to Add or Update Your Cover Photo

Your **cover photo** is the banner-like image displayed at the top of your profile page. This is an opportunity to personalize your profile with a professional or visually appealing image.

Step 1: Accessing the Cover Photo Settings

1. Navigate to your **profile page** as described earlier.

2. Look for the **cover photo section** at the top of your profile.

3. Click on the **"Edit Cover Photo"** button.

Step 2: Uploading a Cover Photo

1. Click **"Upload Cover Photo"** to choose an image from your device.

2. Select an image that meets the following guidelines:

   o **File Format**: PNG, JPG, or JPEG

   o **Recommended Size: 1584x396 pixels** (ideal for full visibility)

   o **File Size Limit: Under 5MB**

   o **Professional and Appropriate**: Ensure the image aligns with company guidelines.

Step 3: Adjusting and Saving Your Cover Photo

1. If needed, drag or resize the image to fit properly within the designated area.

2. Make sure important parts of the image are visible (avoid cropping out key details).

3. Click **"Save"** to update your cover photo.

4. Best Practices for Choosing a Profile Picture and Cover Photo

Profile Picture Best Practices

- **Use a high-quality headshot**: A clear, professional image of your face is ideal.

- **Maintain consistency**: If you use Microsoft 365 apps like Outlook or Teams, keeping the same profile picture across platforms improves recognition.

- **Choose a neutral or professional background**: Avoid distracting or overly personal backgrounds.

Cover Photo Best Practices

- **Align with your professional identity**: Choose an image that reflects your work, industry, or interests.

- **Keep it visually appealing**: Avoid cluttered images; opt for clean, high-resolution visuals.

- **Stay within company branding guidelines**: Some organizations have preferred themes or branded images.

5. Troubleshooting Common Issues

If you encounter problems while updating your profile picture or cover photo, here are some common issues and solutions:

Issue 1: Unable to Upload a Profile Picture

- **Solution**: Ensure the image is in PNG, JPG, or JPEG format and does not exceed the file size limit.

Issue 2: The Profile Picture is Blurry

- **Solution**: Upload a higher-resolution image (**at least 400x400 pixels**).

Issue 3: Cover Photo is Not Displaying Correctly

- **Solution**: Resize the image to the recommended **1584x396 pixels** for the best fit.

Issue 4: Changes Are Not Visible Immediately

- **Solution**: Refresh the page or clear your browser cache. Changes may take a few minutes to update across Microsoft 365.

6. Frequently Asked Questions (FAQs)

Q1: Can I use a GIF as my profile picture or cover photo?

A: No, Microsoft Viva Engage only supports static PNG, JPG, or JPEG formats.

Q2: Can I remove my profile picture if I don't want one?

A: Yes, you can revert to the default initials by selecting **"Remove Profile Picture"** in the settings.

Q3: Can I use a company-branded cover photo?

A: Yes, some organizations provide official templates or branding guidelines for cover photos. Check with your IT or HR department.

Q4: Can other users change my profile picture or cover photo?

A: No, only you (or an administrator in some cases) can update your profile images.

Q5: Will my profile picture sync with other Microsoft 365 applications?

A: Yes, changes to your profile picture will reflect in **Microsoft Teams, Outlook, and other Microsoft 365 services**.

7. Conclusion

Adding a profile picture and cover photo in **Microsoft Viva Engage** is a simple yet powerful way to personalize your presence in your organization's social network. A professional image helps build trust, enhances recognition, and improves collaboration.

By following the steps in this guide, you can ensure your profile is complete, visually appealing, and aligned with your professional identity. Take a few minutes to update your profile today and make your **Viva Engage** experience even more engaging! 🚀

2.2.3 Managing Notification Settings

Microsoft Viva Engage provides a range of notification settings that help users stay informed about relevant updates while avoiding unnecessary distractions. Managing notification settings effectively ensures that you receive timely alerts for important discussions, mentions, and activities without being overwhelmed by excessive notifications.

This section will guide you through the different types of notifications available in Viva Engage, how to customize them based on your preferences, and best practices for keeping your notifications organized.

1. Understanding Viva Engage Notifications

Microsoft Viva Engage offers multiple types of notifications to keep you informed about activity in your communities, posts, and messages. These notifications can be delivered through different channels, including:

Types of Notifications

1. **In-App Notifications** – Appear in the notification center within Viva Engage when someone interacts with your posts, mentions you, or responds to a conversation you are part of.

2. **Email Notifications** – Sent to your registered email address for updates such as mentions, private messages, and important group activities.

3. **Desktop and Mobile Push Notifications** – Appear as pop-ups or banners on your device when using the Viva Engage mobile app or desktop application.

4. **Microsoft Teams Notifications** – If Viva Engage is integrated with Microsoft Teams, you can receive updates directly within Teams.

5. **Digest Emails** – Summary emails sent periodically (daily or weekly) to keep you updated on group discussions and important posts.

2. Customizing Your Notification Settings

To ensure that you receive only relevant notifications, you can customize your notification preferences in Viva Engage. Here's how to adjust your settings:

Accessing Notification Settings

1. **Log into Microsoft Viva Engage.**

2. Click on your **profile picture** in the top-right corner of the Viva Engage interface.

3. Select **Settings** from the dropdown menu.

4. Navigate to the **Notifications** tab in the settings menu.

From here, you can modify how and when you receive notifications for different types of activities.

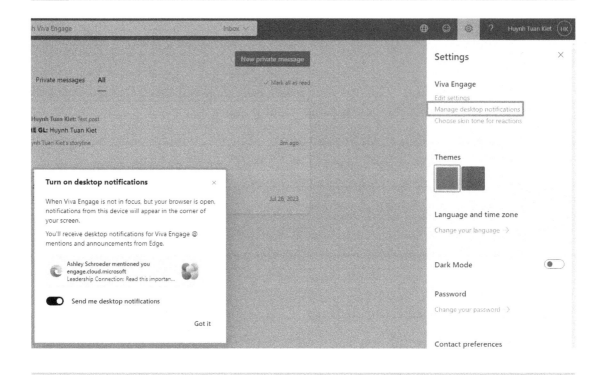

3. Configuring Microsoft Teams Notifications for Viva Engage

If you integrate Viva Engage with Microsoft Teams, you can receive notifications directly within Teams.

Enabling Viva Engage Notifications in Teams

1. Open **Microsoft Teams** and click on **Apps** in the left sidebar.

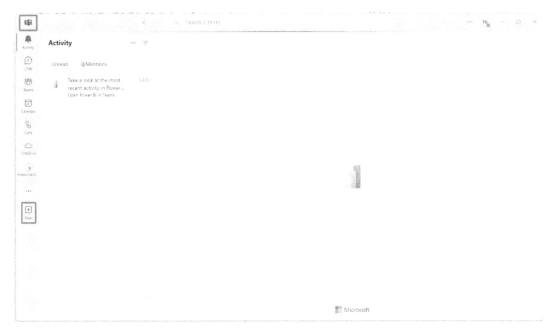

2. Search for and select **Viva Engage**.

3. Click **Add** to integrate Viva Engage with Teams.

4. Go to **Viva Engage settings** within Teams.

5. Enable notifications for:

   o   Mentions

- o Group announcements
- o Replies to your posts

6. Click **Save** to apply changes.

This setup helps consolidate your work notifications into a single platform.

4. Troubleshooting Notification Issues

If you're experiencing issues with notifications, try the following solutions:

Not Receiving Any Notifications

- Check if notifications are disabled in your settings.
- Ensure that email notifications are not going to your spam folder.
- Verify that push notifications are enabled on your device.

Receiving Too Many Notifications

- Reduce the frequency of email notifications (e.g., switch from Immediate to Daily Digest).
- Disable notifications for less important activities.

Viva Engage Notifications Not Working on Teams

- Ensure that the Viva Engage app is properly installed in Microsoft Teams.
- Check if Teams notifications are enabled in Teams settings.

If issues persist, contact your IT department or Microsoft Support for assistance.

Conclusion

Managing notifications in Microsoft Viva Engage is essential for maintaining an efficient workflow while staying informed about key updates. By customizing notification settings based on your preferences, you can reduce distractions and focus on meaningful interactions. Whether using in-app alerts, email updates, or Microsoft Teams notifications, setting up notifications properly ensures you never miss important information while avoiding notification overload.

Now that you have a complete understanding of how to manage notifications in Viva Engage, you're ready to optimize your experience and stay connected with your workplace community effectively. 🚀

2.3 Understanding Viva Engage Groups and Communities

Microsoft Viva Engage is designed to foster collaboration and communication within an organization. One of its core features is **Groups and Communities**, which allow employees to interact, share knowledge, and work together effectively. These groups can be used for various purposes, such as departmental communication, project collaboration, or company-wide discussions.

This section will guide you through the process of **joining existing groups**, **creating new groups**, and **understanding the different types of groups and their permissions**.

2.3.1 Joining and Creating Groups

A. Understanding Groups and Their Purpose

Before joining or creating a group, it's essential to understand their role in **Microsoft Viva Engage**. Groups serve as dedicated spaces where users can post updates, share documents, engage in discussions, and collaborate in real time.

There are different types of groups in Viva Engage, each serving a specific purpose:

1. **Public Groups** – Open to all employees within the organization. Anyone can join without approval.

2. **Private Groups** – Require approval or an invitation to join. These are ideal for confidential discussions or department-specific collaboration.

3. **Official Communities** – Endorsed by the organization and often managed by administrators for broad communication.

4. **Interest-Based Communities** – Groups centered around hobbies, professional interests, or employee resource networks.

Now, let's dive into the step-by-step process of **joining** and **creating** groups in Viva Engage.

B. How to Join a Viva Engage Group

Joining an existing group in Viva Engage is simple and helps you stay connected with relevant discussions and updates.

1. Browsing and Searching for Groups

To find groups to join, follow these steps:

1. **Log in to Microsoft Viva Engage** through a web browser.

2. On the **left sidebar**, locate the **"Discover Communities"** or **"Browse Groups"** option.

3. Use the **search bar** to enter keywords related to the group you want to join (e.g., "Marketing Team" or "HR Announcements").

4. Viva Engage will display a list of matching groups. You can **click on each group** to see its details, members, and recent posts.

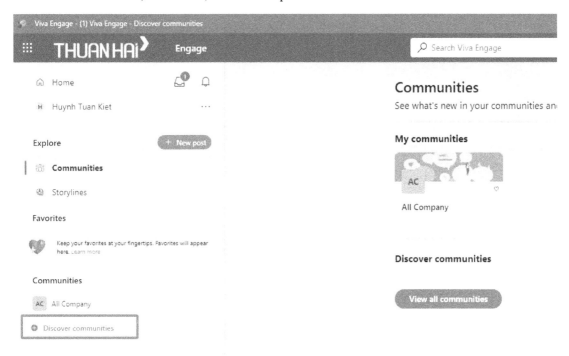

2. Requesting to Join a Group

After finding the right group, follow these steps to join:

- If the group is **Public**, click the **"Join"** button, and you will become a member instantly.

- If the group is **Private**, click **"Request to Join."** The group admin will review your request and either approve or decline it.

- Some groups might require you to **answer a few questions** before joining (e.g., "Why do you want to join this group?").

Once you're a member, you'll receive updates from the group in your feed and can participate in discussions.

3. Setting Notifications for Groups

After joining a group, you might want to manage your notification settings to stay updated without being overwhelmed by too many alerts.

To adjust group notifications:

1. Go to the group page.

2. Click on the **"Settings"** or **"Notifications"** button.

3. Choose how often you want to receive updates (e.g., real-time, daily, or weekly summaries).

This ensures you stay informed about important discussions while avoiding unnecessary distractions.

C. How to Create a New Viva Engage Group

If you can't find a suitable group, you can create your own. Whether it's for a **team project**, **department updates**, or an **interest-based community**, setting up a new group ensures effective communication and collaboration.

1. Steps to Create a New Group

To create a group in Viva Engage:

1. **Log in to Viva Engage** and navigate to the left sidebar.

2. Click on **"Create a Community"** or **"Create a Group"** (depending on your organization's settings).

3. A setup window will appear, prompting you to enter **basic group details**:

   o **Group Name**: Choose a clear and descriptive name (e.g., "Marketing Team Updates" or "Cybersecurity Best Practices").

   o **Description**: Provide a brief overview of the group's purpose.

   o **Group Type**: Select **Public** (anyone can join) or **Private** (membership requires approval).

   o **Cover Image**: Upload a custom banner to make your group visually appealing.

   o **Group Owners**: Assign one or more admins who will manage the group.

4. Click **"Create"** to finalize the setup.

5. You will be directed to the new group's page, where you can start adding members and posting content.

2. Inviting Members to Join Your Group

Once the group is created, you need to invite people to participate.

To invite members:

- Click **"Add Members"** on the group page.

- Enter the names or email addresses of colleagues you want to invite.

- Optionally, include a message explaining the purpose of the group.

- Click **"Send Invite."**

For **public groups**, you can also share a direct link to allow colleagues to join independently.

3. Setting Group Permissions and Rules

To maintain a well-organized group, configure the following settings:

- **Posting Permissions**: Decide whether only admins can post announcements or if all members can create posts.

- **Moderation Controls**: Enable admin approval for posts if necessary.

- **Content Visibility**: Define whether posts are visible only to members or can be seen by external participants (if allowed by company policy).

- **Pinned Posts**: Highlight important announcements at the top of the group feed.

These settings help maintain the group's focus and ensure effective communication.

D. Best Practices for Managing Groups in Viva Engage

To make the most of Viva Engage groups, consider the following **best practices**:

1. Define a Clear Purpose

Each group should have a **specific purpose** to avoid confusion. Whether it's for a project team, a department, or a knowledge-sharing community, make sure members understand the group's objectives.

2. Encourage Active Participation

A group is only valuable if members actively contribute. Encourage engagement by:

- Posting **discussion topics** regularly.

- Using **polls** to gather feedback.

- Recognizing and appreciating members' contributions.

3. Keep Conversations Organized

- Use **hashtags** to categorize discussions (e.g., #ProductUpdates, #HRNews).

- Pin important posts so they remain visible.

- Archive outdated discussions to keep the group relevant.

4. Monitor and Moderate the Group

Group admins should:

- Remove **spam** or **irrelevant posts**.

- Address **inappropriate behavior**.

- Respond to members' questions promptly.

These steps ensure a **professional and productive environment**.

E. Conclusion

Joining and creating groups in **Microsoft Viva Engage** helps teams collaborate efficiently, share knowledge, and build a strong workplace community. By following this guide, you can:

- Find and join relevant groups.

- Create new groups tailored to your team's needs.

- Manage groups effectively for maximum engagement.

In the next section, we will explore how to **customize group settings** to further enhance collaboration. Stay tuned!

2.3.2 Group Roles and Permissions

Understanding Group Roles and Permissions in Microsoft Viva Engage

Microsoft Viva Engage allows users to create and participate in workplace communities that foster collaboration, knowledge sharing, and engagement. Within these communities, different roles and permissions define what users can do. Understanding these roles is essential for effectively managing groups, ensuring smooth communication, and maintaining control over content and interactions.

This section provides a detailed guide on the various roles available in Viva Engage groups, their permissions, how to manage roles, and best practices for maintaining a well-organized and secure group environment.

---

1. Overview of Group Roles in Microsoft Viva Engage

Microsoft Viva Engage offers three main user roles within a group:

1. **Group Admin (Administrator)**

2. **Group Moderator (if enabled by the organization)**

3. **Group Member (Regular User)**

Each role comes with different levels of control and permissions, ensuring that group management remains structured while allowing flexibility in content contribution.

2. Role Descriptions and Permissions

2.1 Group Admin (Administrator)

The **Group Admin** role has the highest level of control within a Microsoft Viva Engage group. This role is responsible for managing group settings, overseeing discussions, and ensuring that content adheres to the organization's policies.

Key Permissions of a Group Admin:

- **Create and delete posts**: Group admins can post messages, upload files, and remove content that violates guidelines.

- **Pin and unpin posts**: Important discussions or announcements can be pinned to keep them visible.

- **Approve and remove members**: Admins control who joins the group and can remove members when necessary.

- **Assign and remove moderator roles** (if applicable): If the organization allows moderator roles, admins can delegate responsibilities.

- **Manage group settings**: This includes changing the group name, description, visibility (public or private), and notification settings.

- **Delete or archive the group**: Admins have the authority to permanently delete or archive inactive groups.

- **Monitor compliance and enforce rules**: Ensuring that discussions align with company policies and addressing inappropriate behavior.

How to Assign a Group Admin Role:

1. Navigate to the group's settings page.

2. Click on "Manage Members."

3. Locate the user you want to promote.

4. Click on the dropdown menu next to their name and select **"Make Admin."**

5. Confirm the selection.

2.2 Group Moderator (Optional Role, if enabled)

Some organizations enable the **Group Moderator** role to help manage content and discussions while giving more flexibility than the admin role. Moderators assist in maintaining a productive and positive group environment.

Key Permissions of a Group Moderator:

- **Approve or reject posts** (if required in the group settings).

- **Delete inappropriate or off-topic content.**

- **Encourage engagement** by responding to comments and guiding discussions.

- **Help enforce community guidelines** and report violations to admins.

How to Assign a Moderator Role (if applicable):

1. Go to the group's settings.

2. Select **"Manage Members."**

3. Find the user you want to assign as a moderator.

4. Click on the dropdown menu next to their name and select **"Make Moderator."**

5. Confirm the selection.

2.3 Group Member (Regular User)

The **Group Member** role represents the majority of users in a Microsoft Viva Engage group. These users participate in discussions, share content, and collaborate with colleagues.

Key Permissions of a Group Member:

- **Post messages and replies.**

- **React to posts using likes and emojis.**

- **Share files, images, and videos.**

- **Participate in polls and surveys.**

- **Mention other users using @username.**

- **Follow discussions and receive notifications.**

3. Managing Group Roles and Permissions

Adjusting Group Permissions

Group admins can adjust permissions based on group needs. To modify settings:

1. **Go to the Group Settings page.**

2. **Select "Manage Permissions."**

3. Adjust the following:

   o **Who can post?** (Admins only or all members).

   o **Who can approve posts?** (If required).

   o **Who can delete messages?** (Admins and moderators).

   o **Who can invite new members?** (Admins or all members).

4. **Save changes.**

Removing or Changing Roles

If a group admin needs to remove or change a role:

1. **Go to "Manage Members."**

2. Find the user whose role needs to be modified.

3. Click on the dropdown menu and choose **"Remove Admin"** or **"Remove Moderator."**

4. Confirm the change.

4. Best Practices for Group Role Management

Defining Clear Responsibilities

- Assign **at least one active admin** to every group to oversee content.

- If moderators are available, **delegate content approval tasks** to maintain efficiency.

- Regularly **review group settings** to ensure roles align with organizational needs.

Maintaining a Safe and Engaging Community

- **Enforce group rules** to prevent spam, harassment, or off-topic discussions.

- Use **moderation tools** to flag inappropriate content.

- Encourage members to **report violations** rather than engage in disputes.

Encouraging Engagement While Maintaining Control

- Empower group members to **contribute freely** but provide guidelines on content expectations.

- Regularly **engage with the community** through pinned posts, Q&A sessions, and polls.

- Use analytics to **monitor engagement trends** and adjust strategies accordingly.

5. Troubleshooting Role and Permission Issues

Common Issues and Solutions

Issue	Possible Cause	Solution
A user cannot post messages.	Posting is restricted to admins only.	Change settings to allow member posting.
A user cannot delete posts.	Only admins/moderators have delete permissions.	Assign moderator privileges if needed.
A member was mistakenly removed from the group.	Admin error or system issue.	Re-invite the user and restore access.
A new admin cannot see group settings.	Role assignment delay or access issue.	Ask them to refresh or log out and back in.

Where to Get Help

- **Microsoft Viva Engage Support Portal** for official documentation.

- **Company IT Admins** for permission-related inquiries.

- **Microsoft Community Forums** for troubleshooting advice.

6. Conclusion

Understanding group roles and permissions in Microsoft Viva Engage is essential for maintaining a well-organized and productive digital workspace. By properly assigning roles, managing permissions, and following best practices, organizations can create a collaborative environment where employees engage effectively while ensuring compliance with internal policies.

By leveraging the correct group structure and role management strategies, Microsoft Viva Engage becomes a powerful tool for workplace communication and knowledge sharing. 🚀

2.3.3 Customizing Group Settings

Microsoft Viva Engage provides a variety of customization options to help group owners and administrators tailor their groups to fit their organization's needs. Customizing group settings allows you to manage privacy, permissions, appearance, and functionalities, ensuring that the group aligns with its intended purpose. In this section, we will explore the different customization options available, how to configure them effectively, and best practices for maintaining an engaging and organized community.

1. Accessing Group Settings

To customize a group in Viva Engage, you must have **admin or owner** permissions for that group. Follow these steps to access the group settings:

1. **Open Microsoft Viva Engage on the Web** and navigate to the group you want to modify.

2. Click on the **gear icon (⚙️) or "Settings"** in the group header.

3. You will see multiple tabs or sections that allow you to configure different aspects of the group.

Once inside the settings menu, you can adjust various elements such as privacy, appearance, membership control, notifications, and integrations.

2. Group Name, Description, and Appearance

Updating the Group Name and Description

A well-defined group name and description help users understand the group's purpose and encourage participation.

- **Group Name:** Should be clear and concise, reflecting the group's focus (e.g., "Marketing Team Updates" or "Product Development Community").

- **Group Description:** Provides more context about the group's purpose, who should join, and what kind of discussions take place.

Adding a Cover Image and Group Icon

Visual elements such as a cover image and icon make the group more appealing and recognizable.

- **Cover Image:**

  - Click **Edit Cover Photo** in the group settings.

  - Upload an image that represents the group (e.g., company branding or team-specific visuals).

  - Use **high-resolution images** to maintain quality.

- **Group Icon:**

  - Choose an icon from available presets or upload a custom logo.

  - Icons help differentiate groups in the Viva Engage interface.

Choosing a Group Theme

Some Viva Engage versions allow group owners to select color themes to match branding or personal preference. Check for options in the **Appearance** section of the settings.

3. Managing Privacy and Membership Settings

Setting Group Privacy: Public vs. Private

Viva Engage offers two primary privacy settings:

- **Public Groups**:
  - Anyone in the organization can join, view, and participate.
  - Best for company-wide announcements, knowledge sharing, and social communities.

- **Private Groups**:
  - Only approved members can join and view discussions.
  - Best for confidential team discussions, sensitive projects, or leadership groups.

How to Change Group Privacy Settings:

1. Go to **Group Settings → Privacy**.
2. Select either **Public** or **Private**.
3. Click **Save Changes** to update the settings.

Controlling Membership Requests and Approvals

For **Private Groups**, admins can decide how members join:

- **Open Requests**: Members request to join and are approved automatically.
- **Admin Approval Required**: Admins must manually approve each request.
- **Invite-Only**: Only group admins can add new members.

To adjust these settings:

1. Navigate to **Membership Settings**.
2. Select the preferred **approval method**.
3. Click **Save**.

Assigning Admin and Moderator Roles

Admins can assign different roles to help manage the group:

- **Group Admins**: Have full control over settings, members, and content moderation.

- **Moderators**: Can manage discussions, approve posts, and remove inappropriate content.

How to Assign Admins and Moderators:

1. Open **Group Members**.

2. Locate the user and click on the **role dropdown**.

3. Select **Admin** or **Moderator**.

---

4. Configuring Posting and Content Controls

Setting Post and Comment Permissions

Group admins can restrict who can post and comment in the group:

- **Anyone can post and comment** (default).

- **Only admins can post, but members can comment**.

- **Only admins can post and comment** (for announcement-based groups).

To configure these settings:

1. Go to **Group Settings → Content Permissions**.

2. Select the desired permissions.

3. Click **Save**.

Enabling Post Approval

In sensitive groups, admins may want to review posts before they go live.

- Toggle **Post Approval On/Off** in **Moderation Settings**.

- When enabled, all posts must be reviewed by an admin or moderator before publishing.

Managing Attachments and External Links

Admins can decide whether members can:

- Upload images, videos, or documents.

- Share external links.

To adjust these settings:

1. Navigate to **Attachment & Link Permissions**.

2. Enable or disable options.

3. Click **Save**.

5. Notifications and Email Preferences

Setting Up Group Notifications

Users can customize their notifications to control how often they receive updates.

Options include:

- **All Activity** (receive alerts for every post).

- **Highlights Only** (get notified about important updates).

- **No Notifications** (mute alerts).

To adjust:

1. Click on **Notification Settings**.

2. Choose preferred **notification frequency**.

3. Click **Save**.

Managing Email Alerts

Viva Engage can send email summaries for group activity. Admins can:

- Enable **daily or weekly digest emails**.

- Allow users to **unsubscribe from emails**.

To configure:

1. Go to **Email Settings**.

2. Select **Email Frequency**.

3. Click **Save**.

6. Integrating with Other Microsoft 365 Tools

Connecting to Microsoft Teams

Viva Engage can be embedded into Microsoft Teams for seamless communication.

Steps to integrate:

1. Open **Microsoft Teams**.

2. Click **Apps** → Search for **Viva Engage**.

3. Select **Add to a Team**.

4. Choose the **Viva Engage group** to integrate.

Linking with SharePoint

Admins can embed Viva Engage discussions into SharePoint pages:

1. Open **SharePoint Site Editor**.

2. Select **Add Web Part** → **Viva Engage**.

3. Choose the **Group Feed** to display.

Using Viva Engage with Outlook

Users can receive and respond to Viva Engage posts directly from Outlook emails.

To enable:

1. Open **Group Email Settings**.

2. Enable **Outlook Integration**.

7. Best Practices for Customizing Viva Engage Groups

Keeping Group Settings Updated

- Regularly review privacy settings and adjust as needed.

- Update group descriptions and visuals to reflect current activities.

Encouraging Engagement

- Use pinned posts to highlight important information.

- Schedule recurring posts to maintain activity.

Moderating Content Effectively

- Assign multiple moderators for large groups.

- Encourage constructive discussions and enforce guidelines.

Conclusion

Customizing group settings in Microsoft Viva Engage helps create an organized and engaging workplace community. By setting up privacy controls, managing membership, configuring content permissions, and integrating with other Microsoft 365 tools, group admins can ensure that their group remains active, secure, and valuable to members.

PART III
Engaging with Posts and Conversations

3.1 Creating and Managing Posts

3.1.1 Writing a New Post

Creating and sharing posts is at the heart of Microsoft Viva Engage. Whether you're making an announcement, starting a discussion, or sharing updates with your colleagues, knowing how to write an engaging and effective post can improve communication and collaboration. This section provides a step-by-step guide on how to compose posts, best practices for making your content more impactful, and ways to enhance visibility and engagement.

1. Understanding the Purpose of a Post in Viva Engage

Before writing a post, it's important to consider its purpose. Viva Engage supports various types of posts, including:

- **General Updates**: Share team or company updates, project progress, or personal work experiences.

- **Discussions**: Engage colleagues in meaningful conversations by asking for opinions, feedback, or ideas.

- **Questions**: Seek information or clarification from your community.

- **Announcements**: Deliver critical information that needs immediate attention.

- **Celebrations and Recognitions**: Acknowledge achievements, milestones, or personal and professional successes.

Choosing the right format and tone for your post helps ensure that your message is clear and engaging.

2. Accessing the Post Creation Tool

To write a new post in Microsoft Viva Engage:

1. **Log in to Microsoft Viva Engage** on your web browser.

2. Navigate to the group, community, or feed where you want to post.

3. Click on the **"Start a Post"** text box at the top of the feed.

4. A new post editor window will appear, allowing you to enter and format your content.

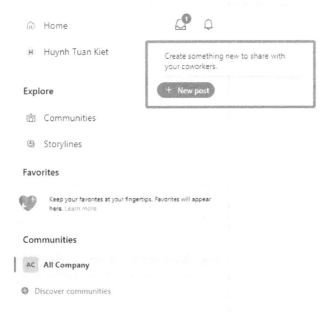

Once you have accessed the post editor, you can start composing your message.

3. Structuring an Effective Post

A well-structured post improves readability and increases engagement. Consider the following components:

3.1 Crafting a Clear and Engaging Opening

The first few sentences of your post determine whether readers will continue reading. To capture attention:

- **Start with a question**: "How do you think our team can improve cross-functional collaboration?"

- **Use a bold statement**: "Exciting news! Our company just launched a new employee recognition program."

- **Mention a key benefit**: "Here's a quick tip that will save you hours in Excel."

3.2 Providing Context and Details

Once you have captured attention, add relevant details to support your message.

- **Explain the purpose**: Why is this post important? What should the reader do with this information?

- **Use bullet points or numbered lists**: These improve readability for long posts.

- **Break text into short paragraphs**: Large blocks of text can be difficult to read on a screen.

3.3 Adding a Call-to-Action (CTA)

Encourage engagement by prompting readers to take action. Some examples include:

- **Ask for feedback**: "What are your thoughts on this update?"

- **Invite participation**: "Comment below if you have experience with this tool."

- **Encourage sharing**: "If you found this helpful, consider sharing it with your team!"

4. Enhancing Posts with Multimedia

To make your post more engaging, consider adding:

- **Images**: Use high-quality visuals relevant to your topic.

- **Videos**: Embed short clips for tutorials or team messages.

- **Documents**: Attach files such as PDFs, Word documents, or PowerPoint presentations.

- **GIFs and Emojis**: Add personality and emotion to your message.

In **Microsoft Viva Engage**, you can upload media by clicking on the **attachment icon** in the post editor.

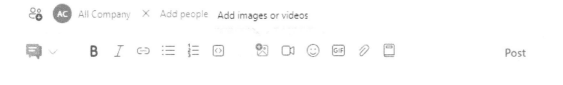

5. Formatting and Customization Options

Microsoft Viva Engage offers various text formatting tools to enhance clarity and emphasis:

- **Bold (CTRL + B)**: Highlight important keywords or phrases.

- **Italics (CTRL + I)**: Add emphasis to specific words.

- **Bullet Points**: Organize information clearly.

- **Numbered Lists**: Present step-by-step instructions.

- **Hyperlinks**: Direct users to additional resources or related discussions.

To apply formatting, highlight the text and choose the desired option from the toolbar in the post editor.

6. Choosing the Right Audience and Privacy Settings

Before publishing your post, ensure it reaches the right audience:

- **Posting in a Group**: If your message is relevant to a specific department or project, post in the appropriate Viva Engage group.

- **Company-wide Announcements**: If your organization allows it, post directly to the company feed.

- **Targeting Specific Individuals**: Use @mentions to notify key people.

Additionally, check the **privacy settings** to determine whether your post should be visible to everyone in the organization or only to members of a specific group.

7. Posting and Managing Published Content

Once your post is ready:

1. Review the content for errors and clarity.

2. Click the **"Post"** button.

3. If necessary, edit or delete the post by clicking on the three-dot menu (⋮) after publishing.

If you need to schedule a post for later, check if your organization has enabled post-scheduling features.

8. Best Practices for Writing Effective Posts

Keep Posts Concise and Relevant

Avoid overly long posts unless necessary. Stick to **3-5 short paragraphs** for readability.

Use Engaging and Inclusive Language

- Avoid jargon that may be unfamiliar to all readers.

- Use positive and encouraging language.

- Be inclusive and respectful in tone.

Encourage Two-Way Communication

- Pose open-ended questions.
- Respond to comments to foster discussion.
- Acknowledge and appreciate contributions from others.

Maintain Professionalism

- Ensure your post aligns with company policies.
- Avoid sensitive topics unless necessary and approved.
- Use proper grammar and spell-check before posting.

9. Troubleshooting and FAQs

Why Can't I Post in a Certain Group?

- You may not have permission to post in restricted or announcement-only groups.
- Check with a group admin for access.

How Do I Edit or Delete a Post?

- Click on the three-dot menu (⋮) next to your post.
- Select **Edit** to make changes.
- Select **Delete** to remove the post permanently.

Can I Pin Important Posts?

- Yes, group admins can pin posts to keep them at the top of the feed.
- Use this feature for FAQs, key announcements, or ongoing discussions.

How Do I Know If My Post is Reaching the Right Audience?

- Check the engagement metrics (likes, comments, and views).
- Adjust content strategy based on interactions.

Conclusion

Writing effective posts in Microsoft Viva Engage is essential for enhancing workplace communication and collaboration. By following best practices, using formatting and multimedia tools, and engaging your audience with clear messaging, you can maximize the impact of your posts.

Ready to take your engagement to the next level? Explore the next section to learn how to incorporate **images, videos, and files** into your posts for even greater impact! 🚀

3.1.2 Adding Images, Videos, and Files

Microsoft Viva Engage is designed to facilitate rich and dynamic workplace conversations. One of its key features is the ability to attach media files—such as images, videos, and documents—to posts. Adding these elements enhances engagement, improves communication clarity, and allows teams to share important information effectively.

This section will provide a **step-by-step guide** on how to attach different types of media to posts, discuss best practices for using these features, and highlight **troubleshooting tips** in case users encounter issues.

1. Why Use Images, Videos, and Files in Posts?

Adding media to your Viva Engage posts enhances your messages in several ways:

✅ **Better Engagement** – Posts with images and videos capture more attention than plain text.
✅ **Improved Clarity** – Visual elements help explain concepts more effectively.
✅ **Collaboration Enhancement** – Sharing documents allows teams to work together seamlessly.
✅ **Stronger Brand Identity** – Using company-branded images and videos reinforces messaging.

Now, let's dive into how to **add each type of media** to a post.

2. Adding Images to a Post

Supported Image Formats

Viva Engage supports various image formats, including:

- **JPEG (.jpg, .jpeg)**
- **PNG (.png)**
- **GIF (.gif)** (for animated content)
- **BMP (.bmp)**

Steps to Upload an Image

1. **Go to Microsoft Viva Engage** and open the group or community where you want to post.

2. Click on the **"Create a Post"** field at the top of the page.

3. Type your message in the text box.

4. Click on the **"Attach"** icon below the text box.

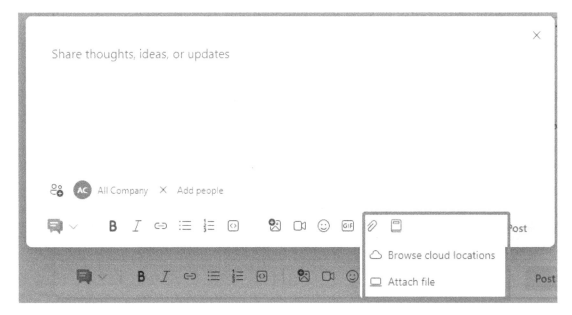

5. Select **"Upload Image"** and choose an image from your computer.

6. Once uploaded, the image will appear as a thumbnail in the post preview.

7. Click **"Post"** to publish your message with the attached image.

Best Practices for Adding Images

*   ⬜ **Use high-resolution images** to ensure clarity.

*   🎨 **Maintain brand consistency** by using company-approved visuals.

*   ✏️ **Resize images** before uploading to avoid distortion.

*   ⬜ **Add captions or descriptions** to provide context.

Editing and Removing Images

*   Click on the uploaded image before posting to preview or remove it.

*   If the post is already published, click the **three-dot menu (...)** → **Edit Post** → **Remove Image**.

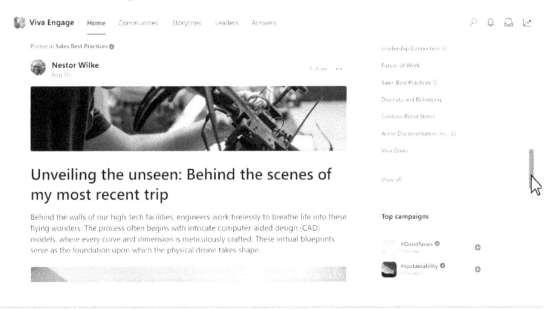

3. Adding Videos to a Post

3.1 Supported Video Formats

Viva Engage allows users to upload videos in the following formats:

*   **MP4 (.mp4) – Recommended**

- **WMV (.wmv)**

- **AVI (.avi)**

- **MOV (.mov)**

3.2 How to Upload a Video

1. Open Microsoft Viva Engage and navigate to the **group or community** where you want to post.

2. Click on the **"Create a Post"** field.

3. Type your message.

4. Click the **"Attach" (🖉) icon** and select **"Upload Video"**.

5. Choose a video file from your device.

6. Wait for the upload to complete (larger files may take longer).

7. Click **"Post"** to publish.

3.3 Embedding Videos from Other Platforms

Instead of uploading a video file, you can **embed a video** from Microsoft Stream, YouTube, or Vimeo.

1. Copy the video **URL** from the external platform.

2. In Viva Engage, click **"Create a Post"**.

3. Paste the video link directly into the text box.

4. Viva Engage will generate a **preview thumbnail**.

5. Click **"Post"** to share the video.

3.4 Best Practices for Adding Videos

- 🎬 Keep videos **short and to the point** (1-3 minutes).

- 🔉 Ensure **clear audio quality** to enhance understanding.

- 🎞 Use **captions** or subtitles for accessibility.

- 🚀 Compress large files before uploading to speed up processing.

3.5 Editing and Removing Videos

- To remove a video before posting, click **"X"** on the preview.

- To delete after publishing, click **"Edit Post"** → **Remove Video**.

4. Attaching Files to a Post

Supported File Types

Viva Engage supports a wide range of document formats, including:

- **PDF (.pdf)**

- **Word (.doc, .docx)**

- **Excel (.xls, .xlsx)**

- **PowerPoint (.ppt, .pptx)**

- **Text (.txt, .csv)**

How to Upload a File

1. Open Viva Engage and navigate to the appropriate group or community.

2. Click the **"Create a Post"** field.

3. Type your message.

4. Click the **"Attach"** (📎) icon → "Upload File".

5. Choose a document from your computer or select a file from **OneDrive**.

6. Wait for the file to upload.

7. Click **"Post"** to share the document.

Sharing Files from OneDrive or SharePoint

Instead of uploading a document directly, you can share a **OneDrive or SharePoint link**:

1. Go to **OneDrive** or **SharePoint** and locate the file.

2. Click **"Share"** and select **"Copy Link"**.

3. Paste the link into your Viva Engage post.

4. Click **"Post"** to share.

Best Practices for Sharing Files

- 📁 **Use OneDrive links** for larger files instead of direct uploads.

- 🔒 **Check permissions** to ensure colleagues can access the file.

- ☐ **Label important documents** for better organization.

- 📑 **Provide a summary** when sharing long reports.

Editing and Removing Files

- Click **"Edit Post"** → **Remove File** before publishing.

- If the post is already live, edit the post and delete the attached file.

5. Troubleshooting Media Upload Issues

Here are some **common problems** and solutions when uploading images, videos, or files:

File Won't Upload

✅ Ensure the file format is **supported**.
✅ Check if the file size **exceeds the maximum limit** (Viva Engage may restrict very large files).
✅ Refresh the page and try uploading again.

Poor Image or Video Quality

✅ Upload high-resolution images (avoid compressed files).
✅ Convert videos to **MP4** format for better compatibility.
✅ Use **photo-editing tools** to enhance image clarity before uploading.

File Not Accessible by Others

✅ If using OneDrive/SharePoint, **adjust sharing permissions**.
✅ Ensure that the file is **not restricted** by IT policies.

6. Conclusion

Adding images, videos, and files in Viva Engage helps create engaging, informative, and visually appealing conversations. By following best practices, ensuring proper formatting, and troubleshooting common issues, users can maximize the effectiveness of their posts.

3.1.3 Using Mentions, Hashtags, and GIFs

Microsoft Viva Engage provides several tools to enhance engagement and visibility in workplace communication. Mentions, hashtags, and GIFs make posts more interactive, searchable, and engaging, fostering collaboration and strengthening workplace culture. This section will guide you through how to effectively use these features in your posts and conversations.

1. Understanding Mentions, Hashtags, and GIFs in Viva Engage

What Are Mentions?

Mentions allow users to tag colleagues or entire groups in posts and comments. This ensures the tagged users receive a notification, increasing visibility and engagement in the conversation.

What Are Hashtags?

Hashtags categorize content, making it easier to find discussions related to specific topics. Using relevant hashtags ensures that posts are discoverable by employees searching for related content.

What Are GIFs and Why Use Them?

GIFs add a visual, expressive element to posts. They are useful for making workplace conversations more engaging, celebrating achievements, or adding a touch of humor to lighten the mood.

2. Using Mentions Effectively in Viva Engage

Mentions are a powerful way to direct messages and involve specific individuals or groups in conversations.

How to Mention Someone in a Post or Comment

1. **Start Typing with "@"**

   o When writing a post or comment, type the **"@"** symbol followed by the person's name (e.g., @John Smith).

2. **Select the User from the Suggestions**

   o Viva Engage will display a dropdown list of matching names. Click on the correct person.

3. **Complete Your Message and Post**

   o After selecting the name, finish your message and click **Post**.

4. **The Mentioned Person Gets Notified**

   o The tagged user will receive an alert in their notifications panel.

Mentioning Groups

To mention an entire group:

- Type @ followed by the group name (e.g., @Marketing Team).

- Select the group from the dropdown list.

- All group members will receive a notification.

Best Practices for Using Mentions

- **Use mentions sparingly** – avoid overusing mentions, as excessive notifications can be overwhelming.

- **Be specific** – mention only relevant individuals or teams.

- **Use mentions for important updates** – ensure key stakeholders are notified about crucial discussions.

Common Mistakes When Using Mentions

- **Misspelling names** – ensure correct spelling for the mention to work.

- **Over-tagging users** – avoid tagging too many people unless necessary.

- **Not verifying group names** – ensure you're selecting the right team to notify the correct audience.

3. Using Hashtags to Organize and Discover Content

Hashtags help structure conversations and allow users to find related posts easily.

How to Add Hashtags in Viva Engage

1. **Type "#" Before a Keyword**

   o In your post, type "#" followed by a relevant keyword (e.g., #CompanyUpdates).

2. **Ensure the Hashtag is Concise and Clear**

   o Use short and meaningful hashtags (e.g., #ProductLaunch, #HRUpdates).

3. **Post the Content**

   o Once posted, the hashtag will become a clickable link, allowing users to find similar posts.

Searching for Hashtags in Viva Engage

1. Click on an existing hashtag to see all related posts.

2. Use the Viva Engage **search bar** to enter a hashtag (e.g., #CustomerFeedback).

3. Browse through the displayed posts and join conversations.

Best Practices for Using Hashtags

- **Use relevant hashtags** – ensure they match the topic of discussion.

- **Limit the number of hashtags** – 2-3 hashtags per post are ideal.

- **Be consistent** – use standard hashtags within your organization to maintain structure.

Examples of Effective Hashtags

- **For company-wide updates:** #CompanyNews, #HRAnnouncements.

- **For specific departments:** #MarketingUpdates, #TechSupport.

- **For events and campaigns:** #AnnualMeeting2025, #NewProductLaunch.

Common Mistakes When Using Hashtags

- **Using too many hashtags** – excessive hashtags make posts difficult to read.

- **Making hashtags too long** – keep them simple (#ProjectUpdate is better than #CurrentProjectStatusUpdate).

- **Using inconsistent tags** – encourage employees to use predefined hashtags for better organization.

4. Enhancing Engagement with GIFs

GIFs can make workplace interactions more dynamic and engaging.

How to Add a GIF in a Post or Comment

1. **Click on the GIF Icon**

   o When creating a post or comment, click the **GIF button** in the text editor.

2. **Search for a Relevant GIF**

   o Type a keyword (e.g., "celebration" or "teamwork") to find matching GIFs.

3. **Select and Insert the GIF**

   o Click on the GIF you want to use, and it will be added to your post.

When to Use GIFs in Workplace Communication

- **Celebrating Achievements** – acknowledge a job well done (🎉 Congrats! with a celebratory GIF).

- **Welcoming New Employees** – make introductions more friendly.

- **Lightening the Mood** – add humor to conversations when appropriate.

Best Practices for Using GIFs Professionally

- **Keep it workplace-appropriate** – avoid offensive or distracting GIFs.

- **Use GIFs sparingly** – too many can make posts less professional.
- **Ensure accessibility** – provide context if necessary for those who may not see animations.

Common Mistakes When Using GIFs

- **Using distracting or irrelevant GIFs** – ensure they match the conversation's tone.
- **Overusing GIFs** – use them strategically to enhance rather than dominate communication.
- **Choosing low-quality or slow-loading GIFs** – pick well-optimized GIFs that load quickly.

5. Combining Mentions, Hashtags, and GIFs for Maximum Engagement

The best way to leverage these tools is by combining them effectively in a single post.

Example of an Engaging Post with Mentions, Hashtags, and GIFs

"Exciting news, everyone! @MarketingTeam has just launched our new campaign! 🎉 Check out the details below and let us know your thoughts. #MarketingUpdates #NewCampaign 🚀"

This post:

- Mentions a relevant team to ensure they see it.
- Uses hashtags to categorize the post for future reference.
- Includes a celebratory GIF to make it more engaging.

5.2 When to Use Each Element

Situation	Mentions	Hashtags	GIFs
Announcing a new initiative	✓	✓	✓
Asking for feedback	✓	✓	✗
Celebrating team success	✓	✗	✓

Situation	Mentions	Hashtags	GIFs
Providing an update	✓	✓	✗
Casual team discussions	✗	✗	✓

6. Conclusion

Using mentions, hashtags, and GIFs effectively in Viva Engage can significantly enhance workplace communication. By tagging the right people, categorizing discussions with hashtags, and adding GIFs appropriately, users can create engaging, structured, and interactive content.

3.2 Interacting with Content

3.2.1 Liking and Reacting to Posts

Microsoft Viva Engage fosters engagement by allowing users to **like and react** to posts, making it easy to express opinions, support colleagues, and enhance workplace communication. Reacting to posts is an essential feature that helps users quickly show appreciation, agreement, or other emotions without needing to write a response. This section will cover the different types of reactions available, how to use them effectively, best practices, and the impact of reactions in workplace collaboration.

1. Understanding Likes and Reactions in Viva Engage

Reactions in Viva Engage serve as a **quick feedback mechanism** for posts and comments. Instead of writing a reply, users can express their thoughts with just a single click.

The Purpose of Likes and Reactions

- Provide **instant acknowledgment** of a post without adding a comment.
- Encourage **engagement and interaction** among team members.
- Show support, appreciation, or agreement in a **non-intrusive** way.
- Help content creators understand how their posts are perceived.

Available Reaction Options in Viva Engage

While Viva Engage may differ slightly across organizations, it generally includes the following reactions:

Nestor Wilke
Jul 13

Seen by 3   •••

Great post on Social Selling - are you doing it to help customers (and find new ones) or for your own vanity project? It's important to know *why* you are doing this and *what* for....customers can see through us if we're only posting for our own metric collection!

https://www.linkedin.com/pulse/social-selling-index-value-va...

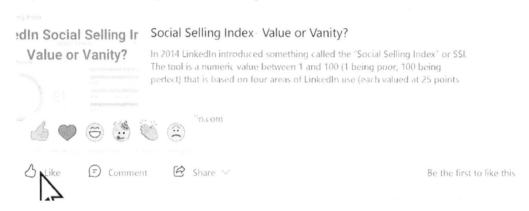

- **Like (👍)** – The standard acknowledgment, showing agreement or appreciation.

- **Celebrate (👏)** – Used to highlight achievements, milestones, or good news.

- **Love (♥️)** – Expresses strong support or admiration for a post.

- **Funny (😄)** – Shows that the content is humorous or entertaining.

These reactions **help add emotional context** to workplace conversations, making interactions feel more dynamic and engaging.

2. How to Like and React to Posts

Liking a Post

The **Like** function is the simplest and most frequently used interaction on Viva Engage. To like a post:

1.   Navigate to the **post** or **comment** you want to engage with.

2. Hover over or click on the **Like (👍) button** below the post.

3. The **thumbs-up icon** will turn blue, indicating that you've liked the post.

4. To remove a like, simply click the **Like button** again.

Using Reactions on a Post

If you want to express a specific reaction beyond a standard "Like," follow these steps:

1. **Hover over the Like button** to see the available reaction options.

2. Select the reaction that best represents your thoughts.

3. The selected reaction will be displayed under the post.

💡 **Tip:** If you accidentally choose the wrong reaction, simply click again and select a new one!

Reacting to Comments and Replies

Reactions are not limited to original posts; they can also be used for **comments and replies** to further encourage discussions.

- Hover over the **comment** you wish to react to.

- Click the **Like button** or hold it to view other reactions.

- Select the appropriate reaction.

This feature helps in recognizing valuable contributions, encouraging discussions, and fostering a more collaborative environment.

---

3. When to Use Likes vs. Other Reactions

While reactions are a great way to interact with posts, it's important to use them appropriately. Here are some **best practices** for using different reactions in the workplace:

When to Use the "Like" Reaction

✅ A post is informative or useful, and you want to acknowledge it.
✅ A colleague shares a status update, and you want to show support.
✅ You agree with an idea but don't have anything to add.

Avoid using "Like" if:

✗ The post is about something sensitive (e.g., job loss, personal struggles).

✗ A different reaction (such as "Insightful") would be more appropriate.

When to Use the "Celebrate" (🎉) Reaction

✓ A team achieves a milestone or completes a project.

✓ A colleague is recognized for outstanding performance.

✓ There's a company-wide event, such as an anniversary or a holiday.

When to Use the "Love" (❤️) Reaction

✓ A post is particularly inspiring or meaningful.

✓ Someone shares a personal achievement, such as a promotion.

✓ A motivational or heartfelt message is posted.

When to Use the "Insightful" (💡) Reaction

✓ The post provides a great idea or learning opportunity.

✓ Someone shares an article, tip, or best practice.

✓ A discussion is thought-provoking and contributes to professional growth.

When to Use the "Funny" (😂) Reaction

✓ A humorous or lighthearted post is shared.

✓ A colleague shares an inside joke relevant to the team.

✓ A workplace meme is posted.

💡 **Tip:** Be mindful when using the "Funny" reaction in professional discussions—it should only be used in appropriate contexts.

---

4. The Impact of Reactions on Workplace Engagement

Encouraging Participation

- Employees who see reactions on their posts feel **recognized and valued**.
- More reactions lead to **higher engagement**, encouraging further discussions.

Boosting Team Morale

- A well-placed **"Celebrate" or "Love" reaction** can boost morale and motivation.

- Encouraging positive reactions helps create a **supportive work culture**.

Enhancing Communication Efficiency

- Reactions allow employees to **express themselves quickly** without needing to type responses.

- They **reduce clutter** in long conversations while still showing engagement.

5. Best Practices for Using Reactions Effectively

✅ Do:

✓☐ Use reactions to provide **quick feedback** without overwhelming a conversation.
✓☐ Choose reactions **thoughtfully** to match the context.
✓☐ Use reactions to **encourage engagement and interaction**.
✓☐ Pay attention to how colleagues **interpret different reactions**.

✖ Don't:

✖ Overuse reactions to the point where they lose meaning.
✖ Use reactions sarcastically or in a way that might confuse others.
✖ React inappropriately to sensitive topics or bad news.
✖ Ignore posts that deserve engagement—sometimes a comment is better than just a reaction!

6. Troubleshooting Common Issues with Reactions

If You Can't See Reaction Options

- Refresh the page or check your **internet connection**.

- Ensure that your **browser is up to date**.

- If using an outdated version of Viva Engage, reactions may not be available.

If You Reacted by Mistake

- Simply hover over the reaction and **select a different one**.

- If needed, remove the reaction completely by clicking on it again.

If Your Reaction Isn't Displaying

- Try reacting again after a few seconds.

- Ensure your **company's Viva Engage settings** haven't disabled reactions.

Conclusion

Liking and reacting to posts in Microsoft Viva Engage is a powerful way to **engage, communicate, and build workplace connections**. By using reactions appropriately, employees can create a more **collaborative, positive, and responsive** work environment.

The next time you read a post in Viva Engage, consider **how your reaction can contribute to the conversation**. Whether it's showing support, celebrating success, or appreciating valuable insights, reactions are a simple yet impactful tool in workplace communication.

3.2.2 Commenting and Replying to Threads

Engaging with posts in **Microsoft Viva Engage** goes beyond simply reading content. Active participation through **comments and replies** fosters collaboration, improves knowledge sharing, and strengthens community engagement. This section will guide you through the different aspects of commenting and replying in Viva Engage, including how to structure meaningful responses, use formatting tools effectively, and manage ongoing conversations efficiently.

1. Understanding the Importance of Commenting and Replying

Comments and replies are essential components of Viva Engage, enabling users to:

- **Provide Feedback** – Acknowledge contributions and share opinions.

- **Ask Questions** – Seek clarification or further information.

- **Engage in Discussions** – Participate in meaningful conversations.

- **Boost Collaboration** – Encourage teamwork and knowledge exchange.

- **Acknowledge Contributions** – Show appreciation for useful posts.

By actively commenting and replying, users contribute to a **more dynamic and engaged workplace** where ideas and knowledge flow seamlessly.

2. How to Comment on a Post

Adding a Comment to a Post

To add a comment to an existing post in Viva Engage:

1. **Locate the Post** – Scroll through your Viva Engage feed or go to a specific group/community.

2. **Click the Comment Box** – Below each post, you will see a field labeled **"Write a comment…"**.

3. **Type Your Comment** – Enter your response in the text box.

4. **Use Formatting Tools (If Available)** – Apply bold, italics, or lists to structure your comment.

5. **Mention People or Use Hashtags (Optional)** –

    o Type **@username** to notify a colleague.

      o   Use **#hashtags** to categorize your response.

6. **Click Post/Send** – Your comment will now be visible to others in the conversation.

Best Practices for Writing Meaningful Comments

A well-crafted comment enhances the conversation and adds value. Consider the following best practices:

- **Be Clear and Concise** – Keep comments short and to the point.

- **Stay Relevant** – Ensure your comment aligns with the topic of the post.

- **Add Value** – Share insights, ask meaningful questions, or provide useful links.

- **Maintain a Professional Tone** – Use respectful and constructive language.

- **Use Emojis and GIFs Appropriately** – Add a human touch but avoid overuse in professional discussions.

Editing or Deleting a Comment

If you need to modify or remove a comment:

1. **Hover over your comment** and look for the **three-dot menu (⋮)**.

2. Select **Edit** to modify the text or **Delete** to remove it permanently.

3. Confirm your action if prompted.

💡 **Tip:** Editing is useful for correcting typos or updating information, while deleting should be used for removing outdated or incorrect comments.

3. How to Reply to a Comment or Thread

Understanding Comment Threads in Viva Engage

A **comment thread** refers to a series of replies within a single conversation, allowing users to engage in deeper discussions.

- **Top-Level Comments** – Direct responses to a post.

- **Replies to Comments** – Responses to a specific comment within the thread.

Replying to a Comment

To reply to a specific comment:

1. **Find the Comment** – Navigate to the post and locate the comment you want to respond to.

2. **Click "Reply"** – Below the comment, you will see a **Reply** button.

3. **Type Your Reply** – Enter your message in the text box.

4. **Format Your Response (If Needed)** – Add bold text, lists, or links for clarity.

5. **Click Send/Post** – Your reply will now be visible beneath the original comment.

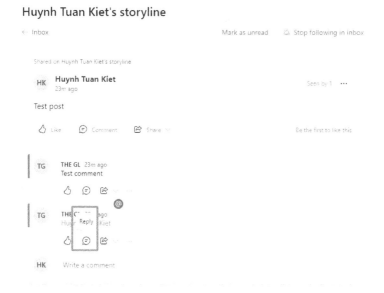

Engaging in an Ongoing Discussion

When participating in an active thread:

- **Acknowledge Previous Comments** – Before replying, read previous responses to avoid redundancy.

- **Use Mentions to Direct Replies** – If responding to a specific person, tag them using **@username**.

- **Keep Replies Concise** – Avoid overly long responses to maintain readability.

- **Respect Different Viewpoints** – Maintain a professional and inclusive tone.

4. Advanced Features for Comments and Replies

Using Rich Text Formatting

Some versions of Viva Engage allow basic text formatting to improve readability.

- **Bold** – text → **text**

- *Italics* –text → *text*

- Inline Code – text → text

- Lists – Use - or 1. for bullet points or numbered lists.

Attaching Files, Images, and Links

Enhance your comments and replies with media and resources:

- **Attach Files** – Upload relevant documents.

- **Insert Images** – Add visuals to clarify points.

- **Embed Links** – Share helpful articles or internal resources.

To attach files:

1. Click the **paperclip icon** (📎).

2. Select the file from your device.

3. Click **Post**.

Using GIFs and Emojis in Comments

- **GIFs** – Click the GIF button and search for an appropriate image.

- **Emojis** – Use ☺ 👍 🎉 to express reactions effectively.

💡 **Tip:** Emojis and GIFs should align with workplace culture—use them professionally.

5. Managing Notifications for Comment Interactions

Enabling or Disabling Comment Notifications

Users can receive alerts for new comments and replies via **email or in-app notifications**.

To adjust notification settings:

1. Click your **profile icon** → **Settings**.

2. Go to **Notifications**.

3. Customize settings for:

   o **Replies to your posts**

   o **Mentions in comments**

   o **Thread updates**

4. Click **Save Changes**.

Following or Unfollowing a Discussion

To stay updated on an important thread:

- Click **Follow Conversation** to receive updates.

- Click **Unfollow** to stop receiving notifications.

6. Moderating Comments and Managing Discussions

Reporting Inappropriate Comments

Admins and users can report comments that violate company policies.

To report a comment:

1. Click the **three-dot menu** next to the comment.

2. Select **Report Comment**.

3. Provide a reason for the report.

Pinning Important Comments

Admins can **pin** key comments for better visibility.

1. Click the **three-dot menu**

2. Select **Pin Comment**.

3. The comment will now appear at the top of the thread.

Closing Comment Threads

In high-traffic discussions, admins may close threads to prevent further replies.

To close a thread:

1. Navigate to the comment thread.

2. Click **Close Discussion**.

7. Best Practices for Engaging in Comment Threads

- **Encourage Constructive Dialogue** – Foster a culture of professional discussions.

- **Acknowledge All Contributions** – Even a simple **"Great point!"** can encourage participation.

- **Use Clear Language** – Avoid jargon or vague responses.

- **Engage Regularly** – Consistent participation helps build a strong workplace community.

- **Set Discussion Guidelines** – If you manage a group, provide engagement rules.

Conclusion

Commenting and replying in **Microsoft Viva Engage** is a powerful way to enhance collaboration, share insights, and build a thriving digital community. By following best practices, using formatting tools effectively, and managing notifications, users can contribute meaningfully to discussions while maintaining professionalism.

3.2.3 Sharing and Reposting Content

Sharing and reposting content in **Microsoft Viva Engage** helps users amplify important messages, foster collaboration, and ensure that valuable discussions reach the right audience. Whether you want to share a company update, highlight a great idea from a colleague, or simply spread useful information across teams, Viva Engage provides several ways to do so.

This section will explore the different methods of sharing and reposting content, when to use each method, and best practices for maximizing engagement.

1. Why Sharing and Reposting Matter

The Role of Sharing in Workplace Communication

In a digital workplace, effective communication is crucial. Sharing and reposting in Viva Engage help:

- **Increase visibility** of important announcements and discussions.

- **Encourage collaboration** by spreading knowledge across different groups.

- **Boost engagement** by involving more team members in ongoing conversations.

- **Break down silos** between departments and ensure everyone stays informed.

Key Differences Between Sharing and Reposting

Before diving into how to share and repost, it's important to understand the key differences:

Feature	Sharing	Reposting
Definition	Allows you to share a post in its original form while adding your own comments or context.	Directly republishes an existing post, keeping the original content intact.
Visibility	The post appears as a new post in the selected group or community.	The post remains in the original location but is bumped up for visibility.
Best Use Case	When you want to **add personal insights** or context before sharing.	When you want to **resurface an important post** without adding comments.

2. How to Share Content in Viva Engage

Sharing content allows you to distribute posts to different groups or individuals.

Sharing a Post to Another Group or Feed

To share a post with another group:

1.   Locate the post you want to share.

2.   Click the **Share** button below the post.

3.   Choose where you want to share it:

     o   A different **group**

     o   Your **personal feed**

4.   (Optional) Add your own comments or additional context.

5.   Click **Post** to share.

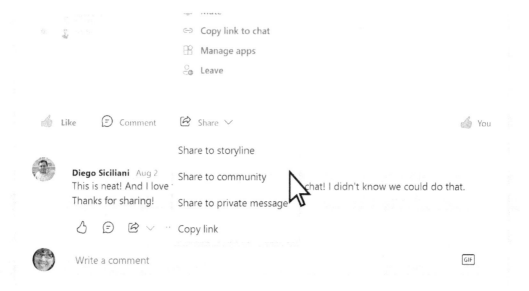

Example:

Imagine your HR department posts an update about a new company benefit. You can share this post with your team's group and add a comment like:

"Exciting news! Our company just introduced a new wellness program. Check out the details below!"

2.2 Sharing Content via Direct Message

Sometimes, you may want to share content privately with specific colleagues.

Steps to share via direct message:

1. Click **Share** on the post.

2. Select **Direct Message** instead of a group.

3. Enter the names of recipients.

4. Add a message if needed.

5. Click **Send**.

This is useful for highlighting important discussions without making them public.

2.3 Sharing External Content to Viva Engage

You can also share articles, reports, or insights from external sources.

Steps to share external content:

1. Copy the **link** to the article or document.

2. Open **Viva Engage** and go to the group where you want to share it.

3. Click **Create Post** and paste the link.

4. Add a caption explaining why it's relevant.

5. Click **Post** to share.

Example:
"I found this great article on industry trends! Thought this might be useful for our upcoming strategy meeting."

3. Repost Content in Viva Engage

Reposting content allows you to **bring attention back to an existing post** without modifying it.

When to Use Reposting

Reposting is ideal when you want to:

- **Resurface an important announcement** for employees who may have missed it.

- **Keep ongoing discussions active** by bringing old but relevant posts back to the top.

- **Highlight valuable insights** without making unnecessary duplicate posts.

4. Best Practices for Sharing and Reposting

Choosing the Right Audience

Before sharing, consider:
Who will benefit from this post?
Is this relevant to my entire organization or just a specific team?
Would a direct message be more appropriate than a public share?

Adding Value When Sharing

Whenever you share a post, try to **add context** or a personal takeaway. Simply resharing without explanation may not drive engagement.

✓☐ **Do:**

- "This is a great update from our HR team—check out the new wellness program details!"

- "Interesting insights on industry trends. What do you think about this approach?"

✗ **Don't:**

- "Check this out." (Too vague, doesn't provide value)

Avoiding Over-Sharing

While sharing content is valuable, avoid **spamming** groups with excessive reposts or redundant shares.

✓☐ **Good sharing frequency:**

- Once every **few days** for major announcements.

- Weekly highlights for key updates.

✕ Avoid:

- Sharing the same post multiple times in a day.

- Reposting old content that is no longer relevant.

-

Using Analytics to Track Engagement

Some Viva Engage versions allow you to **track engagement metrics** on shared posts.

- Check **likes, comments, and views** to see if your shared content is gaining traction.

- If engagement is low, consider **rewording** your shared posts to make them more compelling.

5. Common Mistakes and How to Avoid Them

Mistake 1: Sharing Without Context

Problem: People ignore posts without clear explanations.
Solution: Always add a reason for sharing.

Mistake 2: Sharing Irrelevant Content

Problem: Employees may feel overwhelmed with unrelated posts.
Solution: Share only content that is relevant to the team or community.

Mistake 3: Overusing Reposting

Problem: Constant reposting can frustrate users.
Solution: Only repost when necessary, and provide a reason.

6. Conclusion

Sharing and reposting content in Microsoft Viva Engage is a powerful way to **enhance communication, increase engagement, and ensure important messages reach the**

right audience. By understanding when and how to share posts effectively, you can contribute to a more connected and informed workplace.

By following best practices—such as **adding context, choosing the right audience, and avoiding over-sharing**—you can maximize the impact of your shared content while keeping discussions relevant and engaging.

3.3 Polls, Questions, and Announcements

3.3.1 Creating Polls to Gather Feedback

In workplace communication, gathering feedback and insights is essential for improving collaboration, decision-making, and engagement. Microsoft Viva Engage provides an easy way to create **polls**, allowing users to ask questions and collect responses from colleagues efficiently. This section will guide you through the process of creating polls, best practices for using them effectively, and tips for maximizing engagement.

1. Understanding Polls in Viva Engage

What is a Poll?

A poll is a type of post that enables users to ask a multiple-choice question and receive responses from their audience. It is a quick and structured way to gather feedback without requiring long responses.

Why Use Polls?

Polls in Viva Engage serve several important purposes, such as:

- **Decision-making:** Gather opinions from team members to guide business strategies.

- **Employee engagement:** Encourage participation in discussions by allowing users to vote.

- **Feedback collection:** Understand employee preferences, concerns, and suggestions.

- **Knowledge sharing:** Test employees' understanding of a topic or gauge interest in an event.

2. How to Create a Poll in Microsoft Viva Engage

Steps to Create a Poll

Follow these steps to create a poll in Viva Engage:

1. **Open Viva Engage on the Web** and navigate to the group or community where you want to post the poll.

2. Click on the **"Create Post"** button at the top of the page.

3. Select the **"Poll"** option from the available post types.

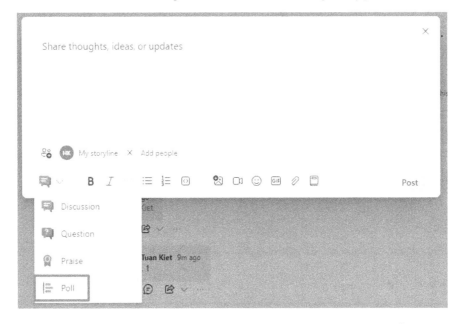

4. In the **question field**, enter the question you want to ask.

5. Provide **multiple-choice options** for respondents to choose from (usually 2–4 choices).

6. (Optional) Adjust settings such as **poll duration** (how long the poll remains open).

7. Click **"Post"** to publish the poll.

3. Best Practices for Creating Effective Polls

- Writing Clear and Concise Questions

A well-crafted question increases participation and ensures meaningful responses. Keep these tips in mind:

- **Be specific:** Avoid vague questions like "Do you like this idea?" Instead, ask, "Which of these project timelines do you prefer?"

- **Use simple language:** Make sure the question is easy to understand for all employees.

- **Keep it neutral:** Avoid biased wording that influences the responses.

Example of a Good Poll Question:
✓ *"Which of the following remote work tools do you find most helpful?"*

Example of a Poor Poll Question:
✗ *"Don't you agree that our new project management tool is amazing?"* (This is leading and biased).

- Choosing the Right Number of Answer Options

- **Too few options** (e.g., Yes/No) may not capture the full range of opinions.

- **Too many options** may overwhelm participants and reduce engagement.

- **Ideally, 3 to 5 options** provide a balanced range of choices.

Example of a Well-Designed Poll:
📋 *"Which communication method do you prefer for daily updates?"*
1. Microsoft Teams Chat
2. Email Updates
3. Viva Engage Posts
4. Video Meetings

- Encouraging Participation

To maximize engagement, try these strategies:

- **Pin important polls** to the top of the group feed so they stay visible.

- **Use mentions (@)** to tag specific team members or departments who should participate.

- **Share the poll in multiple channels** (e.g., Microsoft Teams, email) to reach more employees.

4. Analyzing Poll Results

Viewing and Interpreting Poll Responses

Once your poll receives responses, you can analyze the data to make informed decisions. Viva Engage displays:

- **Total number of votes**

- **Percentage of votes for each option**

- **Who has voted (depending on privacy settings)**

Responding to Poll Results

- If results are clear, use them to **make decisions quickly**.

- If results are split, follow up with **a discussion post** to get more context.

- Share a **summary post** explaining what actions will be taken based on the results.

5. Advanced Polling Features

Using Polls for Employee Engagement

Polls can be used beyond decision-making. Examples include:

- **Icebreaker polls** (*"What's your favorite coffee drink?"*)

- **Fun trivia polls** (*"Guess how many employees joined this year!"*)

- **Well-being check-ins** (*"How are you feeling about remote work?"*)

Integrating Polls with Microsoft Teams and SharePoint

- **Microsoft Teams:** Share your Viva Engage poll in a Teams channel for broader participation.

- **SharePoint:** Embed a Viva Engage poll on your company intranet page to gather insights.

6. Common Challenges and Troubleshooting

Low Participation in Polls

✅ Solution: Promote the poll in different channels, send reminders, or shorten the response time.

Biased or Inconclusive Results

✅ Solution: Reword the question to be more neutral and provide balanced answer choices.

Polls Not Displaying for Some Users

✅ Solution: Check privacy settings and ensure the poll was posted in the correct group.

7. Summary and Key Takeaways

- Polls in Microsoft Viva Engage are an **effective way to gather feedback and drive engagement**.

- To create a successful poll, focus on **clear questions, balanced answer options, and active promotion**.

- Regularly analyze and share poll results to **increase transparency and trust** within the organization.

By using polls strategically, organizations can enhance communication, improve decision-making, and foster a more interactive workplace culture. 🚀

3.3.2 Posting Questions to the Community

Microsoft Viva Engage is designed to foster communication and collaboration within an organization. One of the most effective ways to engage your community and encourage meaningful discussions is by **posting questions**. Whether you're seeking expert opinions, gathering ideas, or troubleshooting a problem, asking the right questions can enhance knowledge sharing and drive valuable interactions.

This section will guide you through the process of posting questions in Viva Engage, best practices for maximizing engagement, and strategies to ensure productive responses.

1. Why Ask Questions in Viva Engage?

Encouraging Collaboration and Knowledge Sharing

Asking questions in Viva Engage helps tap into the collective intelligence of your organization. Employees can share insights, experiences, and best practices, leading to:

- Faster problem-solving

- More innovative ideas

- Greater engagement across teams

Enhancing Learning and Continuous Improvement

By posing thoughtful questions, you create opportunities for professional growth. Team members can learn from experts, clarify doubts, and develop new skills through interactive discussions.

Building a Stronger Workplace Community

Encouraging open-ended discussions through questions helps employees feel heard and valued, promoting a **culture of inclusivity and teamwork**.

2. How to Post a Question in Microsoft Viva Engage

Step-by-Step Guide to Posting a Question

1. **Log into Microsoft Viva Engage** and navigate to the group or community where you want to post your question.

2. Click on the **"Create Post"** button or the **"Ask a Question"** option (if available).

3. In the text box, enter your **question** clearly and concisely.

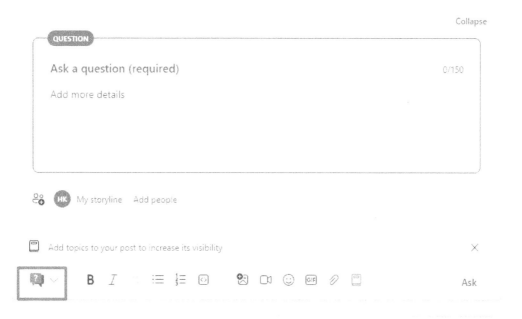

4. Use formatting tools to make your question more readable (bold, bullet points, etc.).

5. Optionally, **add tags** (e.g., #marketing, #ITsupport) to categorize your question.

6. Attach any **relevant files, images, or links** if necessary.

7. Click **"Post"** to publish your question.

Choosing the Right Group or Audience

Before posting your question, consider where it will get the best response:

- **Company-wide groups**: Use these for general inquiries, best practices, or policy-related questions.

- **Departmental groups**: Post here if your question is specific to a team or function.

- **Project-based groups**: Ideal for troubleshooting project-specific issues.

If your organization allows **cross-functional groups**, posting in broader communities can help gain insights from multiple perspectives.

3. Best Practices for Writing Effective Questions

Keep Your Question Clear and Concise

A well-structured question is more likely to receive relevant responses. Follow these guidelines:

- **Be specific**: Instead of "How do I use Viva Engage?" ask, "How can I create a poll in Viva Engage?"

- **Avoid jargon**: Use simple, clear language that everyone can understand.

- **Break it down**: If your question is complex, use bullet points or numbered lists.

Use Open-Ended vs. Close-Ended Questions

Consider whether your question should be **open-ended** (encouraging discussion) or **close-ended** (requiring a yes/no answer):

- **Open-ended:** "What strategies have you used to improve engagement in Viva Engage?"

- **Close-ended:** "Do you prefer email or Viva Engage for internal updates?"

For deeper discussions, open-ended questions usually generate better engagement.

Add Context and Background Information

Provide enough information so respondents can give meaningful answers. For example:
✘ *"How do I manage group settings?"* (Too vague)
✓ *"I'm an admin of a private Viva Engage group. How can I limit who can post announcements while keeping discussions open?"* (Specific and clear)

Tag Relevant People or Groups

Use **@mentions** to direct your question to the right experts:

- **@"JohnDoe"** (if you need insights from a specific person)

- **@"IT Support"** (if addressing a particular team)

This increases visibility and speeds up responses.

Use Hashtags to Categorize Your Question

Adding relevant hashtags like **#HR, #ITSupport, #MarketingTips** helps others find your question more easily.

4. Encouraging Engagement and Quality Responses

Pin or Highlight Important Questions

If your question is **critical** (e.g., policy changes, IT issues), ask an admin to **pin it** at the top of the group.

Engage with Respondents

Once people start responding:

- **Acknowledge contributions** (like or react to their comments).
- **Follow up with clarifying questions** if needed.
- **Summarize key takeaways** after multiple responses.

Accept or Upvote the Best Answer

Some versions of Viva Engage allow marking an answer as **"Best Answer"**. Use this feature to highlight useful responses and help others with similar questions.

5. Examples of Different Question Types

Knowledge-Based Questions

- *"What are some best practices for running virtual town halls using Viva Engage?"*
- *"Can someone explain the difference between Viva Engage and Teams?"*

Problem-Solving Questions

- *"We're struggling with low engagement in our Viva Engage community. Any suggestions?"*
- *"Has anyone found an effective way to integrate Viva Engage with SharePoint?"*

Process-Related Questions

- *"How do I enable post moderation in Viva Engage groups?"*

- *"What's the best way to organize topics in our community discussions?"*

6. Common Mistakes to Avoid

Asking Too Many Questions at Once

⊘ *"How do I create a poll, manage notifications, and delete posts in Viva Engage?"* (Too broad)

✓ Instead, post separate questions or create a **step-by-step discussion thread**.

Posting in the Wrong Group

Make sure your question reaches the right audience. A **technical support question** in a **general announcements group** may not get helpful responses.

Not Following Up on Responses

- If you receive helpful answers, **acknowledge them**.

- If you still need clarification, **ask follow-up questions** instead of reposting.

7. Measuring the Impact of Your Questions

Tracking Engagement Metrics

To see if your questions are effective, check:

- Number of **views** and **responses**.

- The diversity of respondents (are multiple teams engaging?).

- If discussions lead to **actionable solutions** or **improvements**.

Adjusting Your Approach

If engagement is low:

- Try rephrasing your question for clarity.

- Use a different group or broader audience.

- Encourage managers or leaders to contribute first.

Conclusion

Posting questions in Microsoft Viva Engage is a powerful way to drive conversations, improve knowledge-sharing, and strengthen workplace collaboration. By following best practices—crafting clear, engaging questions, tagging relevant users, and encouraging discussion—you can maximize engagement and build a more connected work community.

3.3.3 Making Announcements for Groups

Microsoft Viva Engage provides a powerful way to communicate with teams, departments, and communities within an organization. Among the most effective communication tools in Viva Engage are **announcements**, which allow group admins and leaders to share important updates, company-wide messages, and critical information with group members. In this section, we will explore how to create announcements, customize them for maximum engagement, manage notifications, and track their effectiveness.

1. What Are Announcements in Viva Engage?

An **announcement** in Viva Engage is a special type of post that is highlighted to ensure visibility and reach. Unlike regular posts, announcements:

- Are **pinned to the top** of the group feed for easy access.

- **Trigger notifications** to group members, ensuring they see the message.

- Can be used to **share company updates, team reminders, urgent alerts, or important discussions**.

Only **group admins and moderators** can create announcements. This ensures that announcements are used appropriately and not overused.

2. When to Use Announcements?

Best Use Cases for Announcements

Announcements should be used strategically for **high-priority messages**. Common use cases include:

✓ **Company-wide updates:** New policies, leadership changes, or structural adjustments.

✓ **Project milestones:** Reaching key goals or launching new initiatives.

✓ **Urgent alerts:** Critical IT issues, security updates, or emergency notifications.

✓ **Event reminders:** Important meetings, training sessions, or town halls.

✓ **Employee recognition:** Celebrating achievements, promotions, or anniversaries.

When NOT to Use Announcements

✗ Everyday discussions or casual conversations.

✗ Non-essential updates that do not require high visibility.

✗ Repeated announcements that may cause notification fatigue.

---

3. How to Create an Announcement in Viva Engage?

Creating an announcement in Viva Engage is simple but requires careful planning to ensure clarity and engagement.

Step 1: Navigate to the Group

1. Open **Microsoft Viva Engage** on the web.

2. Go to the **group** where you want to make the announcement.

3. Click on the **Post Box** at the top of the feed.

Step 2: Write a Clear and Engaging Message

When crafting your announcement, keep the following in mind:

★ Be concise but informative: Avoid long paragraphs—get to the point quickly.

★ Use a clear subject line: Example: "🔊*New Remote Work Policy Effective Next Month!*"

★ Use formatting for emphasis: Bold key points, use bullet lists, and keep it scannable.

✓ **Example Announcement:**

🚀 **Exciting News: Our New Hybrid Work Policy is Here!**

Hello Team,

We are thrilled to announce our **new hybrid work policy**, effective **March 1st**. This update provides greater flexibility while maintaining collaboration. Key highlights:

- Work from home up to **three days per week**.

- New meeting guidelines for remote teams.

- Office space upgrades for in-person collaboration.

Check out the full policy document <u>here.</u>
If you have any questions, drop them in the comments!

📅 Join our **Q&A session** on **Friday at 2 PM**.

🎉 Let's embrace the future of work together!

Step 3: Add Media for Engagement

Enhance your announcement with visuals:
☐ **Images** – Infographics, charts, or team photos.
☐☐ **Videos** – A short clip from leadership explaining the update.
📎 **Files/Links** – Attach policy documents, meeting invitations, or resources.

How to add media?

- Click the 📎 **(Attachment) button** to upload files.

- Use the ☐ **(Image) or** 🎥 **(Video) icons** to add media.

- Paste links to external resources (SharePoint, OneDrive, etc.).

Step 4: Mark as an Announcement

1. Before clicking **Post**, look for the **Announcement Toggle** or **Pin Post** option.

2. Select **"Mark as Announcement."**

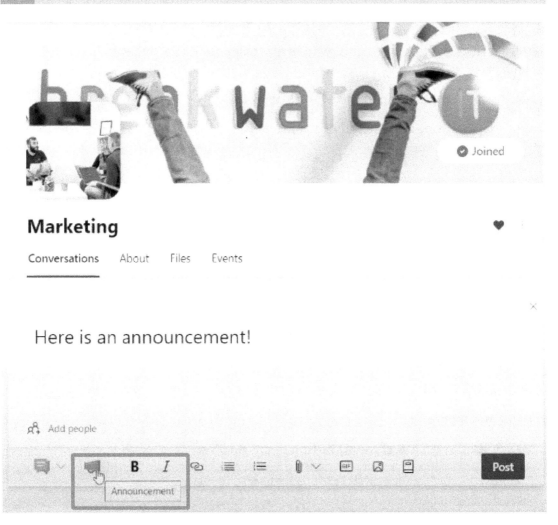

3. Click **Post** to publish.

Your announcement will now appear at the top of the group feed **until unpinned**.

4. Managing Notifications for Announcements

When you create an announcement, **group members automatically receive notifications**. However, you can control how notifications are sent.

Notification Options

🔔 Default Notifications: All group members receive an alert.

📧 Email Alerts: Viva Engage can send an email to all members.

📱 Mobile Push Notifications: Users with the app will get a push notification.

How to Send Email Notifications for an Announcement

To **ensure maximum visibility**, enable email notifications:

1. When creating the announcement, select **"Notify Members via Email."**

2. Group members will receive an **email summary** with the announcement text.

3. Users can click the email to open Viva Engage and respond.

🔊 **Best Practice:** Use email notifications **only for critical updates** to avoid overwhelming users.

---

5. Tracking Engagement and Effectiveness

Once an announcement is live, it's important to monitor its impact.

How to Measure Engagement?

📊 **Post Views:** Check how many users have seen the announcement.

👍 **Reactions:** Gauge sentiment through likes and emojis.

💬 **Comments:** Encourage discussions and answer questions.

🔼 **Shares/Reposts:** See if members are spreading the message.

Using Viva Engage Analytics

Admins can access **Engagement Analytics** to track:

- Number of **unique viewers**.

- Average **time spent** on the post.

- Most common **reactions** and responses.

How to access analytics?

1. Click on the **Announcement Post**.

2. Select **"View Insights" or "Analytics"**.

Tip: If engagement is low, repost the announcement with a different format or send a follow-up reminder.

6. Best Practices for Effective Announcements

Do's and Don'ts

✅ **Do:**
✓☐ Keep announcements **clear and concise**.
✓☐ Use **bold headlines** and formatting for readability.
✓☐ Attach **visuals or videos** for engagement.
✓☐ Encourage **comments and feedback**.

✖ **Don't:**
✖ Overuse announcements (causes notification fatigue).
✖ Post overly **long or complex** messages.
✖ Ignore **follow-up questions** from members.

Timing Matters

☐ **Best times to post announcements:**

- **Morning (8-10 AM):** People check updates early.

- **Lunchtime (12-1 PM):** Higher engagement.

- **Afternoon (3-4 PM):** Good for reminders before the end of the day.

7. Conclusion

Announcements in Microsoft Viva Engage are a **powerful tool** for keeping teams informed, engaged, and aligned. By using announcements strategically, **crafting engaging content**, managing notifications effectively, and tracking engagement, you can ensure your messages reach the right audience at the right time.

🎯 **Key Takeaways:**
Use announcements for high-priority updates.
Enhance posts with images, videos, and documents.

Control notifications to avoid overwhelming users.
Monitor engagement and adjust accordingly.

PART IV
Collaborating with Teams and Colleagues

4.1 Using Viva Engage for Team Collaboration

4.1.1 Sharing Files and Documents

Microsoft Viva Engage is designed to **enhance collaboration and communication** within an organization. One of its most valuable features is the ability to **share files and documents**, allowing teams to easily exchange information, collaborate on projects, and access critical resources in a centralized space.

In this section, we will explore:

- The **types of files** you can share in Viva Engage.

- **How to upload and share files** in groups and private messages.

- Best practices for **organizing and managing shared documents**.

- The integration of **Microsoft 365 tools** like SharePoint and OneDrive for seamless document collaboration.

1. Why File Sharing Matters in Viva Engage?

In any workplace, effective communication goes beyond simple messaging—it requires **the ability to share and access important files effortlessly**. Viva Engage enables employees to:

✓ **Store and share documents** directly in discussions.

✓ **Collaborate on files in real-time** without switching platforms.

✓ **Ensure version control** with Microsoft 365 integrations.

✓ **Reduce email dependency** for file exchanges.

✓ **Improve knowledge sharing** within the organization.

By centralizing document sharing within Viva Engage, teams **streamline collaboration**, **increase efficiency**, and **reduce information silos**.

2. Types of Files You Can Share in Viva Engage

Viva Engage supports various file formats, making it a flexible tool for different workplace needs. You can share:

▪ **Microsoft Office Documents** (Word, Excel, PowerPoint)

⬜⬜ **Images and Graphics** (PNG, JPG, GIF)

⬜⬜ **Videos** (MP4, MOV)

📎 **PDFs and Reports**

💼 **Compressed ZIP Files**

These files can be shared **directly in posts, comments, and private messages**.

3. How to Upload and Share Files in Viva Engage?

Uploading Files in a Viva Engage Group

To share a file in a group:

1▢. **Go to a Group**: Open the Viva Engage group where you want to share the file.

2▢. **Click on the Post Box**: Start a new post.

3▢. **Attach a File**:

Click the 📎 **"Attach File"** icon.

Choose to upload from your **computer**, **OneDrive**, or **SharePoint**.

4▢. **Add a Description**: Provide context or instructions related to the file.

5▢. **Post the Message**: Click **Post** to share the file with the group.

🔊 **Tip:** Use @mentions to **notify specific team members** about the file.

Sharing Files in Private Messages

For one-on-one or small group collaboration, files can be sent via private messages.

1️⃣. Open **Viva Engage Messages**.
2️⃣. Select an **existing chat** or start a **new conversation**.
3️⃣. Click the **"Attach" button (📎)** and select a file.
4️⃣. Add an optional **message or instructions**.
5️⃣. Click **Send** to share the file.

🔊 **Tip:** Private messaging is great for **sensitive documents** or quick file exchanges without cluttering group discussions.

Sharing Files from OneDrive or SharePoint

Instead of uploading a file directly, you can **share a link to a document stored in OneDrive or SharePoint**. This ensures that:

- The **latest version** of the file is always accessible.

- Permissions can be **controlled and managed easily**.

📁 **How to Share from OneDrive/SharePoint?**
1️⃣. In Viva Engage, **create a new post**.
2️⃣. Click **Attach File > Share from OneDrive or SharePoint**.
3️⃣. Select the document from your cloud storage.
4️⃣. Choose the **permissions** (view/edit access).
5️⃣. Post the link in your message.

🔊 **Tip:** Sharing from **OneDrive/SharePoint prevents multiple versions of the same file** from circulating, reducing confusion.

4. Managing Shared Files in Viva Engage

Finding Previously Shared Files

All files shared in a **group** are automatically stored in the **Files** tab of that group.

📌 How to Access Group Files?

1▯. Open the group.
2▯. Click on the **"Files" tab**.
3▯. Browse or search for the document you need.

For **private messages**, shared files can be found within the conversation history.

Editing and Updating Shared Files

Viva Engage integrates with Microsoft 365, allowing **real-time co-editing** of documents.

▢▢ How to Edit a Shared File?

1▯. Click on the **file link** in the post.
2▯. The document opens in **Word, Excel, or PowerPoint Online**.
3▯. Make your edits. Changes **auto-save** and update instantly.

🔊 **Tip:** Avoid **uploading multiple versions** of the same file. Instead, **edit the original document in OneDrive/SharePoint**.

Controlling File Permissions

When sharing documents, it's essential to **manage access rights**:

View Only – Users can read the document but not edit it.
Edit Access – Users can modify the file.
Restricted – Only specific users can access.

🔊 **Tip:** Adjust file permissions **before sharing** to **prevent unauthorized edits**.

Best Practices for File Sharing in Viva Engage

Use Descriptive File Names – Example: "Q1_Sales_Report_2025.xlsx"
Keep Files Organized – Store team documents in **OneDrive or SharePoint**, then share links.
Use Version Control – Avoid creating multiple copies of the same document.
Leverage Real-Time Editing – Co-edit files in Microsoft 365 instead of

downloading/uploading.

Be Mindful of Confidentiality – Restrict access to sensitive information.

5. Common Challenges and Solutions

Challenge	Solution
"I can't find a file someone shared last week."	Use the **Files tab** or **search bar** in Viva Engage.
"I uploaded the wrong document. How do I replace it?"	Delete the post and upload the correct file, or edit the OneDrive/SharePoint link.
"Some users can't edit the file."	Check the **permissions settings** in OneDrive/SharePoint.
"The group has too many duplicate files."	Encourage members to share **links instead of uploading files directly**.

7. Conclusion

Sharing files and documents in Microsoft Viva Engage **enhances collaboration, improves workflow efficiency, and centralizes knowledge** within an organization. Whether sharing a quick update via private messaging or collaborating on a team project in a group, Viva Engage provides seamless integration with Microsoft 365 to ensure **real-time co-editing, proper file management, and easy access**.

By following best practices and leveraging the full potential of Viva Engage's file-sharing capabilities, teams can **work smarter, stay organized, and collaborate effectively**.

4.1.2 Co-editing in Real Time with Microsoft 365 Integration

Collaboration is at the heart of modern workplaces, and Microsoft Viva Engage, when integrated with Microsoft 365, provides seamless real-time co-editing capabilities. This feature allows teams to work together on documents, spreadsheets, and presentations without delays or versioning conflicts. In this section, we will explore how to leverage Viva Engage for real-time co-editing, the tools available, best practices, and troubleshooting common issues.

1. What is Real-Time Co-editing in Viva Engage?

Real-time co-editing refers to the ability for multiple users to simultaneously edit a document while seeing each other's changes in real time. With **Microsoft 365 integration**, this functionality extends to Word, Excel, and PowerPoint files shared within Viva Engage, ensuring that teams can collaborate effectively without the hassle of multiple versions or lost updates.

How It Works

- A team member **uploads or links a Microsoft 365 document** in a Viva Engage post, group, or conversation.

- Other team members **click on the document link** and open it within the Microsoft 365 cloud environment.

- All collaborators **see live updates** as changes are made, with different user cursors and edits appearing instantly.

- The document is **saved automatically**, ensuring that all progress is maintained.

Benefits of Real-Time Co-editing

✅ **Faster Collaboration** – No need to send multiple versions of a document.
✅ **Increased Transparency** – Everyone sees the latest updates as they happen.
✅ **Reduced Errors** – Eliminates versioning issues and outdated files.
✅ **Integrated Workflow** – Users can edit without leaving Viva Engage.

2. Setting Up Real-Time Co-editing in Viva Engage

To enable seamless co-editing within Viva Engage, teams must follow these steps:

Uploading and Sharing a Document for Editing

1. **Go to the Viva Engage Group or Private Message Thread** where collaboration will take place.

2. Click on **Attach File** (paperclip icon).

3. Select **Upload from OneDrive or SharePoint** to ensure real-time co-editing.

4. Choose the document (Word, Excel, or PowerPoint) and **click Upload**.

5. In the post, add context or instructions for collaborators.

6. Click **Post** to share the document with the group.

✦ **Tip:** Always use **OneDrive or SharePoint links** instead of uploading static files to enable live co-editing.

Opening and Editing a Shared Document

1. Click on the **document link** in the Viva Engage post.

2. The file will open in **Word Online, Excel Online, or PowerPoint Online**.

3. Users can **start editing immediately**—changes are saved in real time.

4. Each collaborator's **cursor and edits are visible**, with names indicating who is making changes.

✦ **Tip:** Users can also open the document in the **desktop versions** of Word, Excel, or PowerPoint while still collaborating in real time.

---

3. Key Features of Co-editing in Microsoft 365

Microsoft 365 integration enhances the co-editing experience in Viva Engage with several powerful features:

Live Editing and Autosave

- **Edits appear instantly** to all collaborators.

- The document is **saved automatically**, reducing the risk of data loss.

- Users can **undo changes** using version history.

Commenting and Reviewing

- Users can **leave comments** on specific sections of a document.

- **Mentions (@username)** notify specific users to take action.

- **Track Changes (in Word)** allows for structured edits and approvals.

Version History and Restoring Changes

- Microsoft 365 keeps a **full history of edits**, allowing users to restore previous versions.

- To access: Click **File > Info > Version History** in the document.

- Users can **compare changes** to track progress over time.

Chat and Communication While Editing

- Built-in **Microsoft Teams chat** allows discussion while editing.

- Users can start a **Viva Engage conversation** about the document.

- Comments can include **links, GIFs, or reactions** to provide feedback.

---

4. Best Practices for Effective Co-editing in Viva Engage

Establish Clear Roles and Guidelines

✓ Assign **document owners** to monitor edits.
✓ Use **color-coded highlights** for different team members.
✓ Set **deadlines and expectations** for document completion.

Use Comments Instead of Overwriting Others' Work

✓ Instead of deleting content, use **comments to suggest changes**.
✓ Reply to existing comments to maintain **contextual discussions**.
✓ Mark comments as **"Resolved"** once changes are made.

Avoid Editing Conflicts

✓ Ensure **everyone works on different sections** to prevent overwriting.
✓ Use **Track Changes** for structured editing in Word.
✓ Communicate via **Viva Engage threads or Teams chat** to coordinate edits.

Optimize File Sharing and Permissions

✓ Store documents in **SharePoint or OneDrive**, not local drives.
✓ Set **proper permissions**:

- **"Can Edit"** for active collaborators.

- **"Can View"** for those who need read-only access.
  ✓ Restrict **external access** if working on confidential information.

5. Troubleshooting Common Issues

Despite its efficiency, real-time co-editing can sometimes present challenges. Here's how to resolve them:

Document Not Updating in Real Time

✓ **Solution:** Refresh the document or check internet connectivity.
✓ **Solution:** Ensure all users are accessing the **same document version** in OneDrive/SharePoint.

Unable to Edit a Shared Document

✓ **Solution:** Verify that the file owner has **granted editing permissions**.
✓ **Solution:** Ensure the document is **not in "Read-Only" mode**.

Users Overwriting Each Other's Work

✓ **Solution:** Assign **specific sections** to each collaborator.
✓ **Solution:** Enable **Track Changes** in Word to monitor edits.

Conflicts Between Desktop and Online Edits

✓ **Solution:** Ensure all users are working in **Word Online, Excel Online, or PowerPoint Online**.
✓ **Solution:** If using the desktop app, confirm that **AutoSave** is turned on.

6. Conclusion

Real-time co-editing in Microsoft Viva Engage, powered by Microsoft 365 integration, transforms the way teams collaborate on documents. By using OneDrive and SharePoint for cloud-based file sharing, teams can co-author documents **seamlessly, efficiently, and without version conflicts**.

4.1.3 Using Viva Engage for Knowledge Sharing

In today's fast-paced digital workplace, effective knowledge sharing is essential for organizations to foster innovation, improve collaboration, and enhance productivity. **Microsoft Viva Engage** provides an intuitive platform for employees to share insights, best practices, and valuable resources, making knowledge easily accessible across teams and departments.

This section will explore how Viva Engage facilitates knowledge sharing, best practices for structuring shared knowledge, and how organizations can maximize the benefits of a collaborative learning culture.

---

1. The Importance of Knowledge Sharing in the Workplace

Why Knowledge Sharing Matters

Knowledge sharing helps businesses:

- **Preserve organizational knowledge** – Prevent loss of expertise when employees leave.

- **Enhance productivity** – Reduce the time spent searching for information.

- **Foster innovation** – Encourage employees to contribute new ideas and solutions.

- **Improve collaboration** – Break down silos between teams and departments.

- **Enable continuous learning** – Keep employees updated on best practices and industry trends.

Viva Engage is designed to create a **centralized knowledge-sharing hub**, where employees can contribute, access, and discuss valuable insights.

Types of Knowledge Shared in Viva Engage

Knowledge sharing in Viva Engage typically falls into these categories:

📌 **Best practices** – Tips and strategies for optimizing work processes.
📌 **Company updates** – New policies, industry insights, or leadership messages.
📌 **Project learnings** – Lessons learned from completed initiatives.

★ **Training and tutorials** – How-to guides, videos, and recorded webinars.

★ **FAQs and troubleshooting** – Solutions to common challenges.

By structuring information effectively, employees can **quickly find** and use the knowledge they need.

---

2. How to Use Viva Engage for Knowledge Sharing

Creating a Knowledge Sharing Community

To ensure knowledge is **organized and easily accessible**, companies should create **dedicated communities** within Viva Engage.

Steps to Create a Knowledge Sharing Group:

1. Click **"Create a Community"** on the Viva Engage homepage.

2. Choose a **clear and relevant name** (e.g., "Marketing Best Practices" or "IT Troubleshooting Hub").

3. Set **membership preferences** (open for all or restricted to specific teams).

4. Customize the **group settings** (enable file sharing, pin important posts, and manage permissions).

5. Add **a description and relevant hashtags** to improve searchability.

◄》 **Example:** A company can create a **"Customer Service Insights"** group, where employees share solutions to common customer issues.

Posting Knowledge-Rich Content

To make knowledge sharing effective, posts should be **clear, well-structured, and actionable**.

★ *Tips for Writing Informative Posts:*

✓ Use a **descriptive title** (e.g., "🚀 5 Tips for Writing Engaging Emails")

✓ Keep content **concise and structured** (use bullet points and short paragraphs).

✓ Add **multimedia** (videos, infographics, and screenshots) for better engagement.

✓ Use **hashtags** to improve searchability (e.g., #MarketingTips, #HRBestPractices).

Sharing Documents and Resources

Employees can **upload and share** key documents directly in Viva Engage, ensuring everyone has access to the latest information.

📁 *How to Upload and Share Files:*

1. Click on the **"Attach File"** button when creating a post.

2. Select a document from **OneDrive, SharePoint, or local storage**.

3. Write a **brief description** of the document's purpose.

4. Use **mentions (@) to notify key people** who need the resource.

🎯 **Example:** A sales team can upload a **successful sales pitch deck** so other employees can learn from past wins.

---

3. Engaging with Shared Knowledge

Encouraging Discussions and Q&A

Knowledge sharing works best when employees can **ask questions, provide feedback, and discuss insights**. Viva Engage enables real-time discussions through **comments, reactions, and Q&A threads**.

💡 *How to Encourage Engagement:*

- End each post with an **open-ended question** (e.g., "What are your thoughts on this strategy?").

- Use **polls** to collect feedback from employees.

- Encourage team members to **reply to questions** in the comments.

🔊 **Example:** The IT department shares a post about **cybersecurity best practices** and asks employees to **share personal security tips** in the comments.

Recognizing and Highlighting Valuable Contributions

To motivate employees to contribute, organizations should **recognize valuable contributions** by:

🏆 **Featuring top posts** – Pinning insightful posts at the top of the feed.

🌟 **Giving shoutouts** – Using mentions (@) to appreciate knowledge-sharing efforts.

🔲 **Creating a knowledge champion program** – Rewarding the most active contributors.

🔊 **Example:** A company can create a **"Top Contributor of the Month"** award for employees who actively share valuable insights.

---

4. Integrating Viva Engage with Microsoft 365 for Enhanced Knowledge Sharing

Using Viva Engage with SharePoint

SharePoint serves as a **repository for important company documents**, while Viva Engage acts as a **discussion platform** for sharing and commenting on those documents.

📁 *How to Embed Viva Engage in SharePoint:*

1. Open SharePoint and go to the desired **intranet page**.

2. Click **"Edit" > "Add Web Part"**.

3. Choose **Viva Engage** and select the group you want to display.

4. Employees can now **view and discuss documents directly** in SharePoint.

Using Viva Engage with Microsoft Teams

Microsoft Teams is commonly used for **real-time communication**, while Viva Engage helps with **asynchronous knowledge sharing**.

🔊 *How to Share Viva Engage Knowledge in Teams:*

1. Open the **Viva Engage app within Teams**.

2. Find an insightful post and click **"Share in Teams"**.

3. Choose the relevant **channel or chat** and add a message.

4. Employees can now **discuss the knowledge post in Teams**.

☞ **Example:** An HR team shares **training resources from Viva Engage** in a Teams meeting chat to encourage learning.

5. Measuring the Impact of Knowledge Sharing

Organizations should track knowledge-sharing engagement to **understand what content is valuable** and **improve future contributions**.

Key Metrics to Track:

✦ **Post Engagement** – Number of likes, shares, and comments on knowledge posts.

✦ **File Views and Downloads** – Number of employees accessing shared resources.

✦ **Poll Participation** – How many employees engage in feedback polls?

✦ **Time Spent on Posts** – Identifying which topics retain employee interest.

🔊 *How to Access Analytics in Viva Engage:*

1. Navigate to the **community insights dashboard**.

2. Review engagement trends and identify top contributors.

3. Use insights to **improve content strategy**.

Example: If analytics show that **video tutorials** receive higher engagement than text-based guides, the company can focus on creating more video content.

6. Best Practices for Knowledge Sharing in Viva Engage

✓ **Create a structured knowledge-sharing framework** – Use dedicated groups for different types of knowledge.

✓ **Encourage a collaborative culture** – Motivate employees to share insights and engage in discussions.

✓ **Leverage multimedia content** – Use images, videos, and infographics to make knowledge engaging.

✓ **Use hashtags for better searchability** – Standardize hashtags across departments.

✓ **Monitor and optimize engagement** – Use analytics to refine the knowledge-sharing strategy.

7. Conclusion

Microsoft Viva Engage is a powerful tool for knowledge sharing, enabling employees to collaborate, learn, and contribute valuable insights. By creating structured knowledge-sharing communities, encouraging discussions, integrating with Microsoft 365, and tracking engagement, organizations can build a culture of continuous learning and innovation.

4.2 Private Messaging and Direct Conversations

4.2.1 Sending Messages and Attachments

Effective workplace collaboration requires seamless and efficient communication between team members. **Microsoft Viva Engage** provides a **private messaging** feature that allows users to engage in **direct one-on-one or small group conversations** outside of public group discussions. In this section, we will explore how to send private messages, attach files and media, use message formatting options, and manage privacy settings for effective workplace communication.

---

1. Understanding Private Messaging in Viva Engage

What is Private Messaging?

Private messaging in Viva Engage functions similarly to **direct messaging (DM) in social networks** or **instant messaging tools** like Microsoft Teams. It enables users to:

✓ **Send messages privately** to individuals or small groups.

✓ **Share documents, images, and other media** securely.

✓ **Discuss sensitive topics** outside of public group conversations.

✓ **Collaborate in real-time** without distractions from group discussions.

Private Messages vs. Public Posts

Feature	Private Messages	Public Posts in Groups
Visibility	Only between sender and recipients	Visible to all group members
Best for	Personal conversations, quick Q&As, confidential discussions	Announcements, team discussions, general knowledge sharing
Attachments	Files, images, and links can be shared securely	Files can be shared, but visible to the whole group
Notifications	Recipients receive **direct alerts**	Group members may or may not see the post

Knowing when to use **private messages vs. public posts** ensures clear and effective communication.

---

2. How to Send Private Messages in Viva Engage

Accessing Private Messages

To send a direct message in Viva Engage:

1. **Log in** to Microsoft Viva Engage via your web browser.

2. **Navigate to the Inbox** (usually found in the top-right corner).

3. Click on **"New Message"** or **"Compose"** to start a new chat.

Selecting Recipients

- **Single Chat:** Type the name of the colleague you want to message.

- **Group Chat:** Add multiple recipients to include them in the conversation.

✦ **Tip:** Viva Engage integrates with **Microsoft Entra ID (Azure Active Directory)**, meaning you can search for colleagues using their name or email address.

---

3. Composing and Formatting Messages

Once you've selected your recipient(s), it's time to craft your message.

Writing a Clear and Effective Message

A well-structured message increases clarity and ensures quick responses. Here's a simple framework:

1️⃣. **Greeting:** Start with a friendly introduction (if necessary).
2️⃣. **Context:** Explain the purpose of your message.
3️⃣. **Action:** Clearly state what you need from the recipient.
4️⃣. **Closing:** End with a polite sign-off or next steps.

Example of a Good Message:

Hi Alex,
Hope you're doing well! I wanted to check in about the upcoming **team meeting on Friday**. Could you please send me the latest project updates before then?
Thanks in advance! Looking forward to your response.
Best,
Sarah

⊘ **Example of a Poor Message:**

Hi,
Can you send me that file?

➤ **Tip:** Be specific. Instead of saying **"Can you send me that file?"**, say **"Can you send me the latest budget report in Excel format?"**.

---

4. Attaching Files, Images, and Media

One of the biggest advantages of **private messaging** in Viva Engage is the ability to **attach documents, images, and videos** for seamless collaboration.

Attaching Files

To send an attachment:

1. Click the 📎 **(Attachment) icon** in the message box.

2. Choose **Upload from Computer** or **Attach from OneDrive/SharePoint**.

3. Select the file and click **Send**.

Supported File Types:
📄 **Documents** – Word, PDF, Excel, PowerPoint
☐ **Images** – PNG, JPEG, GIF
🎥 **Videos** – MP4, AVI
📎 **Other files** – ZIP, CSV

➤ **Tip: For large files**, use **OneDrive links** instead of direct uploads to avoid size limitations.

---

5. Sending Images and GIFs for Engagement

Inserting Images

1. Click on the **(Image) icon**.

2. Select an image from your device.

3. Adjust the preview and click **Send**.

Using GIFs and Stickers

- Click the **GIF button** to browse and select an animated image.

- Use **stickers or emojis** to add personality to messages.

- **Example:** "Great job on the presentation! 🎯 🔥"

📌 **Tip:** GIFs and emojis should be used professionally and **avoided in formal discussions**.

---

6. Managing Private Conversations

Editing and Deleting Messages

- **Edit:** Hover over a sent message and click **Edit** to modify it.

- **Delete:** Click **More Options** → **Delete** to remove a message.

💬 **Note:** If the recipient has already seen the message, they may still remember its contents even if deleted.

Muting and Archiving Chats

- **Mute a chat** to stop notifications without leaving the conversation.

- **Archive old chats** to keep the inbox organized.

Blocking Unwanted Messages

If you receive **unwanted or spam messages**, you can:
✅ **Block the sender** to stop future messages.
✅ **Report inappropriate content** to IT administrators.

---

7. Best Practices for Using Private Messaging in Viva Engage

✅ **Do's:**
✓☐ Use private messages for **quick team coordination**.
✓☐ **Be clear and professional** in communication.
✓☐ Share **OneDrive/SharePoint links** for larger files.
✓☐ Mute notifications when **not available** to respond.

✖ **Don'ts:**

✖ Send **urgent business requests** via private messages (use Teams instead).

✖ Spam colleagues with **unnecessary messages**.

✖ Overuse GIFs or emojis in **formal discussions**.

Conclusion

Private messaging in **Microsoft Viva Engage** is a valuable tool for workplace communication. By using direct messages effectively, attaching relevant files, and managing conversations properly, you can enhance **team collaboration** and **productivity**.

4.2.2 Managing Message Threads

Effective communication is crucial in any workplace, and Microsoft Viva Engage provides a streamlined way to manage private messages and direct conversations. While sending messages is straightforward, organizing and managing ongoing **message threads** efficiently can help users stay productive and ensure that important information is easily accessible.

In this section, we will explore:

- What message threads are and why they matter.

- How to organize and manage conversations effectively.

- Best practices for handling multiple conversations.

- Advanced features for improving messaging efficiency.

1. Understanding Message Threads in Viva Engage

What Are Message Threads?

A **message thread** in Viva Engage is a continuous conversation between two or more users in the **private messaging system**. Instead of individual, disconnected messages, conversations are grouped together in a single thread, making it easy to track discussions over time.

Why Are Threads Important?

📌 **Keeps conversations organized** – Instead of scattered messages, everything is in one place.

📌 **Reduces confusion** – Users can follow discussions without searching for older messages.

📌 **Improves collaboration** – Team members can easily refer back to previous discussions.

📌 **Enhances productivity** – Users spend less time looking for information and more time acting on it.

Example:

Imagine a team is discussing a marketing campaign. Instead of creating multiple new messages, they use a single thread to discuss changes, share updates, and attach files related to the campaign.

---

2. How to Manage Message Threads in Viva Engage

Accessing and Navigating Message Threads

1️⃣. **Open Viva Engage on the Web**: Log in with your Microsoft 365 credentials.

2. **Click on the Messaging Icon**: The messaging feature is usually in the **top-right corner** or the side panel.

3️⃣. **Select a Conversation**: Click on any existing conversation to open a thread.

Understanding the Conversation Layout:

- **User Avatar & Name** – Identifies the person you're chatting with.

- **Message Timestamps** – Shows when each message was sent.

- **Reply Box** – Allows you to continue the conversation within the thread.

Deleting a Conversation

If a conversation is **no longer needed**, you can delete it permanently.

☙ *How to Delete a Conversation:*

1. Open the message thread.

2. Click the **three-dot menu.**

3. Select **"Delete Conversation."**

4. Confirm the deletion.

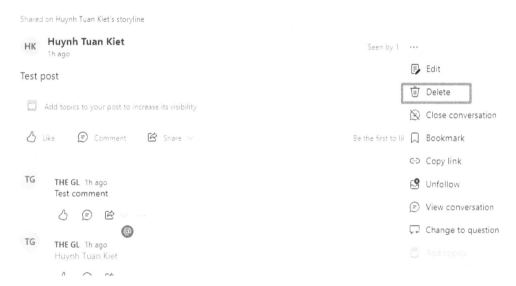

⚠ **Warning:** Deleting a conversation **cannot be undone**. If you might need it later, consider archiving instead.

3. Handling Multiple Message Threads Efficiently

Managing many conversations can become overwhelming. Here are some **best practices** to stay organized:

Using Filters and Search

To quickly find a conversation, use the **search bar** at the top of the messaging window.

🔍 How to Search for a Thread:

- Type a **keyword**, **contact name**, or **topic**.
- Viva Engage will display matching results.

Filters Available:

- **Unread Messages** – View only messages you haven't opened.
- **Pinned Conversations** – Show only important conversations.
- **Mentions** – Find messages where you were @mentioned.

4. Advanced Features for Managing Message Threads

Replying to Specific Messages

In long threads, responding to a specific message prevents confusion.

📧 How to Reply to a Specific Message:

1. Hover over the message.
2. Click **"Reply"** (or long-press on mobile).
3. Type your response.

🔊 **Tip:** Quoting a message helps when answering multiple questions.

Using Mentions (@) to Get Attention

If you're in a group chat, tag someone to **direct their attention**.

📧 How to Mention a User:

- Type **@username** and select the person from the dropdown list.
- They will receive a **notification**.

◀⎞ **Tip:** Use @mentions only when necessary to avoid spamming.

Sending Attachments and Files

You can share documents directly within message threads.

▰ *How to Attach a File:*

1. Click the 📎 **(Attachment) button**.

2. Select a file from **OneDrive, SharePoint, or local storage**.

3. Click **Send**.

◀⎞ **Tip:** If the file is frequently updated, use **SharePoint links** instead of uploading new versions.

Using GIFs, Emojis, and Stickers

Make conversations **more engaging** with visual elements.

- **Click the ▢ Emoji button** to add reactions.

- **Use the GIF button** to find animated responses.

- **Send Stickers** for a fun, informal touch.

◀⎞ **Tip:** Keep GIFs and emojis **professional** in workplace discussions.

Conclusion

Managing message threads in Viva Engage is essential for maintaining clear, organized, and efficient workplace communication. By utilizing features like **pinning important chats, archiving old messages, using mentions, and filtering notifications**, users can navigate multiple conversations with ease.

4.2.3 Using GIFs and Emojis in Chats

Microsoft Viva Engage is designed to **enhance workplace communication** by making conversations more engaging, expressive, and interactive. One of the simplest yet most effective ways to **add personality and emotion** to messages is through the use of **GIFs and emojis**. These elements can help users convey tone, emphasize key points, and create a more human connection in digital interactions.

In this section, we will explore:

- The **importance of GIFs and emojis** in workplace communication

- **How to use them effectively** in Viva Engage chats

- **Best practices and etiquette** for professional environments

1. The Role of GIFs and Emojis in Workplace Communication

Why Use GIFs and Emojis?

While text-based communication is essential, it **lacks the non-verbal cues** of face-to-face conversations, such as body language and tone of voice. GIFs and emojis **fill this gap** by:

✅ **Adding Emotion** – A simple emoji can clarify intent, preventing misunderstandings.
✅ **Making Messages More Engaging** – GIFs make chats more dynamic and fun.
✅ **Encouraging Interaction** – Colleagues are more likely to respond to engaging messages.
✅ **Strengthening Team Culture** – Shared humor and expressive communication foster camaraderie.

When to Use GIFs and Emojis in Viva Engage Chats

Although GIFs and emojis enhance communication, they should be **used appropriately** in a professional setting. Here are some **ideal situations**:

✔ **Acknowledging Messages:** 👍 (Thumbs up) or ✅ (Checkmark) for quick confirmations.
✔ **Celebrating Achievements:** 🎉 (Party Popper) or 🏆 (Trophy) for team wins.
✔ **Expressing Encouragement:** 💪 (Flexed Biceps) or ☺ (Smiling Face) for motivation.
✔ **Lightening the Mood:** A well-placed GIF can reduce tension and foster a positive work environment.

2. How to Use Emojis in Viva Engage Chats

Adding Emojis to Messages

Emojis in Viva Engage can be used in **both direct messages and group conversations**. To insert an emoji:

1. Click on the **chat box** in Viva Engage.

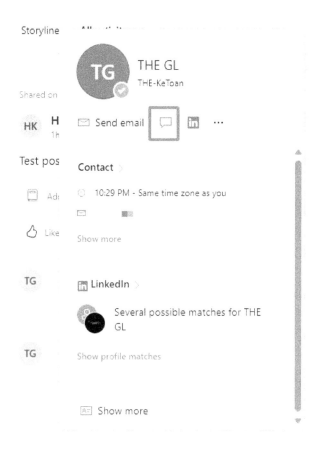

2. Look for the **emoji icon (☺)** in the toolbar.

3. Click on it to open the emoji menu.

4. Choose an emoji **or use a text shortcut** (e.g., :) converts to ☺).

5. Press **Enter** to send your message.

📌 **Shortcut Tip:** Many emojis can be typed directly using **colon codes**. For example:

- :smile: → ☺
- :thumbsup: → 👍
- :fire: → 🔥

Reacting to Messages with Emojis

Instead of typing a response, you can **react to messages** using emoji-based reactions.

Steps to react to a message:

1. Hover over the message.
2. Click the **reaction button** (often a smiley face or thumbs-up).
3. Select an appropriate reaction (👍 ❤️☐ 😄 🎉).

📌 **Use Case Example:**

- If a colleague announces a successful project completion, you can **react with** 🎉 **or** ✋.
- If someone shares an important update, you can use 👍 **to acknowledge receipt**.

3. How to Use GIFs in Viva Engage Chats

GIFs (Graphics Interchange Format) are **short, looping animations** that add humor, energy, and expression to conversations.

Sending a GIF in Viva Engage Chats

To send a GIF in Viva Engage:

1. Open a **direct message or group chat**.

2. Click the **GIF button (☐☐ or GIF)** next to the message input box.

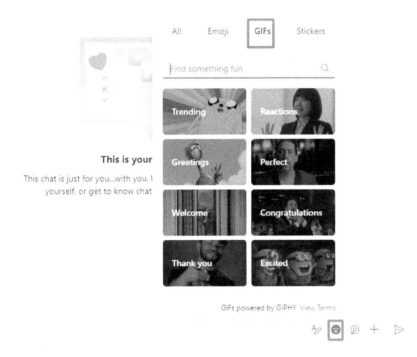

3. Use the **search bar** to find an appropriate GIF (e.g., "Great Job", "Excited", "Thank You").

4. Click on the GIF to insert it into the chat.

5. Press **Enter** to send the message.

📌 **Example Scenarios:**

- **Welcoming a new teammate?** Send a GIF of a waving hand.

- **Congratulating a colleague?** Use a celebratory GIF.

- **Sharing good news?** Send an excited or happy GIF.

Using GIF Shortcuts

If your Viva Engage platform supports keyboard-based GIF integration, you can:

- Type /giphy [keyword] (if enabled) to insert a GIF automatically.

- Some workplaces may allow /gif [keyword] to find and send a GIF.

4. Best Practices for Using GIFs and Emojis in Viva Engage

Dos and Don'ts

✅ **Do:**
✓ Use emojis to **add clarity and friendliness**.
✓ Use GIFs **sparingly** to enhance communication.
✓ Make sure emojis and GIFs **fit the tone of the conversation**.
✓ React to posts with emojis to **show engagement without typing long replies**.

✖ **Don't:**
✖ Overuse GIFs in professional discussions.
✖ Use inappropriate or offensive images.
✖ Replace entire messages with just emojis—keep messages clear.
✖ Send large numbers of GIFs in quick succession (it can be distracting).

Understanding Workplace Etiquette

While Viva Engage encourages **casual and expressive communication**, workplace culture varies. Some teams **embrace GIFs and emojis**, while others **prefer a more formal tone**.

📌 **Check the company's culture:**

- If leadership frequently uses emojis and GIFs, they are likely acceptable.

- If most messages are formal, limit GIFs to casual chats.

📌 **Be mindful of different interpretations:**

- Some emojis can have **multiple meanings** based on culture and context.

- When in doubt, **use universally understood emojis** (👍 ☺ 🎉).

5. Customizing Emoji and GIF Preferences in Viva Engage

If you prefer **not to see GIFs** or want to control how emojis are displayed, Viva Engage allows users to **customize settings**.

Adjusting Emoji Preferences

To disable emoji auto-conversion:

1. Click on **Settings** in Viva Engage.

2. Navigate to **Chat Preferences**.

3. Toggle off **"Convert text-based emoticons into emojis"**.

Disabling GIFs

If your workplace restricts GIFs, admins may have disabled this feature. However, if allowed:

1. Go to **Settings > Content Preferences**.

2. Toggle **"Show GIFs"** on or off.

Conclusion

GIFs and emojis are **valuable tools** that **enhance workplace communication** by adding emotion, engagement, and clarity. However, they should be **used thoughtfully** to maintain professionalism.

PART V
Advanced Features and Integrations

5.1 Connecting Viva Engage with Microsoft Teams

5.1.1 Accessing Viva Engage from Teams

Microsoft Viva Engage integrates seamlessly with Microsoft Teams, allowing users to stay connected, collaborate, and engage with their communities without leaving the Teams environment. By embedding Viva Engage within Microsoft Teams, organizations can enhance workplace communication, boost employee engagement, and streamline information sharing across teams.

This section will provide a comprehensive guide on how to access Viva Engage from Teams, configure it for optimal usage, and leverage its features effectively.

1. Why Access Viva Engage from Microsoft Teams?

Microsoft Teams serves as the central hub for workplace collaboration, and integrating Viva Engage into Teams provides several benefits:

✅ **Seamless Collaboration** – Users can interact with Viva Engage without switching between multiple apps.

✅ **Improved Engagement** – Employees can stay connected to important conversations within their communities.

✅ **Centralized Communication** – Announcements, updates, and discussions can be accessed directly from Teams.

✅ **Better Productivity** – Reduces distractions by keeping all work-related interactions in one place.

By accessing Viva Engage from Teams, employees can **view posts, reply to discussions, create new content, and engage with colleagues** without ever leaving their primary communication tool.

---

2. Ways to Access Viva Engage from Microsoft Teams

There are multiple ways to access Viva Engage within Microsoft Teams:

Using the Viva Engage App in Teams

The Viva Engage app can be installed directly into Microsoft Teams, allowing users to interact with it just like any other Teams application.

Accessing Viva Engage Through the Web Tab in Teams

Users can create a custom **web tab** inside Teams that links directly to Viva Engage, making it easily accessible.

Receiving Viva Engage Notifications in Teams

Users can configure **notifications** in Teams to stay updated on new posts, mentions, and announcements from Viva Engage.

Each method offers different levels of integration, depending on how an organization wants to use Viva Engage within Teams.

---

3. Installing and Configuring the Viva Engage App in Microsoft Teams

The best way to fully integrate Viva Engage into Microsoft Teams is by installing the **Viva Engage app**. Here's how to do it:

How to Install the Viva Engage App in Teams

Step 1: Open Microsoft Teams

- Launch **Microsoft Teams** on your desktop or web browser.

Step 2: Access the Microsoft Teams App Store

- Click on the **Apps** button on the left navigation bar.

- In the **Search Bar**, type **"Viva Engage"**.

Step 3: Install the Viva Engage App

- Click on the **Viva Engage app** in the search results.

- Click **Add** to install it in your Teams workspace.

Step 4: Pin Viva Engage for Quick Access

- Once installed, click on the **More Options (···) menu** on the left sidebar.

- Find **Viva Engage** and right-click on it.

- Select **Pin** to keep it permanently visible on the sidebar.

After installation, Viva Engage will now be easily accessible within Microsoft Teams.

4. Navigating Viva Engage in Microsoft Teams

Once installed, Viva Engage appears as a full-featured application within Teams. Users can navigate it just like the standalone Viva Engage platform.

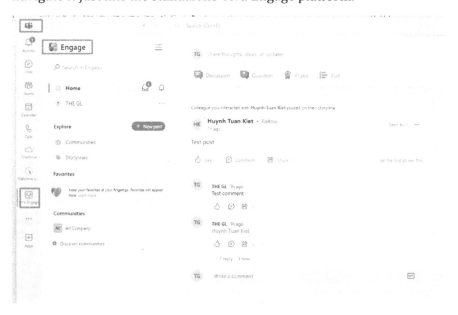

Home Feed

- The **home feed** displays the latest posts, announcements, and discussions.

- Users can **like, comment, and share** posts directly from this view.

Communities & Groups

- Viva Engage communities and groups are accessible under the **Communities tab**.

- Users can **create new groups**, join discussions, and interact with their team members.

Posting and Engaging

- Users can create new posts, ask questions, conduct polls, and share updates.

- All engagement features, including **mentions (@), hashtags (#), GIFs, and file attachments**, work within Teams.

---

5. Adding Viva Engage as a Tab in a Microsoft Teams Channel

For teams that frequently use Viva Engage, it can be **added as a tab** inside a specific Teams channel.

How to Add Viva Engage as a Tab in a Channel

Step 1: Navigate to the Desired Teams Channel

- Open **Microsoft Teams**.

- Go to the **Team and Channel** where you want to add Viva Engage.

Step 2: Add a New Tab

- Click on the **"+" (Add a tab)** button at the top of the channel.

Step 3: Select Viva Engage

- Search for **Viva Engage** in the tab options.

- Select it and click **Add**.

Step 4: Configure the Viva Engage Tab

- Choose the **community or discussion group** to display.

- Click **Save** to finalize.

★ **Tip:** This setup allows teams to have direct access to Viva Engage discussions **within their specific Teams channels**, improving communication and collaboration.

---

6. Configuring Viva Engage Notifications in Teams

To ensure users **never miss important updates**, Viva Engage notifications can be enabled in Microsoft Teams.

How to Enable Notifications for Viva Engage in Teams

Step 1: Open the Viva Engage App in Teams

- Navigate to the **Viva Engage app** inside Microsoft Teams.

Step 2: Go to Settings

- Click on the **Settings (⚙☐) icon** in the top right corner.

Step 3: Customize Notification Preferences

Users can choose to receive notifications for:
✅ **New posts and announcements** in their communities.
✅ **Mentions (@username) and replies** to their posts.
✅ **New conversations in followed groups**.

🔔 **Tip:** Users can **mute notifications** for less critical updates to avoid distractions.

---

7. Common Issues and Troubleshooting

Even with a seamless integration, users may encounter issues when accessing Viva Engage from Teams. Below are some **common problems and solutions**:

Issue: Viva Engage App Not Visible in Teams

◆ **Solution:** Ensure Viva Engage is installed and pinned on the Teams sidebar.

Issue: Notifications Are Not Appearing

◆ **Solution:** Check **notification settings** in both Viva Engage and Microsoft Teams.

Issue: Cannot Post or Engage in Viva Engage

◆ **Solution:** Confirm **user permissions**; some companies restrict posting rights to specific roles.

---

8. Best Practices for Using Viva Engage in Teams

⊙ **Encourage Regular Engagement** – Train employees to check Viva Engage discussions regularly.
✦ **Pin Important Communities** – Keep key communities accessible for quick reference.
⚐ **Use Announcements Wisely** – Avoid overloading employees with unnecessary alerts.
▥ **Leverage Analytics** – Monitor engagement levels and adjust communication strategies accordingly.

---

9. Conclusion

By integrating Viva Engage with Microsoft Teams, organizations can create a more **collaborative, connected, and engaged workplace**. The ability to access Viva Engage from within Teams eliminates the need to switch between platforms, allowing employees to **stay informed, participate in discussions, and collaborate effectively**.

5.1.2 Sharing Viva Engage Posts in Teams

Microsoft Viva Engage is a powerful platform designed to enhance workplace communication, knowledge sharing, and team collaboration. However, when combined with **Microsoft Teams**, it becomes an even more effective tool for organizations that rely on **both synchronous and asynchronous communication**. Sharing **Viva Engage posts** directly in Teams allows users to extend discussions, bring in more stakeholders, and enhance visibility across platforms.

In this section, we will explore why sharing **Viva Engage posts in Teams** is beneficial, how to do it effectively, and best practices for maximizing engagement.

---

1. Why Share Viva Engage Posts in Microsoft Teams?

Integrating Viva Engage posts into Teams offers several advantages for workplace communication:

Enhancing Cross-Platform Communication

- **Teams is for real-time collaboration**, while **Viva Engage is for broader discussions**.

- Sharing a Viva Engage post in Teams ensures **important conversations** are not missed.

- Users who primarily work in **Teams** can engage with Viva Engage content **without switching platforms**.

Increasing Visibility of Important Updates

- Announcements, discussions, and questions in Viva Engage can be **pushed to Teams channels** for greater visibility.

- Users in Teams can **react, comment, and share insights** without logging into Viva Engage separately.

Encouraging Broader Participation

- Some employees may not check Viva Engage regularly but are active in Teams.

- Sharing posts in Teams ensures that discussions reach a **wider audience**, including executives, managers, and frontline workers.

---

2. How to Share a Viva Engage Post in Microsoft Teams

Method 1: Using the Viva Engage Share Button

The easiest way to share a post from Viva Engage into a **Microsoft Teams chat or channel** is by using the built-in share feature.

Steps to Share a Post from Viva Engage to Teams:

1. **Open Viva Engage** in a web browser.

2. Locate the **post** you want to share.

3. Click the **"Share" button** below the post.

4. Select **"Share to Teams."**

5. A **pop-up window** will appear, allowing you to:

   o Choose a **specific Teams channel** or **direct message**.

   o Add an **optional message** explaining why you're sharing it.

6. Click **"Send"** to share the post in Teams.

✓ The post will now appear in the **selected Teams chat or channel**, and members can view and interact with it.

Method 2: Copying and Pasting the Viva Engage Post Link

If the "Share to Teams" option is unavailable, you can manually share the post by **copying the link**.

Steps to Copy and Paste a Viva Engage Post Link into Teams:

1. **Go to Viva Engage** and find the post you want to share.

2. Click the **three-dot menu (⋮)** next to the post.

3. Select **"Copy Link."**

4. Open **Microsoft Teams** and navigate to the chat or channel where you want to share the post.

5. Paste the **copied link** into the message box.

6. Add **context or a short message** to encourage engagement.

7. Press **"Send."**

📌 **Tip:** Use @mentions in Teams to notify specific colleagues about the post.

Method 3: Using the Viva Engage App in Teams

For organizations that **frequently share** Viva Engage posts in Teams, installing the **Viva Engage app** in Teams provides a seamless experience.

How to Share Viva Engage Posts via the Teams App:

1. Open **Microsoft Teams**.

2. Click **Apps** in the left sidebar.

3. Search for **"Viva Engage"** and click **"Add."**

4. Go to the **Viva Engage tab** within Teams.

5. Locate the post you want to share.

6. Click **"Share"** → **"Post to Teams."**

7. Choose a **Teams channel** or **chat** and click **Send.**

✅ This method is ideal for **frequent Viva Engage users** who want quick access from within Teams.

---

3. Best Practices for Sharing Viva Engage Posts in Teams

To ensure maximum engagement and effectiveness, follow these best practices when sharing Viva Engage posts in Teams.

Add Context to Shared Posts

When sharing a post, include a short **introductory message** explaining:
✅ Why the post is important.
✅ Who should respond or engage.
✅ What actions are expected.

📌 **Example Message:**

"🔊 Important update! Our **Q1 Sales Strategy** has been posted in Viva Engage. Take a look at the proposed goals and share your thoughts. Let's align before our next team meeting!"

Use @Mentions for Key Stakeholders

- Mention **specific individuals** (@JohnDoe) or **Teams channels** (@MarketingTeam).

- This ensures **relevant team members** see the post.

📌 **Example:**

"Hey @SalesTeam, check out this discussion on lead generation strategies in Viva Engage. Your input would be valuable!"

Avoid Over-Sharing or Spamming

- Not every post needs to be shared in Teams.

- Use **announcements or major updates** for Teams channels, and keep casual discussions within Viva Engage.

- **Set a schedule** (e.g., weekly updates) instead of sharing posts multiple times a day.

Encourage Engagement in Teams

After sharing a post, **prompt discussions** in Teams:

✅ Ask a **question** related to the post.

✅ Encourage **quick reactions** (👍, ❤️□, 🔥).

✅ Request **feedback or insights**.

📌 **Example Prompt:**

"What do you think about the new HR policy shared in Viva Engage? Comment below or reply in Viva Engage!"

3.5 Monitor Responses and Follow Up

- Keep track of **reactions and comments** in Teams.

- If necessary, **redirect discussions back to Viva Engage** to maintain structured conversations.

- Use the **Viva Engage analytics tool** to check engagement levels.

4. Common Issues and Troubleshooting

Shared Post Does Not Appear in Teams

✅ **Check permissions**: Ensure the Viva Engage post is visible to all members.

✅ **Refresh Teams**: Sometimes, posts may not load instantly.

✅ **Manually copy the link** if the "Share to Teams" feature fails.

Users Do Not Engage with the Shared Post

✅ **Rephrase your message**: Make it more engaging.

✅ **Tag key individuals** to drive participation.

✅ **Follow up** with a reminder if the post is important.

Viva Engage App Not Appearing in Teams

✅ Ensure **your organization has enabled the Viva Engage app** in Teams.

✅ Try **logging out and back in**.

✅ Contact **IT support** if the issue persists.

---

5. Conclusion

Sharing **Viva Engage posts in Microsoft Teams** is an effective way to **bridge the gap between real-time collaboration and ongoing discussions**. By following the steps outlined in this chapter, you can **maximize engagement, improve communication flow, and encourage participation** across your organization.

🎯 **Key Takeaways:**

✔☐ **Use multiple sharing methods** (Share button, link, or Teams app).

✔☐ **Provide context** to shared posts for better engagement.

✔☐ **Leverage @mentions** to notify key team members.

✔☐ **Avoid over-sharing** and keep posts relevant.

✔☐ **Monitor engagement** and adjust sharing strategies as needed.

5.1.3 Setting Up Notifications in Teams

Microsoft Viva Engage and Microsoft Teams are two of the most powerful communication tools within the Microsoft 365 ecosystem. By integrating Viva Engage with Teams, users can streamline their workflows, stay updated on important discussions, and ensure they never miss critical announcements. A key part of this integration is **setting up notifications** so that users receive relevant updates without unnecessary distractions.

In this section, we will explore how to configure notifications, customize them to suit different user preferences, manage notification overload, and use best practices to optimize engagement without causing notification fatigue.

1. Understanding Notifications in Microsoft Viva Engage and Teams

Before configuring notifications, it's important to understand how they work in the Viva Engage and Teams integration.

Types of Notifications

When integrating Viva Engage with Teams, users can receive notifications in multiple ways:

🔔 **Teams Activity Feed Alerts** – Notifications appear in the Teams **Activity tab** when there are updates in Viva Engage.

✉ **Chat Notifications** – Viva Engage can send updates as messages within Teams.

📧 **Email Notifications** – Users can choose to receive email summaries of important updates.

📱 **Push Notifications** – If the Teams mobile app is installed, push notifications will appear on the user's device.

What Triggers Notifications?

Notifications can be triggered by:

✅ **Mentions (@yourname)** – When someone tags you in a Viva Engage conversation.

✅ **Group Announcements** – Admins can send critical messages to group members.

✅ **Replies and Reactions** – When someone interacts with your posts.

✅ **New Posts in Followed Groups** – Updates from communities you follow.

✅ **Polls and Questions** – When you're invited to vote or answer.

Understanding these notification types will help you decide **which ones are essential and which ones should be disabled** to avoid overload.

2. How to Enable and Customize Viva Engage Notifications in Teams

Enabling Viva Engage Notifications in Teams

By default, some notifications from Viva Engage may not appear in Teams. To ensure you receive updates, follow these steps:

1. **Open Microsoft Teams** and go to the **Apps** section.

2. In the **search bar**, type **Viva Engage** and select it from the list.

3. Click **Add** to install the app if it is not already available.

4. Once installed, click on **Viva Engage** in the left panel.

5. Go to **Settings > Notifications**.

6. Toggle **Enable Teams Notifications** to ON.

7. Select which types of notifications you want to receive:

   o **All activity (default)** – Get notified for all major updates.

   o **Mentions only** – Receive alerts only when tagged.

   o **Custom** – Manually choose which notifications to enable.

Configuring Notification Preferences

Once enabled, you can fine-tune your notification settings based on your needs.

- Click on your **Profile Picture** in Teams.

- Select **Settings > Notifications**.

- Scroll down to **Viva Engage Notifications**.

- Adjust settings such as:

   o ☐ **Mute specific groups** – Disable notifications from less relevant groups.

   o ☐ **Set frequency** – Choose **Real-time, Hourly, or Daily digest**.

   o ✉ **Turn off email notifications** – If you prefer Teams alerts only.

Best Practice: If you receive too many updates, try **Daily digest mode**, which consolidates multiple updates into one notification.

3. Managing Notification Overload

Receiving too many notifications can be distracting. Here are some tips to **reduce noise while staying informed**:

Using Notification Prioritization

Viva Engage allows users to prioritize certain types of notifications. To do this:

1. Open **Viva Engage** in Microsoft Teams.

2. Go to **Settings > Notifications**.

3. Under **Notification Priority**, choose:

   o **High Priority** – Mentions, direct messages, company-wide announcements.

   o **Medium Priority** – Group posts, poll invitations.

   o **Low Priority** – Likes, reactions, and general updates.

Tip: Set High Priority notifications to **push alerts** and Low Priority notifications to **email summaries** to minimize distractions.

Turning Off Unnecessary Notifications

If certain notifications are overwhelming, disable them:

1. In **Teams**, go to **Settings > Notifications**.

2. Find the **Viva Engage section**.

3. Toggle OFF:

   o **"Someone reacts to your post"**

   o **"A new post is created in a non-critical group"**

   o **"Someone likes your reply"**

Setting Up Quiet Hours

For better work-life balance, set **quiet hours** to silence notifications during non-working hours:

1. Open **Teams mobile app**.

2. Go to **Settings > Notifications > Quiet Hours**.

3. Choose a start and end time.

4. Optionally, set **Quiet Days** (e.g., weekends).

This ensures Viva Engage notifications won't disturb you outside of work.

4. How to Use Viva Engage Notifications for Team Engagement

While controlling notifications is important, using them **strategically** can improve team engagement.

Encouraging Team Participation

To increase engagement, encourage teams to:

✓☐ **Tag colleagues (@mention) in discussions** to notify them of relevant updates.

✓☐ **Use Announcements instead of regular posts** for high-priority messages.

✓☐ **Leverage Polls and Questions** to trigger interactive responses.

Avoiding Notification Fatigue

To ensure people **don't mute Viva Engage**, follow these best practices:

✓ **Send concise updates** instead of multiple posts.

✓ **Use pinned announcements** to reduce repeated notifications.

✓ **Respect user preferences** – don't overuse @mentions.

Conclusion

Setting up notifications for Viva Engage in Microsoft Teams is crucial for staying updated while avoiding information overload. By carefully configuring notification preferences, prioritizing important alerts, and using best practices to engage teams effectively, organizations can enhance communication without overwhelming employees.

5.2 Viva Engage and Microsoft SharePoint

5.2.1 Embedding Viva Engage in SharePoint Pages

Microsoft Viva Engage and SharePoint are two powerful tools within the Microsoft 365 ecosystem that help organizations foster collaboration, communication, and knowledge sharing. By embedding **Viva Engage in SharePoint pages**, businesses can seamlessly integrate social interactions with structured content, making it easier for employees to engage with company updates, discussions, and knowledge bases—all within a unified platform.

In this section, we will explore **why** embedding Viva Engage in SharePoint is beneficial, **how** to set it up, and **best practices** for optimizing its effectiveness.

1. Why Embed Viva Engage in SharePoint?

Integrating **Viva Engage** into **SharePoint Online** enables organizations to create a more interactive and social intranet experience. Here are some key benefits:

Improved Employee Engagement

Embedding Viva Engage in SharePoint makes it easier for employees to interact with company announcements, discussions, and social feeds without having to switch between different applications. This fosters better engagement and participation.

Centralized Communication Hub

SharePoint serves as a structured content repository, while Viva Engage facilitates real-time discussions and collaboration. By embedding Viva Engage, organizations can create a **one-stop hub** for both formal and informal communication.

Increased Collaboration and Knowledge Sharing

Employees can share ideas, ask questions, and discuss company updates directly from SharePoint pages. This helps break down silos and encourages cross-team collaboration.

Streamlined Information Access

Users can see the latest updates, announcements, and conversations **without leaving SharePoint**, reducing the need for excessive emails or multiple platforms.

Enhanced Internal Branding

Organizations can customize SharePoint pages with embedded Viva Engage feeds to reflect corporate culture, making it easier to communicate the company's vision, mission, and initiatives.

2. How to Embed Viva Engage in SharePoint

Embedding a Viva Engage feed or conversation into SharePoint Online requires **adding the Viva Engage web part** to a page. Follow these steps to integrate Viva Engage into your SharePoint site effectively.

Step 1: Navigate to the SharePoint Page

1. Open **SharePoint Online** in your web browser.

2. Navigate to the **page** where you want to embed the Viva Engage feed.

3. Click the **Settings (⚙□) button** in the top-right corner.

4. Select **"Edit Page"** to enable editing mode.

Step 2: Add a Viva Engage Web Part

1. Click the **"+" (Add a Web Part)** button on the section of the page where you want to place the Viva Engage feed.

2. In the web part search box, type **"Viva Engage"** or **"Yammer"** (since Viva Engage was formerly known as Yammer).

3. Select the **"Viva Engage Conversations"** web part.

Step 3: Configure the Viva Engage Web Part

1. Once added, click the **"Edit Web Part" (▬·□ icon)** on the Viva Engage web part.

2. Choose the **source** of the Viva Engage content:

   o **A specific group** (e.g., HR Updates, IT Announcements).

   o **The entire Viva Engage network** (for broader engagement).

     o   **A specific topic or hashtag** (e.g., #CompanyNews, #Wellness).

3. Customize the feed display settings (number of posts shown, sorting order).

Step 4: Save and Publish the Page

1. Click **"Apply"** to save the changes.

2. Click **"Publish"** to make the updated SharePoint page available to users.

---

3. Best Practices for Embedding Viva Engage in SharePoint

To maximize the impact of your Viva Engage integration, follow these best practices:

Choose the Right Viva Engage Group for Your Audience

- If embedding on a **company-wide intranet homepage**, use **a general announcements group**.

- If embedding in a **department-specific SharePoint site**, choose a **relevant team's Viva Engage group**.

- For **project collaboration pages**, embed **a dedicated project group** where members can share updates.

Organize SharePoint Layout for Better User Experience

- Place the Viva Engage feed **at the top of the page** for high visibility.

- Combine it with other **SharePoint web parts**, such as **News, Quick Links, and Events**.

- Use **column layouts** to balance structured content (documents, policies) with dynamic discussions.

Encourage Employee Participation

- Post a **welcome message** on Viva Engage and pin it to the top of the group.

- Encourage managers and leaders to interact with posts to **drive engagement**.

- Set up **weekly discussion topics** to keep conversations active.

Optimize Notification Settings

- Enable **SharePoint notifications** to alert users about new Viva Engage discussions.

- Configure **digest emails** to keep employees informed without overwhelming them.

4. Troubleshooting Common Issues

Viva Engage Web Part Not Displaying Content

✅ **Solution:** Check if the user has the appropriate **Viva Engage permissions**. Ensure that the group or feed is **public** or that users are **members of the group**.

Slow Page Load Time

✅ **Solution:** Reduce the number of posts displayed in the Viva Engage web part to **5-10 posts** instead of loading the full feed.

Formatting Issues

✅ **Solution:** Ensure the SharePoint page is in **modern mode** and not in **classic mode**, which may cause layout issues.

Comments and Likes Not Syncing

✅ **Solution:** Refresh the page or clear the browser cache to update the embedded feed properly.

5. Advanced Customization: Embedding Viva Engage with SharePoint Framework (SPFx)

For organizations that require **greater customization**, developers can use **SharePoint Framework (SPFx)** to embed and control Viva Engage content dynamically.

Why Use SPFx for Viva Engage Integration?

✅ Enables **custom styling** to match company branding.
✅ Allows integration with **other Microsoft 365 services**.
✅ Provides more **control over user experience and interaction**.

Steps to Embed Viva Engage Using SPFx

1. Use **Visual Studio Code** to create an SPFx web part.

2. Install **Microsoft Viva Engage APIs** and authentication settings.

3. Fetch Viva Engage data using **REST API**.

4. Apply custom CSS styles for better display.

5. Deploy the web part in **SharePoint Online**.

This approach is ideal for IT teams that want **deeper customization** and a seamless user experience.

6. Conclusion

Embedding Viva Engage in SharePoint provides a **powerful way** to bring social collaboration into a structured intranet environment. Whether using the built-in Viva Engage web part or advanced SharePoint Framework customization, businesses can create **engaging, interactive, and informative digital workplaces**.

5.2.2 Using Viva Engage for Intranet Communications

As organizations move towards more integrated, digital communication platforms, **Microsoft Viva Engage** and **Microsoft SharePoint** serve as two critical pillars for fostering a connected workplace. While SharePoint is widely recognized as a powerful tool for managing documents, internal websites, and collaboration hubs, Viva Engage enhances these functions by adding a social layer for communication and interaction. The integration between these two tools creates a dynamic intranet experience that empowers employees to collaborate, share information, and communicate more effectively.

In this section, we will explore how Viva Engage can be used for **intranet communications** within an organization. We'll cover how to leverage SharePoint for content management, how to integrate Viva Engage into SharePoint pages, and the benefits of creating an intranet experience that enhances employee engagement and information flow.

1. Introduction to Intranet Communications with Viva Engage and SharePoint

Before diving into the specifics of integrating Viva Engage with SharePoint, it's essential to understand the role of **intranet communication** in modern organizations.

An **intranet** is a private network that is used within an organization to share information, conduct internal communications, and collaborate on projects. Traditionally, intranets were primarily **document repositories** and **internal communication channels** like newsletters or company announcements. However, with the rise of social collaboration tools like Viva Engage, the intranet has evolved into an **interactive, real-time communication platform**.

Intranet communication is essential for:

- Promoting **organizational transparency** and aligning employees with company goals.

- Fostering a **collaborative culture** where teams can share ideas and solve problems together.

- Ensuring **easy access to information**, policies, and resources across the organization.

- Encouraging **employee engagement** through feedback, interaction, and social recognition.

By integrating Viva Engage into SharePoint, organizations can create a **rich and engaging intranet** that empowers employees to stay informed, connected, and engaged with their workplace.

2. Integrating Viva Engage into SharePoint Pages

One of the primary ways to leverage Viva Engage for intranet communication is by embedding **Viva Engage widgets** and **posts** directly within **SharePoint pages**. This seamless integration brings **social interaction features** directly into your SharePoint intranet experience, allowing employees to engage with the content and each other in real-time.

Embedding Viva Engage Web Parts into SharePoint

To integrate Viva Engage into your SharePoint pages, Microsoft provides **Viva Engage Web Parts**, which can be added to modern SharePoint site pages. These Web Parts allow you to display various types of Viva Engage content such as group feeds, conversations, and posts directly within SharePoint. Here's how to do it:

Step 1: Access Your SharePoint Site

1. Navigate to your **SharePoint site** where you want to add the Viva Engage content.

2. Select the **page** where you want to embed Viva Engage.

Step 2: Add the Viva Engage Web Part

1. Click **Edit** at the top of the page to enter the page editing mode.

2. In the section where you want to add the Viva Engage widget, select the **"+" button** to add a new Web Part.

3. From the list of Web Parts, select **Viva Engage**.

4. Choose the specific Web Part you want to add:

   o **Group Feed:** Displays a group's posts and discussions.

   o **Top Posts:** Displays popular or most engaged posts across Viva Engage.

   o **Recent Conversations:** Displays the latest conversations within a group.

Step 3: Customize the Web Part

After selecting the Web Part, customize it to fit the needs of your intranet page:

- **Choose the group** whose feed you want to display.

- **Filter posts** by date or engagement level.

- **Adjust the layout** (list view, card view, etc.) to align with the design of your SharePoint page.

- **Add a call to action** (CTA) for engagement, like "Join the Discussion" or "See More Posts."

Step 4: Publish the Page

Once you've added and customized the Viva Engage Web Part, click **Publish** to make the page live. Employees visiting this page will now be able to see the latest posts and interact with Viva Engage content directly within SharePoint.

3. Benefits of Using Viva Engage for Intranet Communications

Integrating Viva Engage into your intranet communication strategy offers numerous benefits, helping create a **more connected, collaborative, and engaged workforce**. Let's explore some of the key advantages:

Real-Time Communication and Engagement

Traditional intranet systems often provided static content, such as documents or announcements, but lacked real-time engagement features. Viva Engage brings a dynamic, **social interaction layer** to your intranet, allowing employees to:

- Share **ideas** and **feedback** instantly with posts, comments, and reactions.

- **Engage in discussions** with colleagues from different departments and locations.

- Use **mentions**, **hashtags**, and **emojis** to increase the visibility and engagement of their posts.

By incorporating this interactive feature into SharePoint pages, organizations can keep the conversation flowing and ensure that information is not just shared but **actively discussed and acted upon**.

Promoting Organizational Transparency and Communication

Integrating Viva Engage into your SharePoint intranet helps drive **transparency** within the organization. Key announcements, policy changes, or important initiatives can be posted on Viva Engage and embedded directly into SharePoint, ensuring they reach a broader audience. Employees are encouraged to engage with these posts, ask questions, and provide feedback, leading to **better communication** and clearer understanding of company goals and strategies.

Creating a Culture of Knowledge Sharing

Viva Engage promotes a **culture of knowledge sharing** by allowing employees to create posts, ask questions, share documents, and contribute to discussions. By embedding Viva Engage within SharePoint, organizations can:

- **Encourage cross-team collaboration**, where employees can share knowledge and resources across departments.

- Provide an **interactive platform** where employees can discuss best practices, lessons learned, and industry trends.

- Create **knowledge hubs** by grouping related posts and discussions in specific Viva Engage groups, making it easier to access relevant information.

Facilitating Employee Recognition and Engagement

With Viva Engage embedded in SharePoint, employee recognition becomes more accessible. Leaders can **acknowledge employee achievements**, share company-wide recognition posts, and celebrate milestones directly on the intranet. This boosts employee morale and encourages participation. By engaging with these posts and celebrating their colleagues, employees feel more connected to their workplace and motivated to contribute.

4. Best Practices for Using Viva Engage for Intranet Communications

To maximize the effectiveness of Viva Engage for intranet communications, consider these best practices:

Define Clear Communication Guidelines

While Viva Engage is a great platform for informal communication and social interaction, it's important to have clear guidelines in place for how it should be used within your organization. Establish policies regarding:

- What types of content should be shared.

- What is considered appropriate in terms of tone and language.

- How employees should engage with content (e.g., using respectful comments, providing constructive feedback).

Having these guidelines ensures that Viva Engage remains a productive and respectful space for communication.

Encourage Leadership Engagement

For Viva Engage to truly have an impact on intranet communications, it's important for leadership to engage with the platform regularly. When leaders share updates, recognize achievements, and engage in discussions, employees feel more connected to the company's direction and leadership. Encourage leaders to post regular updates, host Q&A sessions, and recognize employee contributions.

Monitor and Respond to Engagement

Monitor the engagement with posts on your SharePoint-integrated Viva Engage feed. Track how employees are interacting with content and respond to comments or questions in a timely manner. This encourages continued interaction and shows employees that their voices are valued.

Promote Internal Campaigns and Initiatives

Use Viva Engage to promote internal campaigns such as wellness programs, training opportunities, or diversity initiatives. By embedding these posts within SharePoint pages, employees are more likely to notice and engage with them.

5. Conclusion

Using **Viva Engage for intranet communications** through SharePoint offers a unique opportunity for organizations to create a **dynamic and interactive workplace**. The integration of social communication features into the traditional intranet system promotes engagement, collaboration, and transparency, resulting in a more connected and informed workforce. By embedding Viva Engage directly into SharePoint pages, organizations can foster an environment where communication flows freely, knowledge is shared openly, and employees are motivated to stay engaged with company activities and updates.

Leveraging the full potential of this integration can be a game-changer for your organization's internal communications, enabling better collaboration, faster decision-making, and a more empowered workforce.

5.2.3 Sharing SharePoint Files in Viva Engage

In today's collaborative workplace, integrating tools and platforms to ensure seamless communication and information sharing is essential. One of the most powerful integrations in the Microsoft ecosystem is between **Microsoft Viva Engage** and **Microsoft SharePoint**. SharePoint, known for its robust document management capabilities, allows teams to store, share, and manage files effectively. When combined with Viva Engage, SharePoint files can be shared seamlessly, making collaboration smoother and more efficient. In this section, we will explore how to share SharePoint files within Viva Engage, its benefits, and best practices for utilizing this integration to improve teamwork and communication.

1. Why SharePoint Integration is Essential for Viva Engage

The Power of SharePoint

Microsoft **SharePoint** is a platform designed for collaboration and document management. It enables users to store and organize files, share them across teams, and collaborate on content in real time. SharePoint's features, such as versioning, access control, and easy sharing, make it an invaluable tool for teams across industries.

When you integrate **SharePoint with Viva Engage**, you unlock the ability to share files, documents, and resources directly within your team's social network. Viva Engage, a social collaboration tool, offers employees a space to share posts, exchange ideas, and participate in conversations. By combining these two powerful platforms, organizations can increase efficiency, encourage knowledge sharing, and streamline collaboration.

The Benefits of Sharing SharePoint Files in Viva Engage

Sharing SharePoint files within Viva Engage offers several key benefits:

- **Centralized Access**: Employees can access important documents and resources without having to navigate multiple platforms. SharePoint files shared in Viva Engage are easily accessible and organized within the conversation or post.

- **Seamless Collaboration**: Team members can access, comment, and collaborate on shared files in real-time, making it easier to work on documents together and share feedback immediately.

- **Better Engagement**: By embedding files directly into conversations, posts, and announcements, employees are more likely to interact with the content. This drives engagement and ensures that important resources are seen by all relevant stakeholders.

- **Version Control**: SharePoint's versioning system allows teams to track changes, ensuring that everyone is working on the most up-to-date version of a document. Any changes made to a file will be reflected immediately, and team members can access older versions if necessary.

- **Security and Permissions**: Files shared from SharePoint into Viva Engage retain their SharePoint permissions. This means that only users with the appropriate access rights will be able to view, edit, or share the file, maintaining security and privacy standards.

2. How to Share SharePoint Files in Viva Engage

Sharing SharePoint files within Viva Engage is straightforward. Follow these steps to get started:

Step 1: Navigate to the Post or Conversation in Viva Engage

To share a file from SharePoint, start by opening the post, conversation, or group where you want to share the file. You can do this by:

1. Logging into **Microsoft Viva Engage** via your web browser.

2. Going to a specific **group** or **community** you are part of, or you can open a **private conversation** with a colleague.

3. Clicking on the **Post Box** to start a new post or open an existing conversation thread.

Step 2: Access SharePoint Files

1. **Select the Attachment Option**: In the post box, you will see an attachment icon, often represented as a **paperclip** (📎). Click on this icon to begin attaching files.

2. **Choose SharePoint Files**: Once you click the attachment icon, you will be presented with several options to upload files. Select **"SharePoint"** or **"OneDrive"**, depending on your organization's settings. This will open a window where you can browse for files stored in SharePoint.

Step 3: Select Files from SharePoint

1. Navigate to the **document library** within your SharePoint site.

2. Use the search bar to find the **file** or **folder** you want to share.

3. Once you locate the file, select it, and click **"Share"** or **"Attach"** to attach it to your Viva Engage post.

Step 4: Add Context to Your SharePoint File

Before posting the file, you have the opportunity to add context to it. This is important because it provides your colleagues with the necessary information to understand the relevance of the document.

- **Add a description**: Briefly explain what the file is, its importance, and why you're sharing it.

- **Ask questions or prompt discussion**: Encourage colleagues to interact with the file by posing questions or asking for feedback.

- **Tag relevant team members**: Use **mentions** (@) to tag individuals who should specifically review the file or contribute to the conversation.

Step 5: Post and Share the File

Once you've added any necessary context, click **"Post"** or **"Share"** to send the document to the group or conversation. The SharePoint file will appear as a link, and other team members can click on it to view or edit the document directly.

3. Permissions and Security Considerations

When sharing SharePoint files in Viva Engage, it is important to ensure that the appropriate permissions and security measures are in place. Here are some things to keep in mind:

File Permissions in SharePoint

SharePoint files retain the permissions set in **SharePoint** when they are shared in Viva Engage. For example:

- **If a file is private**, only people who have been given access in SharePoint will be able to view or edit the file.

- **If a file is public within the organization**, anyone within the organization with access to Viva Engage can view it.

- **Editing rights**: You can set permissions for users to **view**, **edit**, or **comment** on a file. This control ensures that you can manage who has access to make changes to the document.

Privacy and Confidentiality

When sharing sensitive information, always be mindful of the document's content. It is recommended to:

- **Review permissions** before sharing a file to ensure that confidential information is only visible to the appropriate people.

- Avoid sharing files that contain private data, such as employee information or financial records, in public groups or posts.

4. Best Practices for Sharing SharePoint Files in Viva Engage

To get the most out of this integration and avoid common pitfalls, follow these best practices when sharing SharePoint files in Viva Engage:

Provide Clear Context

When sharing a file, always provide a clear explanation of its purpose. Simply attaching a file without context can leave colleagues unsure about its importance or how to interact with it. For example, if you are sharing a project report, explain what key information the report contains and whether team members need to review it, provide feedback, or take action.

Regularly Update Documents

SharePoint allows for **real-time collaboration** on documents, but it's important to keep your files updated regularly. Encourage team members to stay on top of document changes, and ensure that important files are always accessible and up-to-date.

Use Version Control Wisely

One of the powerful features of SharePoint is its **version control** system. Every time a file is edited or updated, SharePoint saves a new version. When sharing files in Viva Engage, be aware of which version you are sharing. If the document has gone through multiple changes, make sure you share the most current version to avoid confusion.

Encourage Feedback and Discussion

After sharing a file, encourage your colleagues to leave comments or suggestions. You can use Viva Engage's conversation features, such as commenting and tagging, to spark discussions around the file. This interaction makes it easier for team members to collaborate and engage with the document content.

Keep File Organization Simple

When sharing files from SharePoint, consider organizing your content in an easy-to-navigate manner. Use descriptive file names, organize documents into **folders** or **document libraries**, and make sure everyone knows where to find the resources they need. This will reduce confusion and save time when trying to locate important documents.

5. Conclusion

The ability to share SharePoint files directly within **Microsoft Viva Engage** enhances collaboration and communication across teams. By integrating SharePoint with Viva Engage, organizations can simplify the process of sharing important documents and ensure that employees have easy access to the resources they need. Whether you're sharing project reports, team guidelines, or important company updates, this integration enables smooth and efficient file-sharing that supports collaboration, security, and productivity.

By following the steps outlined in this section and adhering to best practices for file sharing, you can ensure that you are using both Viva Engage and SharePoint to their full potential. This powerful combination helps teams work more cohesively, share knowledge more efficiently, and ultimately drive business success through improved communication and collaboration.

5.3 Insights and Analytics in Viva Engage

5.3.1 Tracking Engagement Metrics

As organizations increasingly rely on digital collaboration tools like Microsoft Viva Engage, it is vital to understand how employees and teams interact with the content and activities within the platform. Tracking **engagement metrics** is crucial to gauge the effectiveness of communications, identify areas for improvement, and ensure that the platform meets organizational goals. Microsoft Viva Engage provides powerful tools and features that allow administrators and team leaders to measure engagement, analyze performance, and ultimately make informed decisions to enhance collaboration across the organization.

In this section, we will explore how to track engagement metrics in Viva Engage, what key metrics to focus on, how to analyze these metrics, and how to use insights to improve communication and collaboration within the workplace.

1. Understanding Engagement Metrics

Before diving into the specifics of how to track engagement metrics, it's important to understand what types of metrics are available and what they represent. In general, engagement metrics in Viva Engage offer insights into how people are interacting with posts, comments, messages, and other content within the platform. These metrics are designed to provide a comprehensive view of user activity and content effectiveness.

Key Engagement Metrics in Viva Engage

Here are some of the most important engagement metrics you will encounter in Viva Engage:

- **Post Views**: This metric shows how many users have seen a particular post or announcement. High post views indicate that the content is being seen by a broad audience, but it does not measure how users interact with the content.

- **Reactions**: This refers to the likes, thumbs-up, love, and other emoji reactions that users give to posts and comments. Reactions provide a quick gauge of how users feel about the content being shared.

- **Comments**: The number of comments on a post or thread is a powerful indicator of engagement. Comments suggest that users are not only reading the content but also actively participating in discussions.

- **Shares/Reposts**: When users share or repost content within Viva Engage, it amplifies the reach of the message. Tracking shares can help assess how much a post resonates with the audience and how much users want to spread that message within their own networks.

- **Replies**: Replies to comments or threads indicate that there is an ongoing conversation, which can be a sign of strong engagement. A high number of replies suggests that the content is prompting users to take part in a more meaningful dialogue.

- **Mentions**: The number of times a user is mentioned in posts or comments is another important engagement metric. Mentions can lead to more direct interactions and provide valuable insights into how individuals are participating in the conversation.

- **Post Impressions**: Impressions reflect how often a post appears on users' feeds, regardless of whether they interact with it. This metric helps to understand the visibility of your content.

- **Click-Through Rate (CTR)**: This metric measures how often users click on links included in posts, such as a link to a document, website, or other resources. It is particularly important for understanding how effective content is at driving users to additional materials or external platforms.

2. How to Track Engagement Metrics in Viva Engage

Microsoft Viva Engage integrates seamlessly with the broader Microsoft 365 ecosystem, providing several ways to track engagement metrics. Admins and group owners can access detailed analytics for the content shared in their groups, communities, and across the platform.

Accessing Insights and Analytics

To track engagement metrics, users must first access the analytics dashboard in Viva Engage. Here's how you can access these metrics:

1. **Log into Viva Engage**: Start by logging into your Viva Engage account via the web platform.

2. **Navigate to a Group or Community**: Go to the group or community where you wish to track engagement. If you're an admin or group owner, you will have access to the group's analytics.

3. **Click on the Analytics Tab**: Within the group or community page, look for the **Insights** or **Analytics** tab (depending on your version). This is typically located in the top menu or side navigation.

4. **Review the Analytics Dashboard**: Upon accessing the Analytics section, you will be presented with a dashboard displaying key metrics. These will often include metrics for posts, interactions, engagement by day/week/month, and other relevant data points.

5. **Filter by Content Type**: You can often filter the metrics by content type (posts, comments, polls, etc.) to see specific performance data.

6. **Export Data**: For deeper analysis, you can typically export data to CSV or Excel for further examination or sharing with stakeholders.

Group Insights for Admins

As an admin, you have access to detailed **group-level insights**, which help track how your group is performing over time. This includes:

- **Group Engagement Trends**: Tracking overall engagement across the group. This shows how active your community is, the frequency of posts, comments, and the level of interaction with the content.

- **Top Content**: Analytics can highlight the most popular posts in the group based on views, reactions, and shares. This is valuable for understanding what types of content drive engagement.

- **Member Engagement**: This metric shows which members are the most active in the group. It tracks how frequently members are posting, commenting, and reacting to content. This insight can help admins identify key influencers or contributors within the group.

3. Analyzing Engagement Data

After gathering engagement metrics from Viva Engage, the next step is to analyze the data to extract actionable insights. Here are some steps for effectively analyzing your engagement data:

Identifying Content Trends

By tracking metrics like post views, reactions, comments, and shares, you can start to identify trends in the types of content that drive engagement. For instance, you may discover that posts with **videos** or **interactive polls** tend to get more reactions and comments than plain text posts.

Tip: Use this insight to tailor future content. If certain types of posts are consistently receiving more engagement, consider posting similar content in the future to keep your audience engaged.

Understanding Audience Sentiment

Analyzing the reactions and comments on posts can provide valuable insights into how your audience feels about specific topics. For instance, if a particular post receives overwhelmingly positive reactions (heart emoji or thumbs up), it indicates that the content is well-received.

Conversely, if the post receives negative or neutral reactions, you may need to reconsider the tone or approach for future posts. Use comments to gain further context—are users asking for clarification? Are they debating certain points? This kind of sentiment analysis helps improve communication strategies.

Improving Post Frequency and Timing

Engagement metrics can help you identify the **best times** to post and the optimal frequency for posting. For example, you may find that posts published in the **morning** tend to generate more interaction compared to posts made later in the day. Similarly, tracking weekly or monthly engagement can help you understand if you should post more frequently or if certain days of the week see higher activity.

4. Leveraging Analytics to Improve Communication

Once you have access to your engagement metrics and insights, the next step is to leverage these findings to **optimize communication and content strategies** within your organization.

Tailor Content Based on Engagement Insights

For example, if you notice that posts with **interactive content** such as polls, surveys, or questions receive higher engagement than traditional posts, consider making these elements a regular part of your content strategy. Additionally, keep in mind what times or days show higher engagement and schedule posts accordingly to maximize visibility.

Experiment with Content Formats

Based on the engagement data, experiment with different content formats to see what works best. For instance, if **video content** gets more attention than text-heavy posts, plan on creating more engaging videos for upcoming announcements or updates.

Use Data to Improve Group Interactions

By understanding the engagement levels of various group members, you can foster a more interactive community. Reach out to highly engaged members to encourage more participation from others. Recognize and acknowledge contributors by tagging them or thanking them for their contributions in group discussions.

Continuous Improvement

Tracking engagement metrics is not a one-time exercise. It's an ongoing process that should be used to refine and optimize your communication approach. Use the insights gained from analytics to inform future decisions and adapt your strategies as necessary.

---

5. Conclusion

Tracking engagement metrics in Microsoft Viva Engage is a powerful tool that helps teams, admins, and organizations assess the effectiveness of their communications and collaboration efforts. By leveraging Viva Engage's analytics features, you can make data-driven decisions that enhance user engagement, improve content quality, and foster better communication across teams.

Regularly reviewing engagement data allows you to **adapt** your strategies, **refine** your content, and ensure that your organization's use of Viva Engage remains effective and relevant.

By combining these insights with a proactive approach to content creation and communication, you can help ensure that Microsoft Viva Engage plays a central role in fostering a connected and engaged workplace.

5.3.2 Understanding Group Insights

In the world of modern workplaces, communication and collaboration are the cornerstones of success. Microsoft Viva Engage, as an integrated platform within the Microsoft 365 ecosystem, is designed to foster dynamic interactions and encourage seamless communication across teams and organizations. For businesses and teams to thrive, understanding how to measure and optimize this communication is essential. This is where **Group Insights** in Viva Engage come into play.

Group Insights provide valuable metrics and data about your group's activity, engagement, and overall interaction patterns. These insights allow administrators and group leaders to assess the health of a community, track content performance, and optimize strategies for improving team collaboration. In this section, we will dive deep into **Group Insights**, exploring how to access these insights, what data they provide, and how to use this information to boost engagement and improve communication.

1. What Are Group Insights in Viva Engage?

Group Insights refer to the data and analytics provided for groups within Microsoft Viva Engage. This data includes vital information about group member activity, engagement with posts, interactions, and more. Group insights help administrators understand:

- **How active the group is**—how often members are posting, commenting, or reacting to posts.

- **Which posts perform the best**—gauging which types of content are most engaging to the group.

- **Member participation levels**—seeing which members are most engaged, and how the group is growing over time.

These insights offer a holistic view of the group's activity, allowing admins to make informed decisions on how to manage, moderate, and improve the group's dynamics.

2. How to Access Group Insights in Viva Engage

Accessing Group Insights in Viva Engage is a straightforward process, but it requires appropriate permissions. Only **group admins** and **group owners** have access to this feature. Here's how to navigate to Group Insights:

1. **Login to Viva Engage:**

   o Go to the Viva Engage website and log in with your Microsoft 365 credentials.

2. **Navigate to the Group:**

   o On the left-hand panel, click on the **Groups** icon and select the specific group you want to review insights for.

3. **Access Group Insights:**

   o Once you are in the group, click on the **Settings** menu (represented by a gear icon) in the upper-right corner of the screen.

   o From the dropdown menu, select **Group Insights**.

   o Alternatively, some groups may have a dedicated tab for **Analytics** directly within the group's homepage interface.

Once you've accessed the Group Insights page, you'll be presented with a variety of data points and graphs that provide a comprehensive overview of your group's activity.

3. Key Metrics in Group Insights

Total Engagement

The **Total Engagement** section provides an overview of how engaged your members are within the group. This metric tracks the cumulative number of interactions with posts, including:

- **Likes** or **Reactions**: Shows how often members have reacted to posts with likes, emojis, or other available reactions.

- **Comments**: Tracks the number of comments made on posts within the group.

- **Shares**: Provides insight into how often posts are shared across other platforms or groups within Viva Engage.

Total engagement metrics give you a snapshot of the group's level of activity and involvement.

Post Performance

Post Performance shows the popularity of individual posts within the group. This section helps admins understand which content resonates most with the group members. Key indicators include:

- **Top Posts by Reactions**: Which posts have received the highest number of likes or reactions.

- **Top Posts by Comments**: Which posts have generated the most discussion and interaction from members.

- **Post Views**: Tracks how many times a post has been viewed by group members.

- **Shares and Reposts**: Shows the number of times a post has been shared with others or reposted within the group.

Understanding post performance is crucial for adjusting content strategies and delivering the type of content that gets the best engagement.

Member Participation

Member Participation metrics show how involved each individual member is within the group. This metric helps identify active contributors and potential areas for encouragement. Key data includes:

- **Most Active Members**: Lists members who are engaging most frequently by posting, commenting, liking, or sharing.

- **Member Activity Trends**: Visual representation of a specific member's participation over time—whether their involvement is increasing, decreasing, or remaining stable.

- **Group Growth**: Provides data on how the number of members has grown over time, helping you identify trends in group expansion.

These insights allow admins to acknowledge highly engaged members and encourage others to participate more frequently.

Engagement Over Time

Engagement Over Time is a crucial metric that provides insights into the group's activity across different timeframes. It can be presented as a graph showing engagement on specific days, weeks, or months. Key points include:

- **Activity Spikes**: Pinpoint days or times when engagement was particularly high.

- **Drop-offs**: See if engagement has dropped, which may indicate the need for more stimulating content or group activities.

- **Long-Term Trends**: Track engagement over longer periods to understand whether the group is trending upwards or downwards.

Tracking engagement over time is valuable for identifying seasonal or situational trends in group activity, such as periods of high participation during special events or announcements.

4. Interpreting Group Insights

Understanding the data presented in Group Insights is essential to making informed decisions for improving engagement and collaboration within your group. Here are some ways to interpret and act upon the data:

Identifying Engagement Opportunities

If you notice that certain types of posts are getting more reactions and comments, this is a clear signal of what content your group values. Use this information to:

- **Create more similar content**: Replicate the successful posts to maintain engagement levels.

- **Involve group members**: Encourage users to share their experiences, ideas, or expertise on topics that are resonating with others.

- **Adjust content timing**: If posts at certain times of the day or week receive higher engagement, try to post more during those periods.

Identifying Inactive Members

Group Insights help you spot **inactive members** who are not engaging with posts, even if they are part of the group. When you notice a member's activity declining over time, you can:

- **Reach out directly**: Send a private message to encourage them to participate.

- **Ask for feedback**: If a member hasn't been participating, it could be due to a lack of interest or unclear expectations, so gathering feedback could help improve group dynamics.

Monitoring Group Health

By tracking engagement metrics and participation trends, you can monitor the overall **health** of the group. Low engagement could signal that the group is losing interest or that the content is not meeting the members' needs. On the other hand, a group with high engagement suggests that the community is active and thriving.

- **Take corrective actions**: If a group's activity drops, consider initiating new discussions, bringing in fresh content, or organizing group events like Q&A sessions or virtual meetups.

- **Foster inclusivity**: Ensure that the group is open to diverse voices and discussions, which can lead to higher participation rates.

5. Actionable Strategies Based on Insights

Tailoring Content to Member Preferences

One of the biggest advantages of Group Insights is that they allow you to tailor content to what your group members actually want. If certain types of posts (e.g., questions, polls, or event invitations) are receiving more reactions, it's important to:

- Prioritize these formats in the future.

- Experiment with different types of content to see what works best.

- Use member feedback from comments or surveys to create more relevant content.

Recognizing and Rewarding Active Members

Active members are the backbone of any successful group. Group Insights can help identify these members by tracking their interactions with posts. To keep them motivated:

- **Acknowledge top contributors**: Regularly highlight and thank them for their contributions.

- **Involve them in leadership roles**: Offer them the opportunity to become group moderators or content creators.

- **Provide incentives**: Create reward programs that recognize and celebrate the efforts of active participants.

Conclusion

Group Insights in Viva Engage is an invaluable tool that allows group admins and team leaders to track, measure, and optimize communication within their groups. By understanding key metrics such as engagement, post performance, and member participation, you can make data-driven decisions to enhance collaboration and keep the group healthy and vibrant.

The goal is to **use this data to foster better interactions, create more engaging content**, and **support team members in meaningful ways**. Armed with these insights, you can ensure that your group remains an active, collaborative, and engaging space for all members.

5.3.3 Using Data to Improve Communication

In today's digital workplace, communication is key to maintaining productivity, collaboration, and employee engagement. However, the sheer volume of content shared across communication platforms can make it challenging to assess whether the messages are reaching their intended audience or achieving the desired outcomes. This is where **data analytics** comes in. Microsoft Viva Engage, with its robust **insights and analytics capabilities**, enables organizations to use data to refine communication strategies, enhance engagement, and continuously improve how teams collaborate.

In this section, we will explore how to **use data from Viva Engage** to **optimize communication** within your organization. We'll cover the key metrics you can track, how to interpret those metrics, and how to apply the insights gained to improve workplace communication effectively.

1. Key Metrics to Track in Viva Engage

Viva Engage provides a variety of data points to measure engagement and communication effectiveness. The key metrics that can help improve communication include:

Post Engagement Metrics

These metrics focus on how users are interacting with content within the platform. They offer insight into how well your posts are resonating with your audience.

- **Likes/Reactions:** These indicate the initial level of engagement. A high number of likes suggests that your content resonates with your audience.

- **Shares/Reposts:** Sharing content signifies that users find it valuable enough to distribute to others. High sharing activity usually indicates strong communication.

- **Comments:** Comments are often a sign of deeper engagement. Tracking the number of comments and analyzing their content can give you a good sense of whether the post sparked discussions or prompted questions.

- **Views/Impressions:** This shows how many people have seen the content. While views are important, it's essential to consider them alongside other metrics like comments and shares for a fuller picture of engagement.

Actionable Insight: If your posts receive lots of likes but little comments, it could indicate that the content is not encouraging discussions or dialogue. In such cases, you may want to include more **call-to-actions** (CTAs) in your posts, prompting users to share their thoughts or questions.

Group Engagement Metrics

Group activity and engagement are crucial for understanding the effectiveness of communication within teams and communities.

- **Active Members:** Track how many members in the group are actively participating in conversations. This can help gauge the health of the group's dynamic.

- **New Members Joining:** This metric can help assess whether your group is growing and attracting new members. A steady increase in group membership is often a sign of effective communication and relevance.

- **Post Frequency and Consistency:** The regularity of posts made by group members indicates the level of communication happening. Frequent posts usually reflect an engaged group, while less frequent posting may suggest stagnation or disengagement.

- **Mentions:** The number of times a post is mentioned or tagged by others. Frequent mentions can suggest that the content is important or highly relevant.

Actionable Insight: If your group engagement metrics show that posts are infrequent or group participation is low, it may be an indication that the content is not aligned with the interests of the members. You can improve engagement by tailoring content to specific group interests or initiating discussions based on members' needs.

User Profile Analytics

Viva Engage allows you to track user profiles and participation. Analyzing this data can provide insights into individual engagement levels, helping to identify influencers or team members who require more encouragement or support.

- **Top Contributors:** Identify the most active members who contribute regularly to discussions. These individuals can be used as examples or even leaders in driving communication within groups.

- **Engagement Levels by Role or Department:** Understanding engagement by different departments or roles can help identify where communication may need improvement. For example, if a particular team is consistently disengaged, it might indicate that your content is not relevant to their work.

Actionable Insight: If you find that specific departments are not engaging, consider tailoring content for those specific teams. Alternatively, you could organize targeted sessions or send personalized communications that directly address their needs or challenges.

Feedback and Sentiment Analysis

Another important aspect of using data to improve communication is understanding the **sentiment** around your posts and discussions. Analyzing **comments** and **feedback** can provide valuable insights into how your audience is feeling about the content.

- **Sentiment Scores:** Tools integrated with Viva Engage can analyze the tone of comments and reactions. Positive, neutral, or negative sentiments can give you an overall view of how well your communication is being received.

- **Survey Responses:** If you've posted surveys or polls, the feedback received can provide direct insight into how your team feels about certain topics.

Actionable Insight: If the sentiment around a post is predominantly negative, it may be worth revisiting the message or the way it was communicated. Negative feedback is an opportunity to improve clarity, tone, and relevance.

2. Interpreting the Data for Actionable Insights

Once you've gathered the relevant data, it's essential to interpret it effectively. Here are some steps to help you make sense of the analytics and gain actionable insights:

Identifying Communication Gaps

By analyzing the **engagement metrics**, you can identify if any gaps exist in your communication. For example, if posts are receiving many views but few reactions or comments, it may suggest that the content is not resonating deeply with the audience. This gap can be an opportunity to refine the message or adjust the content type.

Actionable Insight: Consider using more **interactive content**, such as polls, questions, or announcements, to provoke responses. Additionally, incorporating **storytelling** or real-world applications may help make the content more relatable.

Enhancing Content Strategy

Data-driven insights can help improve your content strategy. For instance, if you notice that certain types of content, such as images or videos, are driving more engagement, you can focus more on these formats to increase impact.

*Actionable Insight:*If posts containing videos are getting higher engagement, consider creating more video content, such as **tutorials, interviews, or behind-the-scenes footage**.

Personalizing Communication

By analyzing individual user data, you can tailor your communications to better meet the needs of specific individuals or groups. For example, if you see that certain employees are highly active in groups but others are not participating, you can send personalized messages to encourage their involvement or ask for feedback on why they may be disengaged.

Actionable Insight: Create **targeted communication campaigns** that address the unique needs or preferences of different user groups. Personalized messages can encourage higher participation and create a more engaged community.

Measuring the Impact of Announcements and Polls

When you make a significant announcement or post a poll, tracking the responses and subsequent interactions is critical to understanding its success. For example, you might track if the announcement led to **increased engagement** or if the poll sparked more discussions.

Actionable Insight: If an announcement about a new company policy leads to increased comments and shares, it may indicate that employees care deeply about the topic. Conversely, if a post doesn't generate much interaction, it may suggest that the message needs to be revisited or that it is not as relevant as initially thought.

3. Best Practices for Using Data to Improve Communication

Once you've gathered and analyzed the data, it's essential to apply best practices to improve communication based on the insights gained.

Make Data-Driven Decisions

Use the data as a foundation for all communication strategies. Regularly monitor engagement and adapt your approach based on what works and what doesn't.

Regularly Review Analytics

Set aside time to periodically review the insights in Viva Engage. By consistently monitoring the data, you can make timely adjustments and continuously refine your communication approach.

Foster a Culture of Feedback

Encourage team members to share their feedback on the content they find valuable. Incorporating feedback into your communications strategy ensures that the content remains relevant and meaningful to your audience.

Conclusion

In today's workplace, communication must be data-driven to be effective. By leveraging **Viva Engage's insights and analytics**, you can track engagement metrics, interpret the data for actionable insights, and adjust your communication strategies accordingly. This will not only improve internal communication but also foster a more engaged, informed, and productive workforce. By continuously using data to improve your communication strategies, your team can stay aligned, motivated, and prepared to face the challenges of the modern workplace.

PART VI
Best Practices for Effective Communication

6.1 Building an Engaging Viva Engage Community

6.1.1 Encouraging Participation and Discussions

Building a thriving community on **Microsoft Viva Engage** requires more than just setting up groups and posting content. It involves actively **encouraging participation and fostering meaningful discussions** that keep users engaged, informed, and connected. A well-managed community serves as a dynamic space for collaboration, knowledge sharing, and professional growth.

In this section, we'll explore **effective strategies** to encourage participation and discussions, ensuring that your Viva Engage community remains an active and valuable resource for all members.

1. Understanding the Importance of Participation and Discussions

Active participation and discussions are the backbone of any successful digital workplace community. Here's why they matter:

- **Boosts Employee Engagement:** Engaged employees are more likely to contribute ideas, share insights, and stay connected with the organization's goals.

- **Encourages Knowledge Sharing:** Discussions facilitate the exchange of expertise and best practices, reducing information silos within the company.

- **Enhances Collaboration:** Active participation helps teams work together efficiently, regardless of location or department.

- **Strengthens Company Culture:** A well-engaged community promotes transparency, inclusivity, and a sense of belonging.

- **Improves Decision-Making:** Leaders and managers can gather real-time feedback, allowing them to make more informed business decisions.

Encouraging participation requires a strategic approach that includes content planning, engagement techniques, and community management.

2. Strategies to Encourage Active Participation

Encouraging participation in Viva Engage involves a combination of **content strategy, leadership involvement, incentives, and engagement techniques**. Below are several ways to boost interaction and foster meaningful discussions.

Leading by Example

One of the best ways to encourage participation is by demonstrating active engagement yourself. Community leaders, managers, and moderators should set an example by:

- Regularly posting **updates, insights, and thought-provoking questions**.

- Responding to comments and acknowledging contributions from community members.

- Sharing relevant company news and encouraging feedback.

- Using mentions (**@mentions**) to directly involve individuals in discussions.

💡 **Tip:** Employees are more likely to participate if they see leadership actively engaging in conversations.

Posting Thought-Provoking Questions

A great way to spark discussions is by asking questions that invite employees to **share their opinions, experiences, or insights**. Some examples include:

- **"What's one productivity tip that has helped you manage your workload better?"**

- "What's a challenge you've faced in remote work, and how did you overcome it?"

- "What's the best piece of career advice you've ever received?"

💡 **Tip:** Use **open-ended questions** rather than simple yes/no queries to encourage richer discussions.

Recognizing and Encouraging Contributions

Acknowledging and appreciating contributions can motivate employees to participate more. Some effective methods include:

- **Liking and commenting** on posts to show appreciation.

- Featuring a **"Post of the Week"** or **"Top Contributor"** to highlight valuable contributions.

- Creating **employee spotlight posts** to showcase individual expertise or achievements.

💡 **Tip:** A simple "Great insight, @JohnDoe!" or "Thanks for sharing, @JaneSmith! What do others think?" can go a long way in fostering engagement.

Using Polls and Surveys

Polls are an **interactive way to engage employees** and gather opinions quickly. Some effective ways to use polls include:

- Gathering feedback on new company policies.

- Asking for input on upcoming initiatives.

- Running fun, informal polls (e.g., "What's your favorite productivity tool?").

💡 **Tip:** Keep polls **short and relevant**, and always follow up with a discussion based on the results.

Encouraging Storytelling

People connect more deeply with **real stories and experiences**. Encourage employees to share their personal stories related to:

- Workplace achievements and lessons learned.

- Memorable projects and key takeaways.

- Challenges they've faced and how they overcame them.

💡 **Tip:** Create **storytelling prompts** such as "Tell us about a time you successfully solved a tough problem at work."

Creating Engaging Content Formats

Not all employees engage in the same way, so it's important to **diversify content formats**. Some ideas include:

- **Video updates from leadership** (short clips sharing insights or news).

- **Infographics** summarizing key ideas.

- **GIFs and memes** for lighthearted engagement.

- **Case studies and success stories** to highlight best practices.

💡 **Tip:** A mix of **text, visuals, and videos** keeps the community lively and appealing to different types of users.

Hosting Virtual Events and Q&A Sessions

Live discussions, AMAs (**Ask Me Anything** sessions), and webinars create opportunities for real-time engagement. You can:

- Invite senior leaders for **Q&A sessions** to discuss company updates.

- Organize virtual coffee chats to **foster informal interactions**.

- Host panel discussions with **subject matter experts**.

💡 **Tip:** Record sessions and upload key takeaways to ensure **continued engagement** from those who couldn't attend live.

3. Overcoming Common Engagement Challenges

Even with the best strategies, some challenges may arise when encouraging participation. Here's how to tackle them:

Low Participation Rates

Solution:

- Identify and engage **early adopters** (enthusiastic employees who can encourage others).

- Offer **small incentives**, such as recognition or professional development opportunities, to those who engage regularly.

- Ask for direct feedback: **"What topics would you like to see discussed more?"**

One-Way Communication

Solution:

- Avoid making every post a **top-down announcement**.

- Frame posts in a way that **invites conversation** rather than just delivering information.

- Encourage **peer-to-peer discussions** by prompting employees to tag colleagues in conversations.

Disengaged Employees

Solution:

- Personalize content by **tailoring discussions to different departments** or job roles.

- Identify **inactive members** and reach out with **personalized invitations** to join specific discussions.

- Share success stories about how engaging in Viva Engage has helped **employees grow professionally**.

---

4. Measuring Engagement and Adjusting Strategies

To ensure that your participation strategies are effective, regularly track engagement metrics such as:

- **Post reach and impressions** (how many employees are seeing posts).

- **Number of comments, shares, and reactions** (how actively users engage).

- **Participation trends over time** (whether engagement is increasing or declining).

- **Top contributors** (who are the most active members in discussions).

💡 **Tip:** If engagement is low, **experiment with different content types** and **re-evaluate discussion topics** based on employee feedback.

5. Conclusion

Encouraging participation and discussions in **Microsoft Viva Engage** requires a combination of **active leadership, engaging content, interactive techniques, and ongoing encouragement**. By fostering an open and dynamic communication culture, organizations can unlock the full potential of Viva Engage, leading to better collaboration, innovation, and employee engagement.

By implementing these best practices, your Viva Engage community will become a **thriving hub** where employees **share knowledge, support one another, and stay connected**— ultimately creating a more vibrant and communicative workplace. 🚀

6.1.2 Recognizing and Rewarding Engagement

Building a thriving community in Microsoft Viva Engage requires more than just participation—it requires motivation and encouragement. Recognizing and rewarding engagement is a powerful strategy to keep employees actively involved, inspire meaningful contributions, and create a positive, collaborative environment. By acknowledging user contributions, organizations can reinforce positive behaviors and cultivate a culture of engagement and knowledge sharing.

This section will explore the **importance of recognition, different methods to reward engagement, best practices for implementation**, and **how to measure the impact of engagement initiatives** in Viva Engage.

1. The Importance of Recognition in Viva Engage Communities

Recognition is a key driver of engagement in any social or workplace platform. When employees feel that their contributions are valued, they are more likely to continue participating actively. Here's why recognition matters:

Boosts Participation

Employees are more likely to engage in discussions, share insights, and contribute valuable content when they know their efforts will be acknowledged.

Strengthens Workplace Culture

Public recognition fosters a **positive work culture**, promoting collaboration and teamwork across departments.

Encourages Knowledge Sharing

Recognizing employees who share valuable insights or answer questions encourages others to contribute their expertise, leading to a richer knowledge base within the organization.

Increases Employee Satisfaction and Retention

When employees receive appreciation for their engagement, they feel a stronger connection to the company, which can enhance job satisfaction and reduce turnover.

2. Strategies for Recognizing and Rewarding Engagement in Viva Engage

Recognition can take many forms, from simple acknowledgments to structured reward programs. Here are several strategies for effectively recognizing and rewarding engagement in Viva Engage.

Public Acknowledgment in Posts and Comments

One of the simplest yet most effective ways to recognize engagement is through **public acknowledgment**. This can be done by:

- **Tagging employees** in posts to highlight their contributions.

- **Replying to comments** with personalized appreciation.

- **Using reactions (such as likes, applause, or hearts)** to acknowledge valuable input.

Example: *"Great insight, @JohnDoe! Your analysis of market trends really helps the team stay ahead. Thanks for sharing!"*

This type of acknowledgment is quick but impactful, reinforcing positive behavior and encouraging others to participate.

Leader and Executive Recognition

When recognition comes from company leaders or executives, it carries even greater weight. Some ways to implement this include:

- Having **managers or executives** comment on or share outstanding posts.

- Creating a **"Leader Spotlight" post** where top contributors are mentioned and celebrated.

- Using **video messages** from leadership to thank employees for their contributions.

Example: A monthly post from the CEO highlighting the **"Top Engaged Employees"** in Viva Engage can create excitement and a sense of achievement.

Employee of the Month and Recognition Badges

Many organizations use **recognition badges or awards** to highlight engagement. These can be:

- **Badges for top contributors** (e.g., "Most Helpful Member," "Top Knowledge Sharer," or "Engagement Champion").

- **A "Contributor of the Month" award**, where employees who actively engage in discussions, share valuable content, or help others are publicly recognized.

- **Digital certificates or profile badges** that highlight engagement achievements.

Example: Microsoft Viva Engage allows companies to integrate **badging systems** where employees can earn **virtual awards** displayed on their profiles.

Gamification: Points and Leaderboards

Gamification is an effective way to make engagement **fun and rewarding**. Organizations can:

- Assign **points** for different types of engagement (e.g., posting content, commenting, sharing, answering questions).

- Create **leaderboards** displaying the most engaged employees each month.

- Offer **small incentives or recognition perks** for employees who reach certain milestones.

Example: *"Jane has earned 500 engagement points this month and is our Top Contributor! Keep up the great work!"*

Recognition Through Internal Newsletters or Meetings

Another way to showcase engagement is through **company-wide communications**, such as:

- Featuring **top contributors in internal newsletters**.

- Announcing **employee achievements in team meetings**.

- Showcasing **highly engaged teams in corporate emails or town halls**.

Example: A quarterly newsletter section titled *"Engagement Spotlight"* can feature employee contributions and testimonials.

Personalized Appreciation Messages

A simple **direct message from a manager or leader** thanking an employee for their engagement can be very effective. Personalized messages can:

- Show employees that their contributions are noticed.

- Encourage continued participation.

- Strengthen the relationship between leadership and employees.

Example Message: *"Hi Sarah, I noticed how actively you've been engaging in Viva Engage and sharing valuable insights with the team. Your contributions are making a real impact. Keep up the great work!"*

Small Incentives and Rewards

While recognition itself is powerful, adding small **tangible rewards** can further motivate employees. Some reward ideas include:

- **Gift cards or vouchers** for top contributors.

- **Extra time off or flexible work hours** for consistent engagement.

- **Exclusive company swag** (T-shirts, mugs, notebooks, etc.).

- **Professional development opportunities** (e.g., a free course, conference tickets).

Example: A monthly contest where the **top three engaged employees** receive a **small reward**, such as a coffee voucher, can boost participation.

Encouraging Peer-to-Peer Recognition

Encouraging employees to recognize each other fosters a more **collaborative and supportive environment**. Viva Engage allows:

- Employees to **tag and thank colleagues** in posts.

- The use of **peer recognition badges** where employees can "nominate" coworkers for engagement awards.

- The creation of a **shout-out or appreciation group** where employees celebrate each other's contributions.

Example: *"Big thanks to @Emily for always answering our finance-related questions! Your expertise is invaluable to the team."*

---

3. Measuring the Impact of Recognition Initiatives

To ensure your recognition efforts are effective, it's important to track their impact. Viva Engage offers **analytics and insights** to measure how recognition affects engagement.

Tracking Engagement Growth

Monitor whether engagement levels **increase after implementing recognition initiatives**. Metrics to track include:

- Number of **active users** in Viva Engage.

- Growth in **comments, shares, and reactions**.

- Increase in **post contributions**.

Employee Sentiment and Feedback

Gather employee feedback through:

- **Surveys or polls** to assess if employees feel recognized and valued.

- **Direct interviews or focus groups** to understand how recognition impacts motivation.

Monitoring Retention and Participation Rates

Employee engagement and retention often go hand in hand. If engagement and participation improve, it may also lead to **higher employee satisfaction** and reduced turnover.

Example: An HR team might compare engagement metrics before and after implementing a recognition program to measure its success.

4. Best Practices for Implementing Recognition in Viva Engage

To ensure success, here are some best practices:

Be Consistent

Recognition should be **ongoing and frequent**, not just a one-time effort.

Align Recognition with Company Values

Tie recognition back to company values to reinforce desired behaviors.

Personalize Acknowledgments

Generic recognition feels less meaningful. **Make it specific and personal** to each employee's contribution.

Encourage Company-Wide Participation

Ensure all levels of the organization—from leadership to employees—are **actively participating in recognition efforts**.

5. Conclusion

Recognizing and rewarding engagement in Viva Engage is a powerful way to **motivate employees, boost participation, and foster a positive workplace culture**. Whether through public acknowledgment, leader involvement, gamification, peer-to-peer appreciation, or small incentives, recognition plays a key role in maintaining an engaged and thriving Viva Engage community.

By implementing a structured approach to recognition and consistently tracking its impact, organizations can create a **more engaged, collaborative, and motivated workforce**, driving better communication and stronger team connections.

6.1.3 Creating a Positive Work Culture

A positive work culture is the foundation of a thriving and engaged workplace. It fosters collaboration, innovation, and a sense of belonging among employees. With **Microsoft Viva Engage**, organizations can create a **digital community** that promotes inclusivity, transparency, and a strong team spirit. However, simply having a platform for communication is not enough—companies must actively cultivate an environment that **encourages positivity, recognition, and meaningful interactions**.

This section explores how to use Viva Engage to **build a positive work culture**, including key strategies, best practices, and real-world applications that will help employees feel valued, heard, and connected.

---

1. The Importance of a Positive Work Culture

Before diving into how Viva Engage can support a positive work culture, it's essential to understand why a **healthy workplace environment** matters. A **positive work culture** results in:

- **Higher employee engagement:** Employees who feel connected to their workplace are more motivated and productive.

- **Better collaboration:** A culture of open communication encourages teamwork and knowledge sharing.

- **Stronger company loyalty:** Employees who feel valued and supported are more likely to stay with the company.

- **Increased innovation:** An inclusive and supportive culture allows employees to freely share ideas without fear of criticism.

- **Lower stress levels:** When employees experience a **supportive digital environment**, workplace stress and conflicts decrease.

Viva Engage provides the perfect digital space to **nurture these cultural values** while ensuring that all employees—whether remote, hybrid, or in-office—feel included and connected.

2. Strategies for Creating a Positive Work Culture Using Viva Engage

To **foster a culture of positivity** within Viva Engage, companies must take deliberate actions. Here are some key strategies:

Promote Open and Transparent Communication

A positive culture thrives when employees feel **informed and involved**. Viva Engage allows organizations to **share updates, company news, and leadership messages** in an engaging way.

Best Practices:

- **Encourage leadership participation**: Leaders should actively engage by posting regular updates, responding to employee feedback, and recognizing achievements.

- **Create an "Ask Me Anything" (AMA) series**: This allows employees to interact directly with leadership, fostering trust and transparency.

- **Use storytelling**: Instead of just posting announcements, share real-life stories about company successes, customer impact, and employee contributions.

★ *Example:* A company could create a monthly "Leadership Corner" post where executives share company updates and invite employees to ask questions.

Recognize and Celebrate Employee Achievements

One of the strongest ways to create a **positive workplace culture** is by recognizing employees' hard work and accomplishments. **Public recognition boosts morale and motivation**.

Best Practices:

- **Employee Spotlights:** Dedicate a weekly or monthly post to recognizing outstanding contributions.

- **Peer-to-Peer Recognition:** Encourage employees to shout out their colleagues using the **@mention feature**.

- **Celebrate milestones:** Use Viva Engage to recognize **work anniversaries, promotions, and project completions**.

📌 *Example:* A manager posts a "Thank You Thursday" message each week, recognizing different team members for their contributions.

Encourage Inclusivity and Diversity

A **positive culture** is one where every employee feels **seen, heard, and valued**. Viva Engage can be used to support inclusivity through **dedicated spaces for employee resource groups (ERGs), diversity discussions, and cultural celebrations**.

Best Practices:

- **Create ERG communities**: Set up Viva Engage groups for women in leadership, LGBTQ+ employees, cultural affinity groups, and other diversity-focused initiatives.

- **Host virtual cultural events**: Celebrate different traditions and awareness months through **posts, videos, and employee spotlights**.

- **Ensure diverse voices are heard**: Encourage employees from all backgrounds and roles to participate in discussions.

📌 *Example:* A company could create a **#CulturalCelebrations** community where employees share their unique traditions, recipes, or stories.

Foster Social Connections and Fun

Work is not just about productivity—**building personal connections** strengthens collaboration and overall job satisfaction. Viva Engage provides an opportunity to **create a sense of community beyond work-related discussions**.

Best Practices:

- **Casual conversation groups:** Set up communities for shared interests, such as **fitness, book clubs, pets, or travel**.

- **Host fun challenges:** Encourage employees to participate in challenges like **photo contests, wellness challenges, or trivia games**.

- **Create a virtual break room:** Establish a **"Watercooler Chat"** where employees can have informal conversations.

✦ *Example:* A company launches a **"Pet of the Month" contest** where employees share photos of their pets, and colleagues vote for the winner.

Provide Learning and Growth Opportunities

A culture that prioritizes learning and development creates a more **engaged and satisfied workforce**. Viva Engage can support **knowledge sharing, mentorship programs, and skill-building initiatives**.

Best Practices:

- **Host "Lunch and Learn" sessions**: Use Viva Engage to organize short training sessions where employees can learn from experts.

- **Encourage mentorship and coaching**: Create **mentorship groups** where senior employees can guide junior team members.

- **Share industry insights**: Post articles, videos, and discussions about trends and best practices in your field.

✦ *Example:* A company creates a **"Tech Tips Tuesday"** series where IT experts share short tutorials on software and digital productivity.

3. Best Practices for Sustaining a Positive Culture on Viva Engage

Building a **positive work culture** on Viva Engage is not a one-time effort—it requires **ongoing maintenance and participation**. Here's how to **sustain** it:

Set the Right Tone from the Start

Ensure that **all communications within Viva Engage align with your company's values**. Establish a **culture of respect, inclusivity, and encouragement**.

◆ **Action Tip:** Create **community guidelines** that promote **respectful discussions, constructive feedback, and professional engagement**.

Ensure Leadership Involvement

Leaders play a crucial role in setting the tone for company culture. Their **active participation** in Viva Engage **encourages employees to engage more**.

✦ **Action Tip:** Encourage **managers and executives** to post regularly, respond to employee questions, and acknowledge contributions.

Keep Content Fresh and Engaging

A stagnant platform leads to disengagement. Ensure that content remains **varied, interactive, and up-to-date**.

✦ **Action Tip:** Use a **content calendar** to plan engaging posts, such as **employee spotlights, leadership messages, polls, and fun challenges**.

Monitor Engagement and Adjust Strategies

Regularly track **engagement metrics** to assess the effectiveness of your initiatives.

✦ **Action Tip:** Use **Viva Engage analytics** to monitor participation, comments, and reactions. If engagement declines, adjust the approach.

Foster a Safe and Supportive Environment

Employees should feel **safe expressing their ideas and concerns** without fear of negativity or criticism.

✦ **Action Tip:** Assign **moderators** to ensure that discussions remain **respectful and professional**.

Conclusion

A positive work culture is the backbone of an engaged, motivated, and collaborative workforce. By leveraging Microsoft Viva Engage, organizations can foster meaningful connections, recognize employee contributions, promote inclusivity, and create a thriving digital community.

By implementing these best practices, businesses can turn Viva Engage into more than just a communication tool—it becomes a space where employees feel valued, inspired, and connected. A positive culture drives productivity, boosts morale, and ultimately contributes to business success.

6.2 Writing Impactful Posts and Updates

6.2.1 Best Practices for Clarity and Engagement

Writing impactful posts and updates in **Microsoft Viva Engage** is essential for fostering **meaningful communication, driving engagement, and ensuring clarity** in the workplace. Whether you are announcing company-wide updates, encouraging discussions, or sharing insights, crafting well-structured, engaging content can **enhance collaboration and knowledge-sharing** across teams.

This section explores best practices for **clarity and engagement** when creating posts and updates in Viva Engage. By following these guidelines, you can ensure that your messages are **clear, compelling, and effective** in reaching your audience.

---

1. The Importance of Clear and Engaging Communication in Viva Engage

Before diving into best practices, it's important to understand why clarity and engagement matter in workplace communication:

✅ **Ensures Message Understanding** – Clear messaging reduces misunderstandings and misinterpretations.
✅ **Encourages Participation** – Engaging posts invite colleagues to **comment, share, and interact**.
✅ **Builds Community and Collaboration** – A well-written post fosters a culture of **knowledge-sharing and teamwork**.
✅ **Enhances Productivity** – Well-structured content ensures employees quickly grasp key points, saving time and effort.

By incorporating **structured writing techniques, a conversational tone, and interactive elements**, you can significantly **boost engagement and participation** in Viva Engage.

---

2. Best Practices for Clarity in Viva Engage Posts

2.1 Use Clear and Concise Language

When crafting posts in Viva Engage, keep your language **simple, direct, and free from unnecessary complexity**. Avoid jargon, technical terms (unless relevant), and overly long sentences.

Use plain language:
Instead of:
✗ *"It has come to our attention that a significant number of our esteemed colleagues are experiencing challenges with the newly implemented workflow optimization framework."*
Try:
✓ *"We've noticed that many team members have questions about the new workflow process. Here's a quick guide to help!"*

Be direct and avoid filler words:
✗ *"We would like to take this opportunity to inform you that the IT department will be conducting routine maintenance."*
✓ *"IT will conduct routine maintenance on Friday from 6 PM to 9 PM."*

Action Tip:
Before posting, read your message out loud. If it sounds overly complicated, simplify it for **better clarity**.

2.2 Structure Your Post for Readability

A well-structured post helps readers absorb information quickly. Use formatting techniques to **improve readability**:

✓ **Use short paragraphs** – Large blocks of text can be intimidating. Keep paragraphs **two to three sentences long**.
✓ **Use bullet points and lists** – Helps break down information clearly.
✓ **Use bold text for key points** – Draws attention to important details.

Example of a Well-Structured Post:

🚀 **Team Update: New Remote Work Guidelines!**

◆ **When?** Starting next Monday, the new policy takes effect.

◆ **Key changes:**

✓ Employees may work remotely up to **3 days per week**.

✓ Office attendance is required for **team meetings and client presentations**.

✓ Work schedules should be updated in Viva Engage for better coordination.

Let us know if you have any questions in the comments! 👆

This post is **short, structured, and easy to scan**, ensuring **clarity and quick understanding**.

2.3 Include a Clear Call-to-Action (CTA)

A **CTA (Call-to-Action)** tells your audience **what to do next**—whether it's commenting, sharing, or taking an action. Without a clear CTA, users might **read your post but not engage**.

Examples of effective CTAs:

- "Comment below with your thoughts!"

- "Click the link to register for the webinar."

- "Tag a colleague who might find this helpful."

- "Vote in the poll and share your feedback."

By **encouraging interaction**, you create a more dynamic and engaged Viva Engage community.

3. Best Practices for Engagement in Viva Engage Posts

Make Your Posts Interactive

A static post may inform, but an interactive post **engages**. Consider incorporating:

✓ **Polls** – Great for gathering opinions or feedback.

✓ **Questions** – Encourage users to share their thoughts.

✅ **GIFs & Emojis** – Make posts visually engaging.

✅ **Mentions (@name)** – Tagging colleagues invites participation.

Example of an Engaging Post:

🎯 **We need your input!**

Our team is working on improving the onboarding experience for new hires. **What was the most helpful part of your onboarding journey?**

💬 Drop your thoughts in the comments!

Tag a new colleague who might have fresh insights! 🏆

This **question-based** post **sparks discussion** and encourages participation.

Use a Conversational Tone

Formal corporate language can feel distant. Instead, write **as if you were talking to a colleague**—friendly, warm, and engaging.

✅ **Examples of a conversational tone:**

- Instead of *"All employees are requested to submit their reports before the designated deadline."*
  → Try *"Hey team! Don't forget to submit your reports by Friday. Thanks!"*

- Instead of *"We appreciate your cooperation in adhering to the guidelines."*
  → Try *"Thanks for following the guidelines! You're awesome!"*

Action Tip:
Use "you" and "we" to create a **personal** connection with readers.

Leverage Visual Content

Posts with **images, videos, or infographics** receive **higher engagement** than text-only posts.

✅ **Use images to reinforce key messages.**
✅ **Post short videos (1-2 mins) for announcements.**
✅ **Include infographics to simplify complex information.**

Example of a Post with Visuals:

🌟 **Meet Our Employee of the Month!** 🌟

🎉 Congrats to **@JohnDoe** for his outstanding work on the new client project! 🎉

John streamlined processes, reduced turnaround time by **20%**, and received **amazing feedback from the client**.

👏 Let's give John a big round of applause in the comments! 👏

[Insert a photo of John receiving his award]

Visual elements **grab attention** and make posts more engaging!

---

4. Common Mistakes to Avoid

Even with best practices, some mistakes can reduce engagement and clarity. Avoid:

✖ **Overly long posts** – Keep it concise and to the point.
✖ **Using too much jargon** – Write for **everyone**, not just specialists.
✖ **Lack of engagement prompts** – Always **include a CTA**.
✖ **Ignoring feedback** – Respond to **comments and reactions** to keep the conversation going.

Conclusion

Clear and engaging posts in Viva Engage help create **a vibrant, interactive workplace community**. By focusing on **clarity, structure, interaction, and visuals**, you can make your messages **more effective and impactful**.

🚀 **Key Takeaways:**
✅ Keep language **simple and concise**.

✅ Use **bullet points, bold text, and formatting** for easy reading.

✅ Include a **clear CTA** to drive engagement.

✅ Use **questions, mentions, and polls** to spark conversations.

✅ Incorporate **visuals** to boost engagement.

By applying these strategies, you'll **transform your workplace communication**, ensuring that your messages are not only **seen** but also **engaged with and acted upon**. Happy posting! 🎉

6.2.2 Using Visual Content Effectively

In the modern digital workplace, written communication alone is not always enough to capture attention and drive engagement. Visual content plays a critical role in making posts more engaging, memorable, and effective. Whether you are sharing an update, announcing a new initiative, or encouraging discussion within your Viva Engage community, incorporating images, videos, GIFs, and other visuals can enhance the clarity and impact of your message.

This section will explore the importance of visual content, the different types of visuals you can use, best practices for creating and integrating visual elements, and how to analyze their effectiveness in Microsoft Viva Engage.

1. Why Visual Content Matters in Workplace Communication

Visual content is a powerful tool for communication because it helps convey information quickly, improves retention, and makes content more appealing. Here's why using visuals effectively in Viva Engage is essential:

Capturing Attention in a Busy Workplace

Employees receive countless messages daily, from emails to chat notifications. A text-heavy post may be easily overlooked, but an engaging image, infographic, or video can immediately draw attention and encourage people to stop and engage with the content.

Example:

- Instead of a long paragraph about an upcoming company event, a visually appealing **flyer or poster** with key details can make the announcement more noticeable.

Enhancing Understanding and Retention

Studies show that people remember **visuals better than text**. A well-designed graphic or an explanatory video can simplify complex information and make it easier for employees to retain key messages.

Example:

- A **chart or infographic** explaining company goals for the quarter is more effective than a long text description.

Increasing Engagement and Interaction

Posts with **images and videos receive significantly more engagement** than plain-text posts. Employees are more likely to **like, comment on, and share** posts that contain appealing visual elements.

Example:

- A GIF or meme related to an ongoing company project can encourage informal discussions and boost team morale.

2. Types of Visual Content to Use in Viva Engage

There are multiple types of visual content that you can incorporate into your Viva Engage posts to maximize impact. Each serves a different purpose, and choosing the right type depends on the context and goal of your communication.

Images and Photos

Images are the most commonly used form of visual content and can instantly enhance the appeal of your posts.

- **Screenshots:** Helpful for demonstrating features, tutorials, or step-by-step instructions.
- **Team Photos:** Great for humanizing content, celebrating milestones, or showcasing team culture.

- **Stock Images:** Useful when an appropriate photo isn't available, but should be selected carefully to avoid looking generic.

- **Branded Graphics:** Custom-designed images with company branding can reinforce messaging and maintain consistency.

Best Practices:
Use **high-quality images** to maintain professionalism.
Keep images **relevant** to the content.
Avoid overly **text-heavy** images—if needed, use infographics instead.

Infographics and Data Visualizations

Infographics are an excellent way to present **complex data, statistics, or step-by-step guides** in an easily digestible format.

When to Use:
When summarizing survey results or key performance metrics.
To illustrate a workflow or company process.
To break down industry trends or best practices.

Example:

- Instead of writing out the results of an employee engagement survey, create an **infographic showing key statistics** with simple icons and charts.

Best Practices:
Keep text concise and use **visual hierarchy** to highlight key points.
Choose **consistent colors and fonts** aligned with company branding.
Avoid clutter—use white space effectively to improve readability.

Videos

Videos are highly engaging and can effectively deliver messages in an interactive format.

When to Use:
To demonstrate a new tool, feature, or software update.

To share leadership messages or company updates in a **more personal way**.
To promote an upcoming event or campaign in an engaging format.

Example:

- Instead of writing a lengthy post about new company policies, a **short video from leadership** explaining the changes can make the message more impactful.

Best Practices:
Keep videos **short** (ideally under 2 minutes) to retain engagement.
Add **subtitles** to improve accessibility.
Use **captivating thumbnails** to encourage clicks.

GIFs and Memes

GIFs and memes add an element of fun and **boost informal engagement**. They are effective for fostering a friendly work culture.

When to Use:
To celebrate team achievements with humor.
To make workplace reminders (e.g., meeting schedules) more entertaining.
To encourage participation in polls or discussions.

Example:

- A GIF of a clapping audience when announcing a major team success can make the post more lively and engaging.

Best Practices:
Ensure **GIFs align with company culture** (avoid unprofessional content).
Use sparingly—excessive use can dilute the message.

Slide Decks and Documents

If you need to share more **detailed information**, consider embedding **PowerPoint slides, PDFs, or interactive documents** in your posts.

When to Use:
To provide detailed guides or training materials.
To summarize meeting notes or project updates.
To share policy changes or company-wide reports.

Best Practices:
Keep slides **visually engaging**—avoid walls of text.
Include **summaries** or key takeaways for easy skimming.

3. Best Practices for Using Visuals Effectively in Viva Engage

While visuals enhance communication, using them **correctly** is key to achieving the best results. Below are some best practices to maximize their impact.

Maintain Visual Consistency

Maintaining a **consistent style, color scheme, and branding** across visual content creates a professional and cohesive experience.

✓ Use company **brand colors and fonts**.
✓ Keep designs simple and uncluttered.
✓ Ensure images are **high quality** and appropriately sized.

Optimize for Mobile Viewing

Many employees access Viva Engage from their **mobile devices**, so ensure that visuals are mobile-friendly.

✓ Use **legible fonts** and avoid tiny text.
✓ Ensure images are **not too wide**, so they display properly.
✓ Test videos on both **desktop and mobile** for clarity.

Balance Text and Visuals

While visuals are powerful, they should **complement** text rather than replace it entirely.

✓ Keep **descriptive captions** short and to the point.

✓ Use visuals **to emphasize** key messages, not replace them.

✓ Avoid overwhelming users with **too many elements in one post**.

4. Measuring the Effectiveness of Visual Content

Once you've incorporated visuals into your posts, it's important to **analyze their impact** to refine your approach.

📊 **Track Engagement Metrics:**

- Compare likes, comments, and shares on posts **with vs. without visuals**.

- Analyze the **time spent on video posts** to determine interest.

📌 **Experiment and Adjust:**

- Try **different types of visuals** (e.g., GIFs vs. infographics) and see what works best.

- Collect feedback from employees to improve future content.

Conclusion

Using visual content effectively in **Viva Engage** can greatly enhance communication, increase engagement, and ensure that messages are **noticed, understood, and remembered**. By strategically incorporating **images, infographics, videos, and other visual elements**, organizations can create a more dynamic and interactive workplace communication environment.

By following best practices—maintaining **visual consistency**, optimizing for **mobile users**, and measuring **impact**—you can ensure that your visual content enhances workplace communication and contributes to a more engaged workforce.

6.2.3 Scheduling Posts for Maximum Reach

In today's digital workplace, effective communication is critical to keeping employees informed, engaged, and connected. Microsoft Viva Engage provides organizations with a dynamic platform for sharing updates, announcements, and discussions. However, simply creating content is not enough—**timing** plays a crucial role in ensuring that your posts **reach the right audience at the right time** for maximum impact.

This section explores best practices for **scheduling posts strategically**, leveraging Viva Engage's built-in features, and ensuring that your content gets **maximum visibility and engagement**.

1. Why Scheduling Posts Matters

Scheduling posts is an essential part of any effective communication strategy. By strategically planning when to publish updates, you can:

- **Maximize Engagement:** Posts published at optimal times receive more views, likes, and comments.

- **Ensure Consistency:** Regularly scheduled posts help keep the community active and engaged.

- **Reach Global Audiences:** For organizations with international teams, scheduling ensures messages are received at the right time in different time zones.

- **Improve Content Planning:** Planning ahead allows for better coordination of messages and prevents information overload.

Let's dive into how to **leverage Viva Engage to schedule posts** effectively.

2. Understanding Audience Behavior and Optimal Posting Times

To schedule posts for maximum reach, you first need to understand **when your audience is most active** on Viva Engage. Several factors influence the **best times** to post, including **work schedules, company culture, and regional differences**.

Identifying Peak Engagement Hours

Analyzing **engagement trends** can help determine the best time to post content. Consider:

- **Standard Working Hours:** Employees typically check updates in the morning (8-10 AM) and after lunch (1-3 PM).

- **Mid-Week Activity Peaks:** Engagement levels often increase on **Tuesdays, Wednesdays, and Thursdays**, while Mondays and Fridays may have lower interaction.

- **Time Zones and Remote Teams:** If your organization operates across multiple regions, scheduling posts at **overlapping work hours** ensures a broader reach.

Actionable Tip: Use Viva Engage's **engagement analytics** to track when users are most active and adjust your scheduling accordingly.

Considering the Type of Content

Different types of content perform better at different times:

Content Type	Best Posting Time
Announcements & Company News	Early morning (8-10 AM) – employees start their day
Interactive Discussions	Midday (11 AM-1 PM) – active engagement time
Training & Educational Content	Mid-afternoon (2-4 PM) – quieter period, better focus
Social/Community Posts	Late afternoon (4-6 PM) – employees winding down

By aligning **post timing** with content type, you can **boost visibility and engagement**.

3. How to Schedule Posts in Viva Engage

Microsoft Viva Engage offers tools for **planning and scheduling posts**, ensuring that content goes live at the right time. While Viva Engage does not have a built-in "schedule post" feature (as of now), you can achieve this by:

Using Microsoft Planner and Power Automate

You can use **Microsoft Planner** and **Power Automate** to schedule posts in Viva Engage:

1. **Create a Post Draft:** Write your post in advance.

2. **Use Microsoft Planner:** Set up a task with a reminder for when you want to publish.

3. **Automate Posting with Power Automate:**

    o   Create a **workflow** that triggers a Viva Engage post at a scheduled time.

    o   Connect it with SharePoint or Outlook Calendar for automatic scheduling.

Integrating Viva Engage with Outlook for Scheduled Announcements

If you're making an important announcement, you can:

- Draft a **Viva Engage post**

- Schedule an **email reminder** in Outlook linking to the post

- Use Outlook's **delayed send feature** to notify employees at the right time

Actionable Tip: For organizations using **Microsoft Teams**, consider setting up **Teams notifications** that alert users when a scheduled Viva Engage post is published.

4. Strategies for Maximizing Post Engagement

Scheduling posts is only part of the strategy—**how** you present the content also matters. Here are some best practices:

Use Engaging Headlines and Previews

- Keep titles **short and compelling** (e.g., "🚀 Exciting News: New Training Program Launching!").

- Use **questions** or **action-driven language** (e.g., "How Can We Improve Collaboration? Let's Discuss!").

- Provide a **preview or teaser** of upcoming content to generate anticipation.

Leverage Multimedia for Better Visibility

Posts with **images, videos, and GIFs** receive **higher engagement** than text-only content. Consider:

- **Adding eye-catching visuals** to stand out in feeds.

- **Using short videos** (under 2 minutes) to increase engagement.

- **Including infographics or charts** for clarity.

Encourage Interaction with Call-to-Actions (CTAs)

A well-placed CTA encourages users to engage with your post. Examples:

- **For announcements:** "What do you think about this update? Share your thoughts below!"

- **For discussions:** "Vote in our poll and help shape our next project!"

- **For training content:** "Save this post for future reference!"

Cross-Promote Across Platforms

To **increase reach**, share your scheduled Viva Engage posts in:

- **Microsoft Teams Channels**

- **Company newsletters**

- **Internal SharePoint pages**

- **Email digests**

Actionable Tip: Tag relevant teams or departments using **@mentions** in your post to ensure they see it.

---

5. Measuring the Success of Scheduled Posts

Once your scheduled posts go live, it's important to **analyze their performance**. Viva Engage provides valuable insights into:

Engagement Metrics to Track

- **Views and Impressions:** How many people saw the post?

- **Likes and Reactions:** What is the audience sentiment?

- **Comments and Replies:** Are people engaging in discussions?

- **Shares/Reposts:** Is the content being spread across the organization?

Adjusting Your Strategy Based on Data

If engagement is **low**, consider:

- Posting at a **different time** based on user activity.

- Making posts **shorter and more direct**.

- Using more **visual elements**.

- Encouraging leaders or managers to **comment and engage** first to drive discussions.

Conclusion

Scheduling posts strategically in Viva Engage can significantly **increase visibility, engagement, and impact**. By understanding audience behavior, using available tools for scheduling, and optimizing content with visuals and CTAs, you can ensure that your posts reach the **right people at the right time**.

To recap:

✅ **Analyze engagement trends** to find the best times to post.
✅ **Use Microsoft Planner and Power Automate** to automate post scheduling.
✅ **Optimize content** with compelling headlines, multimedia, and CTAs.
✅ **Monitor performance metrics** and adjust your approach accordingly.

With a **data-driven** and **well-planned** approach, your scheduled posts on Viva Engage can drive meaningful conversations and enhance internal communication across your organization. 🚀

6.3 Managing and Moderating Communities

6.3.1 Setting Community Guidelines

Creating a strong and engaging community on **Microsoft Viva Engage** requires more than just regular posts and discussions—it demands a well-defined set of **community guidelines**. Clear guidelines help set expectations for behavior, foster a **positive and inclusive** environment, and ensure that members feel safe and encouraged to participate.

This section will guide you through the **importance of community guidelines**, key elements to include, and practical steps to implement and enforce them effectively.

1. Why Are Community Guidelines Important?

Community guidelines serve as the foundation of a well-moderated and productive Viva Engage community. Without them, discussions can become unstructured, and conflicts may arise. Here are some key reasons why setting community guidelines is essential:

Establishing Clear Expectations

Guidelines define what is **acceptable behavior** within the community. When members understand the rules, they are more likely to engage respectfully and constructively.

Encouraging Positive Interactions

A set of well-thought-out guidelines promotes healthy discussions, discourages toxic behavior, and ensures that everyone feels comfortable contributing.

Preventing Misinformation and Misuse

Clear rules help prevent **the spread of misinformation, spam, and irrelevant content**, ensuring that discussions remain **valuable and informative**.

Supporting Diversity and Inclusion

A well-managed community fosters **diversity** and **inclusion**, ensuring that all members—regardless of their backgrounds—feel welcome and respected.

Ensuring Compliance with Organizational Policies

Guidelines ensure that all discussions align with **company values, privacy policies, and professional standards**, reducing the risk of inappropriate or sensitive content being shared.

2. Key Elements of Effective Community Guidelines

Creating effective community guidelines requires a **balance between structure and flexibility**. Below are the key elements that should be included in your Viva Engage community guidelines:

Respectful Communication

Encourage members to be respectful in their interactions. A clear guideline on **respectful discussions** prevents conflicts and promotes a **collaborative environment**.

✓*Example:*
"Treat all members with courtesy and respect. Disagreements are natural, but personal attacks, harassment, or discrimination will not be tolerated."

Relevant and Meaningful Content

Members should post content that is relevant to the community's purpose. This ensures that discussions remain **useful and engaging**.

✓*Example:*
"Posts should be related to professional topics and discussions relevant to our workplace and community interests. Off-topic discussions, excessive self-promotion, and spam are not allowed."

No Harassment or Discrimination

To maintain an inclusive and **safe space**, it's crucial to have a **zero-tolerance policy** against harassment, discrimination, and hate speech.

✓*Example:*
"We do not tolerate harassment, hate speech, or discrimination based on race, gender,

religion, nationality, disability, or any other personal characteristic. If you experience or witness inappropriate behavior, please report it immediately."

Avoiding Spam and Promotional Content

Unnecessary promotions, excessive self-advertising, and spam can reduce the **value of the community** and drive members away.

✅*Example:*
"Avoid posting repetitive content, excessive promotions, or irrelevant advertisements. If you'd like to share a resource or external link, ensure it adds value to the discussion."

Data Privacy and Confidentiality

To maintain workplace security, members should not share **confidential or sensitive company information**.

✅*Example:*
"Do not share proprietary company information, internal documents, or confidential discussions without proper authorization. Protecting data security is a priority for all members."

Constructive Feedback and Healthy Discussions

Encourage members to provide feedback **in a constructive manner**. Discussions should **focus on problem-solving** rather than negative criticism.

✅*Example:*
"We encourage open and honest discussions, but please provide feedback in a constructive and professional manner. Instead of complaining, suggest solutions."

Copyright and Intellectual Property

Make sure that all shared content respects **copyright laws** and **intellectual property rights**.

✅*Example:*
"When sharing external content (articles, images, videos), ensure that you have permission to do so or provide proper attribution to the original creator."

Reporting Violations and Moderation Policy

Members should know how to report inappropriate behavior and understand what actions will be taken when guidelines are violated.

✓*Example:*
"If you see any posts or comments that violate community guidelines, report them to the moderators. Repeated violations may result in content removal, warnings, or restricted access to the community."

3. Implementing Community Guidelines in Viva Engage

Once you've created your community guidelines, the next step is to communicate and enforce them effectively. Here's how:

Posting the Guidelines in a Visible Location

- Pin the guidelines to the top of the community page.

- Include them in new member welcome messages.

- Create a short video or infographic explaining the rules.

Reinforcing Guidelines Through Regular Communication

- Occasionally re-share the guidelines to remind members.

- Highlight positive examples of community engagement to reinforce good behavior.

Encouraging Member Acknowledgment

- Ask new members to agree to the guidelines when joining.

- Conduct periodic awareness sessions about proper community etiquette.

Setting Up Automated Moderation

- Use Viva Engage's moderation tools to automatically detect offensive language or spam.

- Set up keyword filters to flag inappropriate content before it gets posted.

Training Moderators and Community Leaders

- Assign trusted members as moderators to help enforce the guidelines.

- Provide training on handling reports, diffusing conflicts, and encouraging engagement.

4. Handling Violations and Enforcing Guidelines

Even with clear guidelines, violations may still occur. Here's how to handle them effectively:

Addressing Minor Infractions Privately

If a user unintentionally violates a guideline, send them a private message explaining the issue.

✓ Example Message:
"Hi [User], we noticed that your recent post contained promotional content, which goes against our community guidelines. We encourage discussions related to [community topic]. Let us know if you have any questions!"

Deleting Inappropriate Content

If a post or comment is harmful, misleading, or offensive, moderators should remove it immediately and notify the user.

Implementing Escalation Policies

For repeated violations, establish a **three-strike policy**:

1. **First offense** → Private warning

2. **Second offense** → Temporary suspension or restricted posting

3. **Third offense** → Permanent removal from the community

Encouraging a Culture of Self-Regulation

- Encourage members to **self-moderate** and flag inappropriate content.

- Foster a culture where **community members support and correct each other** respectfully.

5. Conclusion

Setting clear and well-structured community guidelines is the key to building a thriving Viva Engage community. Guidelines create a safe, respectful, and productive environment, allowing employees to engage meaningfully and collaborate effectively.

By following best practices—defining expectations, reinforcing policies, training moderators, and handling violations effectively—organizations can ensure that Viva Engage remains a valuable communication tool that enhances workplace collaboration and engagement.

6.3.2 Handling Inappropriate Content

A vibrant and engaging Viva Engage community thrives when members feel safe, respected, and encouraged to participate in meaningful discussions. However, like any online platform, inappropriate content can occasionally surface, disrupting the positive atmosphere and discouraging engagement. Whether it's offensive language, harassment, misinformation, or spam, **handling inappropriate content** effectively is crucial to maintaining a healthy and professional communication environment.

In this section, we will explore how to identify, manage, and prevent inappropriate content in Viva Engage. We will also discuss the role of **moderators and administrators**, as well as best practices for ensuring a safe and productive space for collaboration.

1. Understanding Inappropriate Content in Viva Engage

Before discussing how to manage inappropriate content, it's important to define what constitutes such content. Inappropriate content can take many forms, and organizations may have different policies on what is acceptable. Generally, inappropriate content falls into the following categories:

Offensive or Harassing Language

- Hate speech, discrimination, or derogatory remarks based on race, gender, religion, or other personal attributes.

- Personal attacks, bullying, or intimidation against individuals or groups.

- Use of profanity or language that is offensive or unprofessional.

Misinformation and Fake News

- Sharing false or misleading information that can create confusion or harm credibility.

- Spreading rumors or speculation that could damage the organization's reputation.

Spam and Irrelevant Content

- Excessive self-promotion, such as repeatedly posting promotional material unrelated to the community's purpose.

- Posting irrelevant or disruptive content that does not contribute to meaningful discussions.

- Sharing malicious links, phishing attempts, or unauthorized advertisements.

Confidential or Sensitive Information

- Posting proprietary company information that should remain private.

- Sharing personal employee details without consent.

- Leaking internal discussions or confidential project details.

Explicit or Inappropriate Media

- Posting images, videos, or other media that contain graphic, violent, or explicit content.

- Sharing materials that violate corporate policies or workplace standards.

Understanding these categories helps moderators, admins, and community members quickly identify when content crosses the line and needs to be addressed.

2. Strategies for Managing Inappropriate Content

Once inappropriate content is identified, it's essential to handle it swiftly, professionally, and fairly. Here are the key steps for managing such content in Viva Engage:

Establish and Enforce Community Guidelines

Setting clear and well-defined community guidelines is the first step in preventing and managing inappropriate content. These guidelines should outline acceptable behavior and what constitutes inappropriate content.

- Display guidelines prominently in the community description or pinned posts.

- Ensure all members understand the rules upon joining.

- Regularly review and update policies as needed.

Example Guideline Statement: *"All members are expected to communicate respectfully. Hate speech, personal attacks, and misinformation will not be tolerated. Repeated violations may result in removal from the community."*

Monitoring Content Proactively

Rather than waiting for issues to arise, proactive monitoring helps keep conversations productive. There are several ways to monitor and moderate content effectively:

- Regularly Review Posts and Comments: Assign community moderators to review new posts and discussions to detect issues early.

- Enable Content Filtering Tools: Viva Engage offers built-in filtering options to automatically flag inappropriate content based on keywords or reporting.

- Encourage Self-Regulation: Community members should be empowered to report inappropriate posts when they see them.

Best Practice: Rotate moderation duties among different team members to ensure continuous oversight without burdening a single individual.

Responding to Inappropriate Content

When inappropriate content is identified, moderators should respond promptly and professionally. The response should be appropriate to the severity of the issue:

Minor Offenses (Accidental Violations)

For minor violations, such as irrelevant posts or mild unintentional language misuse, a gentle reminder is often enough.

✓ **Action:** Send a private message reminding the user of the guidelines.
✓ **Example Message:** *"Hi [User], we noticed your recent post doesn't align with our community guidelines. Please ensure that discussions stay relevant to the group. Let us know if you have any questions!"*

Moderate Offenses (Repeated Violations)

For repeated offenses or borderline inappropriate behavior, a stronger warning may be necessary.

✓ **Action:** Issue a formal warning and notify the user of potential consequences.
✓ **Example Message:** *"Hi [User], we have noticed that some of your recent comments do not align with our community standards. This is a formal warning—please be mindful of your language and ensure that future discussions remain respectful. Further violations may result in restrictions."*

Severe Offenses (Harassment, Hate Speech, or Explicit Content)

For serious violations such as hate speech, personal attacks, or explicit content, immediate action is required.

✓ **Action:**

- Remove the content immediately.

- Suspend or remove the user, depending on company policy.

- Escalate the issue to HR or management if necessary.

✓ **Example Message (Public Announcement for Transparency):** *"A recent post was removed due to a violation of our community standards. We take workplace respect seriously and encourage all members to maintain a positive and professional environment. If you have concerns, please contact an administrator."*

Educating the Community on Proper Conduct

A strong communication culture requires ongoing education on workplace behavior. Consider the following strategies:

- Conduct Training Sessions: Offer periodic workshops on digital etiquette and respectful communication.

- Use Positive Reinforcement: Acknowledge and reward members who contribute positively to the community.

- Provide a Reporting System: Ensure all members know how to report inappropriate content and that reports are taken seriously.

Example Training Topic: *"How to Foster Inclusive and Respectful Discussions in Viva Engage"*

3. Preventing Inappropriate Content in the Future

Rather than just reacting to inappropriate content, organizations should implement long-term strategies to prevent issues before they occur.

Assigning Moderators and Admins

Having dedicated moderators ensures that content is reviewed and maintained regularly.

✓ **Tips for Choosing Moderators:**

- Select active and responsible community members.

- Provide training on how to handle violations.

- Establish a moderation workflow to ensure consistency.

Automating Content Moderation

Microsoft Viva Engage provides AI-powered tools to help detect and remove inappropriate content automatically.

✓ Features to Use:

- Keyword Filters: Block specific offensive terms.

- Auto-Flagging: Automatically notify admins when concerning content is posted.

- Pre-Approved Posts: Require admin approval for first-time posters.

Fostering a Positive Community Culture

A healthy community culture reduces the likelihood of inappropriate behavior.

✓ Ways to Promote Positive Engagement:

- Encourage constructive discussions by setting the right tone in leadership posts.

- Recognize and reward positive contributions (e.g., "Member of the Month").

- Lead by example—moderators should model professional and respectful behavior.

Conclusion

Handling inappropriate content in Viva Engage requires a proactive and strategic approach. By setting clear guidelines, monitoring discussions, responding appropriately, and fostering a respectful community, organizations can maintain a safe and productive environment.

By leveraging Viva Engage's moderation tools, assigning responsible community leaders, and promoting **positive engagement**, companies can ensure that their workplace communication remains professional, respectful, and engaging for all employees.

6.3.3 Assigning Moderators and Admin Roles

Managing a successful Viva Engage community requires strong leadership, clear responsibilities, and effective moderation. Assigning moderators and administrators is a crucial step in ensuring that the community remains engaged, organized, and free from disruptions. Properly managed communities encourage healthy discussions, foster collaboration, and create an inclusive and positive work culture.

This section will cover:

- The differences between administrators and moderators.

- The roles and responsibilities of each position.

- Best practices for assigning and managing moderators/admins.

- Tips for effective community governance.

1. Understanding the Different Roles in Viva Engage

Before assigning roles, it's important to understand the **hierarchy of permissions** in Viva Engage. The platform allows different levels of access, each with specific responsibilities and controls.

Administrators (Admins)

Who They Are: Admins are the highest-level managers within a Viva Engage community. They have the authority to oversee the entire platform, configure settings, and enforce policies.

Key Responsibilities:

- Creating and managing communities: Admins can establish new communities and set permissions.

- Defining policies and guidelines: Admins ensure that all users follow the organization's communication policies.

- Configuring platform settings: They can adjust privacy settings, integration options, and system-wide features.

- Monitoring analytics and engagement: Admins track key performance metrics and adjust strategies accordingly.

- Managing user permissions: They can assign and revoke moderator or admin privileges.

- Handling escalations: If an issue arises that moderators cannot resolve, admins step in.

Access Level: Admins have **full control** over Viva Engage and can modify settings that affect all users.

Moderators

Who They Are: Moderators help manage specific communities or groups within Viva Engage. They focus on day-to-day engagement, content management, and community health.

Key Responsibilities:

- Encouraging discussions: Moderators stimulate conversation and ensure active participation.

- Enforcing community guidelines: They monitor discussions and flag inappropriate content.

- Approving or removing posts: Moderators review content to maintain relevance and quality.

- Resolving disputes: If conflicts arise, they step in to mediate and maintain a positive environment.

- Responding to member queries: They answer questions and provide guidance to users.

- Organizing events and activities: Some moderators may plan virtual events to keep members engaged.

Access Level: Moderators have limited control, usually within specific groups or communities. They can manage content and members but cannot change system-wide settings.

Community Members

While they don't have **special permissions**, active community members play a critical role in shaping the culture. Admins and moderators should work to **empower members** by encouraging participation and recognizing valuable contributions.

How to Assign Moderators and Admins Effectively

Assigning the right people to these roles is essential for a well-functioning Viva Engage community. Here's how to ensure that moderators and admins are selected wisely:

Choosing the Right People

When selecting moderators and admins, consider the following criteria:

- Experience and expertise: Select individuals who are knowledgeable about the topic or purpose of the community.

- Engagement levels: Look for active participants who frequently contribute to discussions.

- Communication skills: Moderators should be approachable and able to handle discussions diplomatically.

- Trustworthiness: Since they will have permissions to moderate and manage content, they must be responsible and fair.

- Conflict resolution abilities: Choose people who can handle disagreements professionally and maintain a respectful atmosphere.

Best Practice: Consider creating an application process where interested employees can volunteer and explain why they would make a good moderator.

Assigning Roles in Viva Engage

Once you've chosen the right candidates, follow these steps to assign roles:

For Administrators

1. Go to Viva Engage Admin Center: Navigate to the admin settings.

2. Select "Manage Roles": Look for the option to edit user roles.

3. Add or promote a user: Enter their name or email and select "Administrator."

4. Set permissions: Choose whether they have full access or limited control over certain areas.

5. Confirm and save changes: The new admin will receive a notification about their role.

For Moderators

1. Go to the specific community or group where you want to add a moderator.

2. Click "Manage Members" and search for the user.

3. Assign the moderator role by selecting the appropriate permission.

4. Notify the new moderator so they understand their responsibilities.

3. Best Practices for Moderators and Admins

Having the right people in place is just the first step. To ensure effective management, follow these best practices:

Establish Clear Guidelines

Moderators should have a clear understanding of:

- **What type of content is allowed**

- **How to handle inappropriate behavior**

- **When to escalate issues to admins**

Tip:
Create a **moderator handbook** that outlines responsibilities, best practices, and example scenarios.

Provide Training for Moderators

Training ensures that moderators can confidently handle their responsibilities.

Training Topics to Cover:

- How to moderate discussions effectively.

- Best practices for engagement.

- Managing disputes and user complaints.

- Using analytics to track community success.

Tip:
Host a **quarterly training session** where moderators can discuss challenges and share best practices.

Monitor Performance and Provide Feedback

Admins should regularly check in with moderators to review their effectiveness.

- **Use Viva Engage analytics** to track engagement and see how well moderators are fostering discussions.

- **Offer feedback and coaching** to improve their moderation skills.

- **Recognize and reward moderators** for their contributions.

Tip:
Hold a **monthly moderator check-in meeting** to discuss strategies, address challenges, and share updates.

Rotate Moderators Periodically

If a moderator is inactive or no longer engaged, consider rotating new members into the role.

- Conduct **bi-annual reviews** of moderator effectiveness.

- Encourage moderators to **step down gracefully** if they can't continue their duties.

- Allow other engaged community members to **apply** for the role.

Encourage Transparency and Inclusivity

- Moderators should be **transparent** in their actions (e.g., explain why a post was removed).

- Encourage **diverse voices** to participate in discussions.

- Prevent **bias** by applying rules fairly to all members.

Tip:
Create a **public FAQ or pinned post** that explains the role of moderators and the community guidelines.

4. Common Challenges and How to Overcome Them

Even with well-structured roles, challenges may arise. Here's how to address them:

Challenge	Solution
Lack of participation from moderators	Set clear **engagement expectations** and follow up regularly.
Conflicts between moderators and users	Train moderators on **conflict resolution techniques** and escalation procedures.
Difficulty managing large communities	Assign **multiple moderators** and divide responsibilities (e.g., one handles content, another manages disputes).
Users questioning moderation decisions	Maintain **transparency** and offer an appeal process for removed content.

Conclusion

Assigning moderators and admin roles in Viva Engage is essential for fostering an engaged, professional, and inclusive workplace community. By carefully selecting qualified individuals, providing them with training, and continuously monitoring their effectiveness, organizations can ensure that their communities thrive.

By implementing these best practices, you can create a well-managed Viva Engage environment where employees feel heard, respected, and motivated to participate.

PART VII
Security, Privacy, and Compliance

7.1 Understanding Viva Engage Security Features

7.1.1 Data Encryption and Protection

Introduction

In today's digital workplace, security is a top priority for organizations that rely on cloud-based platforms for communication and collaboration. Microsoft Viva Engage, as part of the Microsoft 365 ecosystem, is designed with **robust security measures** to protect sensitive business data and ensure that organizations can communicate safely and effectively.

One of the most critical components of this security framework is **data encryption and protection**. Encryption ensures that information shared within Viva Engage—whether it's messages, files, or user interactions—remains secure and accessible only to authorized individuals.

In this section, we will explore:

- **How data encryption works in Viva Engage**

- **How Microsoft protects data in transit and at rest**

- **Best practices for organizations to enhance security**

By understanding these principles, IT administrators, security teams, and end-users can better safeguard corporate communication and mitigate risks related to data breaches or unauthorized access.

1. What is Data Encryption?

Encryption is the process of **converting readable data into an unreadable format** to prevent unauthorized access. Only users with the proper decryption key can revert the data back to its original form. In Microsoft Viva Engage, encryption is applied in multiple ways to secure communication and files shared within the platform.

Encryption ensures that:

- Data remains **confidential** and cannot be accessed by unauthorized users.

- Information is **integrity-protected**, meaning it cannot be altered during transmission.

- Data remains **available** to authorized users while being protected from cyber threats.

Microsoft employs industry-standard encryption algorithms, such as **Advanced Encryption Standard (AES-256)**, which is widely regarded as one of the most secure encryption methods.

2. How Viva Engage Encrypts Data

Viva Engage follows Microsoft's Zero Trust security model, which assumes that no entity—inside or outside the organization—should be trusted by default. This means that data encryption is enforced both in transit and at rest to ensure end-to-end security.

Data in Transit Encryption

Data in transit refers to information that is actively moving between users, devices, or cloud servers. This includes messages, files, and any other content that is sent or received within Viva Engage.

To protect this data, Microsoft uses Transport Layer Security (TLS) encryption, ensuring that any communication remains secure against interception or unauthorized access.

♦ Key encryption measures for data in transit in Viva Engage:

- TLS 1.2+ encryption for securing web sessions and API calls.

- HTTPS (HyperText Transfer Protocol Secure) enforcement for all Viva Engage communications.

- End-to-end encryption when exchanging messages within Microsoft 365 applications.

✓ Security Benefits:

- Prevents man-in-the-middle (MITM) attacks, where an attacker tries to intercept communication.

- Ensures that even if data is intercepted, it remains encrypted and unreadable.

- Guarantees secure connections between Viva Engage and integrated Microsoft 365 services.

Data at Rest Encryption

Data at rest refers to information that is stored on servers, databases, or user devices but is not actively being transmitted. This includes messages, documents, and media files uploaded to Viva Engage.

Microsoft uses Azure Storage Encryption (ASE) to encrypt data at rest, ensuring that even if unauthorized access to storage infrastructure occurs, the data remains protected.

◆ Key encryption measures for data at rest in Viva Engage:

- AES-256 encryption for stored data.

- BitLocker encryption for devices and local storage.

- Automatic key management via Microsoft's Key Management Service (KMS).

✓ Security Benefits:

- Ensures that all stored content remains encrypted by default.

- Protects against unauthorized access, even in the event of physical data theft.

- Helps organizations meet regulatory compliance requirements.

3. Microsoft's Security Framework for Data Protection

Viva Engage follows Microsoft's enterprise security policies, which are designed to meet global security standards. Here are key security measures Microsoft applies to keep Viva Engage data protected:

Multi-Factor Authentication (MFA) and Access Controls

Microsoft provides strong access control mechanisms to prevent unauthorized logins. Multi-Factor Authentication (MFA) requires users to verify their identity through an additional step, such as a mobile app or biometric authentication.

✅ How to enable MFA for Viva Engage:

- IT administrators can enforce Conditional Access Policies within Microsoft Entra ID (formerly Azure AD).

- Users can enable Authenticator App verification to prevent unauthorized logins.

◆ Why it matters:

- Prevents unauthorized access even if passwords are compromised.

- Reduces the risk of phishing attacks and credential theft.

Role-Based Access Control (RBAC)

Organizations using Viva Engage can manage user permissions using Role-Based Access Control (RBAC). This ensures that employees only have access to the data they need based on their role.

✅ Types of permissions in Viva Engage:

- Administrators: Have full control over security policies and access management.

- Group Owners: Can manage group-specific settings and member permissions.

- Regular Users: Can create posts and interact with content based on assigned permissions.

◆ Why it matters:

- Prevents unauthorized data modifications or leaks.

- Ensures that sensitive content is restricted to specific roles or departments.

4. Best Practices for Organizations to Enhance Security

While Microsoft provides built-in security features, organizations should adopt best practices to further protect their data in Viva Engage.

Enforcing Data Retention Policies

Organizations should define data retention and deletion policies to manage how long messages and files remain accessible in Viva Engage.

✅ **How to do this:**

- Set up automatic data expiration for messages.

- Use Microsoft Purview compliance policies to control data storage duration.

- Regularly audit old content and delete unnecessary data.

Implementing Security Awareness Training

Many security breaches happen due to human error. Organizations should conduct security awareness training to educate employees about:

- Recognizing phishing attempts.

- Safeguarding sensitive information.

- Reporting suspicious activity within Viva Engage.

✅ **How to implement this:**

- Schedule quarterly security training for employees.

- Use simulated phishing tests to educate users on detecting cyber threats.

- Encourage employees to report security concerns via Viva Engage's reporting feature.

Enabling Audit Logs and Monitoring

Organizations should regularly monitor activity logs to detect suspicious behavior. Microsoft 365 Compliance Center allows IT teams to track:

- Login attempts and failures.

- Unusual data downloads or shares.

- Potential security threats based on user behavior analytics.

✅ **How to enable:**

- Activate Microsoft Defender for Cloud Apps to track user actions.

- Review audit logs in Microsoft Purview for security compliance.

- Set up real-time alerts for unauthorized access attempts.

Conclusion

Data encryption and protection are fundamental to ensuring secure communication within Microsoft Viva Engage. By leveraging industry-leading encryption protocols, robust access controls, and advanced compliance tools, organizations can safeguard their internal communications against threats.

To further enhance security, IT administrators and security teams should:
✓☐ Enable multi-factor authentication (MFA).
✓☐ Monitor audit logs for suspicious activities.
✓☐ Educate employees about security risks.
✓☐ Implement role-based access controls.

By applying these best practices, organizations can build a secure and compliant environment where employees can communicate, collaborate, and innovate with confidence.

7.1.2 Managing User Access and Permissions

Effective management of user access and permissions is crucial in maintaining a secure and efficient environment within Microsoft Viva Engage. By controlling who can view, contribute, and manage content, administrators ensure that sensitive information is protected and that users have the appropriate level of access to perform their roles. In this section, we will explore the different access and permission levels available in Viva Engage, how to assign and modify permissions, and best practices for maintaining a secure and organized communication platform.

1. Overview of User Access and Permissions in Viva Engage

User access and permissions in Viva Engage are designed to provide flexibility while safeguarding organizational data. Access control in Viva Engage can be broadly categorized into:

- **Global Access:** Overall access to the Viva Engage platform.

- **Group-Specific Access:** Permissions within individual groups and communities.

- **Content-Level Permissions:** Control over individual posts, files, and conversations.

These layers of access control allow administrators to customize the user experience and secure information based on organizational policies.

2. Types of Users and Roles in Viva Engage

Global Roles

Global roles apply to the entire Viva Engage platform and define the broad capabilities a user has:

- **Admin:**
    - Full control over the platform, including settings, user management, and content moderation.
    - Can create, delete, and manage groups.
    - Access to analytics and reporting features.

- **Member:**
    - Standard users who can participate in discussions, create posts, and join groups.

- o Limited access to settings and no control over platform-wide configurations.

- **Guest:**

  - o External users with restricted access, typically invited for collaboration on specific projects or topics.

  - o Limited to viewing and participating in designated groups.

Group Roles

Within each group or community, users can have specific roles that dictate their abilities:

- **Group Admin:**

  - o Full control over group settings, membership, and content moderation.

  - o Can make announcements and pin important posts.

- **Moderator:**

  - o Can approve posts, manage discussions, and moderate content.

  - o Supports group admins in maintaining a positive environment.

- **Member:**

  - o Can create posts, comment, and participate in group activities.

  - o Cannot change group settings or moderate other users.

- **Viewer (Read-Only):**

  - o Can only view group content without participating or commenting.

  - o Ideal for informational or broadcast-only groups.

Content-Level Permissions

Permissions can also be set at the content level, allowing users to:

- Restrict visibility of specific posts or files.

- Enable or disable comments on individual posts.

- Limit sharing and downloading of sensitive documents.

3. Assigning and Managing User Access

3.1 Assigning Global Roles

Global roles are typically assigned by platform administrators through the Viva Engage admin center.

Steps to Assign Global Roles:

1. Navigate to the **Admin Center** in Viva Engage.

2. Select **User Management**.

3. Search for the user by name or email address.

4. Click **Edit Role** and select **Admin**, **Member**, or **Guest**.

5. Confirm the changes by clicking **Save**.

Best Practices:

- Limit the number of **global admins** to reduce security risks.

- Regularly review user roles to ensure they align with current responsibilities.

3.2 Managing Group Roles

Group roles can be adjusted by group admins or moderators directly within the group settings.

Steps to Assign Group Roles:

1. Go to the **group** where you want to manage roles.

2. Click on **Members** in the group navigation panel.

3. Locate the user and click the **Role Dropdown** next to their name.

4. Select **Admin**, **Moderator**, **Member**, or **Viewer**.

5. Save changes to apply the new role.

Best Practices:

- Assign **multiple moderators** for large or active groups to ensure efficient management.

- Use **viewer roles** for broadcast or informational groups to prevent unauthorized posts.

3.3 Setting Content-Level Permissions

Content-level permissions are managed directly on posts or documents.

Restricting Post Visibility:

- When creating a post, click on the **visibility settings** (usually a lock or globe icon).

- Choose **Everyone**, **Group Members Only**, or **Specific People**.

- Save to restrict visibility accordingly.

Controlling Document Access:

- Upload the document and click the **permissions icon**.

- Set permissions for **viewing**, **editing**, or **downloading**.

- Enable or disable **commenting** on the document.

Best Practices:

- Use **specific people** visibility for sensitive information.

- Disable **downloading** for confidential documents to prevent unauthorized sharing.

4. Monitoring and Auditing User Access

Effective access management also involves ongoing **monitoring and auditing**. Viva Engage provides tools for tracking user activity and ensuring compliance with organizational policies.

4.1 Monitoring User Activity

Admins can view **activity logs** to track actions such as:

- Group creation and deletion.

- Role assignments and changes.

- Content uploads and deletions.

Accessing Activity Logs:

1. Go to the **Admin Center**.

2. Select **Activity Logs**.

3. Filter by **date**, **user**, or **action type**.

4. Review logs for any unauthorized or suspicious activity.

4.2 Auditing Group Membership

Regularly auditing group membership ensures that only authorized users have access to sensitive information.

Steps for Group Auditing:

1. Navigate to the **Group Settings**.

2. Click on **Members**.

3. Export a list of current members for review.

4. Remove any unauthorized or inactive members.

4.3 Reporting Suspicious Activity

Admins and members should be vigilant in reporting any unusual behavior or unauthorized access.

Reporting Process:

1. Click on the **user's profile** or the specific **content** in question.

2. Select **Report** from the dropdown menu.

3. Provide details of the suspicious activity and submit the report.

4. Admins will be notified to review and take appropriate action.

5. Integrating with Microsoft 365 for Enhanced Security

Viva Engage integrates seamlessly with Microsoft 365's security features, enhancing access control and compliance.

5.1 Using Azure Active Directory (AAD) for Single Sign-On (SSO)

Azure Active Directory (AAD) provides **Single Sign-On (SSO)** capabilities, streamlining user access while improving security.

Benefits of SSO Integration:

- Centralized management of user identities.
- Simplified login process with one set of credentials.
- Enhanced security through multi-factor authentication (MFA).

5.2 Applying Conditional Access Policies

Conditional Access in AAD allows admins to enforce policies based on user location, device compliance, and more.

Examples of Conditional Policies:

- Require **MFA** for users accessing Viva Engage outside the corporate network.
- Block access from **non-compliant devices**.
- Restrict access to specific **IP ranges** or geographical locations.

5.3 Integrating with Microsoft Defender for Cloud Apps

Microsoft Defender for Cloud Apps offers additional monitoring and protection capabilities.

Features of Defender Integration:

- **Real-time monitoring** of user activity for suspicious behavior.
- Automated **alerts and reports** for potential security breaches.
- Integration with **Microsoft Information Protection** for data classification and labeling.

6. Best Practices for Managing User Access and Permissions

Principle of Least Privilege

Grant users the **minimum level of access** required for their role to reduce security risks.

Regularly Review and Update Roles

Conduct **quarterly reviews** of user roles and group memberships to ensure continued relevance and security.

Educate Users on Access Policies

Provide **training and resources** on the importance of access control and how to report unauthorized access.

Implement Multi-Factor Authentication (MFA)

Enforce **MFA** for all admin and sensitive accounts to add an extra layer of security.

---

7. Conclusion

Managing user access and permissions in Microsoft Viva Engage is essential for maintaining a secure, compliant, and efficient communication environment. By understanding the different roles, properly assigning permissions, and leveraging Microsoft 365 integrations, organizations can protect sensitive information while enabling effective collaboration. Regular monitoring, auditing, and adherence to best practices further enhance the security and integrity of the platform.

7.1.3 Compliance with Organizational Policies

Introduction

In today's digital workplace, organizations must ensure that their communication platforms comply with internal policies, industry regulations, and legal requirements. Microsoft Viva Engage provides robust features that help businesses maintain compliance with their security, governance, and privacy policies. Understanding these compliance features is crucial for IT administrators, security teams, and end-users to protect sensitive data, ensure regulatory adherence, and maintain a secure digital workspace.

This section will cover:

- The importance of compliance in Viva Engage

- How Viva Engage aligns with organizational policies

- Key compliance features and best practices for maintaining a secure communication environment

1. Understanding Compliance in Viva Engage

Why Compliance Matters in Workplace Communication

Compliance is an essential component of any enterprise communication platform because it helps:

- Protect sensitive information: Prevents unauthorized access to confidential business data.

- Maintain regulatory adherence: Ensures that communication follows legal and industry standards, such as GDPR, HIPAA, and ISO/IEC 27001.

- Prevent data breaches: Reduces the risk of security incidents by enforcing access controls and monitoring usage.

- Foster a safe and professional environment: Ensures that discussions and shared content remain professional and aligned with company guidelines.

By ensuring compliance, organizations can reduce legal risks, protect brand reputation, and improve employee trust.

How Viva Engage Aligns with Organizational Policies

Microsoft Viva Engage is built within the Microsoft 365 ecosystem, which means it follows the same security and compliance standards as SharePoint, Teams, and OneDrive. Viva Engage integrates with:

- Microsoft Purview Compliance Center: A centralized hub for data governance, auditing, and security policies.

- Microsoft Defender for Office 365: Protects against cyber threats, such as phishing and malware.

- Azure Active Directory (Azure AD): Manages user authentication and role-based access control.

By leveraging these tools, organizations can ensure that all conversations, file sharing, and user interactions within Viva Engage adhere to internal policies and external regulations.

2. Key Compliance Features in Viva Engage

Viva Engage offers several built-in features to help organizations enforce compliance policies and manage risks. These include:

Data Retention and Archiving

Organizations often need to store and retrieve historical communication data for legal and auditing purposes. Viva Engage integrates with Microsoft 365 retention policies, enabling businesses to:

- Retain messages and files for a specified period to meet legal or business requirements.

- Archive inactive groups and discussions without losing historical data.

- Set automatic deletion policies to remove outdated information based on company guidelines.

Example Use Case: A financial institution must comply with SEC (Securities and Exchange Commission) regulations, requiring them to store employee communications for at least five years. Using Microsoft 365 retention policies, they can ensure that Viva Engage conversations are archived securely.

Data Loss Prevention (DLP) Policies

Data Loss Prevention (DLP) policies prevent unauthorized sharing of sensitive data in Viva Engage. With Microsoft Purview DLP, organizations can:

- Identify and block confidential data (e.g., credit card numbers, personal identification numbers).

- Apply encryption rules to protect sensitive files shared in conversations.

- Send alerts to administrators when policy violations occur.

Example Use Case: A healthcare company using Viva Engage must comply with HIPAA (Health Insurance Portability and Accountability Act). DLP rules can prevent employees from sharing patient records in public groups, ensuring compliance with data protection laws.

Content Moderation and Monitoring

To maintain a professional communication environment, organizations can use content moderation tools in Viva Engage, including:

- Keyword Filtering: Blocks messages that contain offensive or inappropriate language.

- Automated Flagging: Uses AI-powered monitoring to detect compliance violations.

- Manual Review: Admins can review flagged posts before they are published.

Example Use Case: A multinational corporation wants to ensure that all internal communications remain professional and inclusive. Using automated keyword filtering, they prevent employees from posting messages that contain offensive language or discriminatory remarks.

eDiscovery and Legal Hold

For organizations subject to legal investigations or compliance audits, Microsoft 365 provides eDiscovery and legal hold features. These tools allow businesses to:

- Search and retrieve messages related to compliance investigations.

- Preserve critical records to meet legal obligations.

- Restrict message deletion to prevent tampering with evidence.

Example Use Case: A company facing a lawsuit related to employee misconduct needs to review past communications. Using Microsoft Purview eDiscovery, they can search for relevant conversations in Viva Engage and present them as legal evidence.

Role-Based Access Control (RBAC)

Organizations can restrict access to sensitive information by assigning specific user roles and permissions in Viva Engage. Through Azure Active Directory (Azure AD), administrators can:

- Define different access levels for employees, managers, and external partners.

- Restrict sensitive conversations to authorized personnel only.

- Control who can create, delete, or edit content within the platform.

Example Use Case: A government agency using Viva Engage needs to ensure that only senior executives can access classified discussions. Using role-based access control, they limit access to approved personnel only.

3. Best Practices for Ensuring Compliance in Viva Engage

To maximize the security and compliance benefits of Viva Engage, organizations should follow these best practices:

Implement Clear Communication Policies

- Define acceptable use guidelines for employees.

- Establish rules for sharing sensitive information.

- Educate employees about potential compliance risks.

Regularly Audit and Monitor Activity

- Conduct routine compliance checks using Microsoft 365 analytics.

- Review user activity logs to detect unusual behavior.

- Ensure that all compliance policies are up-to-date with industry regulations.

Train Employees on Security and Compliance

- Provide training on data protection policies and best practices.

- Teach employees how to report compliance violations.

- Encourage a culture of security awareness and responsible communication.

Leverage AI and Automation for Compliance Monitoring

- Use Microsoft Defender to automatically flag suspicious activities.

- Enable AI-powered sentiment analysis to detect inappropriate conversations.

- Automate data retention and deletion policies to reduce manual workload.

4. Conclusion

Compliance with organizational policies is a critical aspect of workplace communication, ensuring that businesses meet legal requirements, protect sensitive data, and foster a secure communication environment. Microsoft Viva Engage, with its integration into Microsoft 365's compliance ecosystem, provides robust tools for data security, governance, and regulatory adherence.

By leveraging data retention, DLP policies, content moderation, eDiscovery, and role-based access controls, organizations can ensure that communication remains compliant, professional, and risk-free. Following best practices such as regular audits, employee training, and automated compliance monitoring will further strengthen compliance efforts, making Viva Engage a reliable platform for secure and compliant workplace communication.

7.2 Privacy Settings and User Controls

7.2.1 Controlling Who Can See Your Posts

Privacy and security are critical when using a workplace communication platform like Microsoft Viva Engage. While fostering open communication and collaboration is the primary goal, not all information should be visible to everyone. Certain discussions may be sensitive, requiring controlled visibility to ensure that only the right individuals or groups can access them.

This section explores how to control post visibility in Viva Engage, including understanding privacy settings, audience targeting, and best practices for keeping information secure while still promoting engagement.

1. Understanding Visibility and Audience Settings in Viva Engage

Before sharing a post on Viva Engage, it's important to understand who can see your content and how to adjust your audience settings accordingly. Viva Engage offers multiple layers of visibility controls, allowing users to:

- Share posts with specific groups or communities.

- Restrict visibility to certain individuals within an organization.

- Adjust privacy settings based on whether a community is public or private.

Public vs. Private Communities

Viva Engage operates primarily through communities (formerly known as "groups"), where users can post updates, share documents, and engage in discussions. The privacy setting of a community directly impacts who can see your posts:

- Public Communities: Anyone in the organization can view posts, even if they are not a member of the community.

- Private Communities: Only approved members of the community can see and interact with posts.

✦ Best Practice: If you're sharing general company news or updates that should reach a broad audience, posting in a public community is ideal. However, for confidential discussions, use private communities where access is limited.

2. How to Control Post Visibility in Viva Engage

Choosing the Right Audience for Your Post

When you create a post in Viva Engage, you have options to **define the audience** before publishing. These options ensure that the right people see the message while keeping sensitive information restricted.

Option 1: Posting in Public Communities

- Default setting: **Anyone in the organization can see and engage** with the post.

- Ideal for: General announcements, company-wide discussions, or updates relevant to all employees.

Option 2: Posting in Private Communities

- Only members of the specific community can see the post.

- Ideal for: Discussions related to **specific teams, projects, or departments** where confidentiality is important.

Option 3: Mentioning Specific Users

- You can tag specific individuals using **@mentions** to ensure they see the post.

- Ideal for: Directing content to key stakeholders without limiting the audience of the post itself.

Option 4: Creating a Private Message Instead of a Post

- If the information is **only meant for a few individuals**, consider sending a **private message** instead of posting in a community.

- Ideal for: **One-on-one or small-group conversations** that don't require broad visibility.

📌 Best Practice: Always double-check your audience before posting, especially when discussing confidential or sensitive topics.

3. Adjusting Visibility Settings for Existing Posts

After posting content, you may realize that the visibility settings need adjustments. Viva Engage allows users to modify post visibility in some cases:

Editing a Post's Audience

- If a post is shared in a public community, you cannot make it private afterward. Instead, you would need to delete and repost it in a private community.

- If a post is within a private community, you can control who joins the community, indirectly managing who sees the content.

Deleting or Hiding a Post

- If you've posted something in the wrong place, you can delete it and repost in the correct group.

- Admins and moderators may also remove posts if they violate company policies.

📌 Best Practice: Before posting, always preview your audience selection to avoid mistakes.

4. Managing Post Visibility in External Networks

Some organizations use Viva Engage's External Networks feature, allowing collaboration with partners, vendors, or external clients. When posting in an external network, consider the following:

- External networks have separate privacy settings from internal company communities.

- Users outside the organization can view and respond to posts in external networks.

- Sensitive information should never be shared in an external network unless it is specifically permitted.

✦ Best Practice: When working with external collaborators, use document-sharing permissions (e.g., in OneDrive or SharePoint) instead of posting sensitive content directly.

5. Best Practices for Maintaining Privacy on Viva Engage

To ensure a balance between collaboration and privacy, follow these best practices:

Be Mindful of the Community Type

Before posting, check if the community is public or private. If a conversation needs to be confidential, ensure you're posting in the appropriate private group.

Use Clear Labels for Sensitive Content

If a post contains confidential information, use a label like [Internal Use Only] in the title to remind users of its sensitivity.

Regularly Review Your Posts and Permissions

It's a good habit to periodically review past posts and ensure that only the intended audience has access. If needed, delete or relocate posts with sensitive content.

Encourage Employees to Adjust Their Notification Settings

Users should tailor their notification preferences to ensure they receive updates on relevant discussions while avoiding unnecessary exposure to non-critical content.

Report Privacy Concerns to Admins

If an employee accidentally shares confidential information in a public space, notify an admin immediately to take corrective action.

✦ Best Practice: Organizations should train employees on privacy settings within Viva Engage to ensure company-wide security and compliance.

Conclusion

Microsoft Viva Engage is a powerful platform for workplace communication, but privacy and security must always be considered when posting content. By using public and private community settings, selecting the right audience, and following best practices, employees can ensure their messages reach only the intended audience while maintaining confidentiality where needed.

By understanding and properly managing post visibility, organizations can create a secure, collaborative, and efficient communication environment within Viva Engage.

7.2.2 Managing Data and Content Visibility

Introduction

Privacy and data visibility are crucial aspects of digital workplace communication, especially when using enterprise collaboration tools like Microsoft Viva Engage. With a growing emphasis on **data security, user privacy, and compliance**, organizations must ensure that their communication platforms are configured correctly to balance transparency with confidentiality.

In this section, we will explore how **data and content visibility** can be managed within Viva Engage. We will cover different types of content visibility settings, user controls, administrator settings, and best practices for maintaining a secure and compliant environment.

1. Understanding Data Visibility in Viva Engage

Data visibility in Viva Engage determines **who can see specific content**, including posts, comments, files, and discussions. Microsoft has built Viva Engage with **role-based access control (RBAC)** and **granular visibility settings** to allow users and administrators to manage content access efficiently.

Types of Content Visibility in Viva Engage

There are several levels of content visibility in Viva Engage, each serving different purposes within an organization:

- **Public Content:** Available to all users within the organization. Anyone can view, react, comment, or share these posts.

- **Private Content:** Restricted to specific users or groups. Only those with explicit permission can access it.

- **Restricted Access (Admins Only):** Certain administrative or policy-related content may only be accessible to system administrators or compliance officers.

- **External Content:** Content shared with external users (if permitted by company policies).

Understanding how these content types function is key to ensuring that **sensitive or confidential data** remains secure while allowing for effective collaboration.

2. Managing Visibility Settings for Posts and Conversations

Users and administrators in Viva Engage have control over the visibility of posts and discussions.

Setting Post Visibility

When creating a post, users can choose from the following visibility options:

1. **Public Posts** – Visible to all employees within the organization.

2. **Group-Specific Posts** – Restricted to members of a particular **Viva Engage group**.

3. **Private Messages** – Visible only to selected recipients.

4. **Announcements** – Can be targeted to a specific audience, such as a department or leadership team.

Best Practices for Managing Post Visibility:

✓ Use public posts for general discussions or company-wide updates.

✓ Limit sensitive or confidential discussions to private groups.

✓ Avoid sharing personally identifiable information (PII) or proprietary data in open forums.

Editing and Deleting Posts for Privacy Control

In Viva Engage, users can:

- **Edit posts** to correct errors or remove sensitive information.

- **Delete posts** if content was shared inappropriately or is no longer relevant.

Administrators may also have the ability to **remove or archive posts** if they violate company policies or compliance standards.

3. Managing File and Attachment Visibility

Uploading and Sharing Files Securely

Viva Engage allows users to upload and share files, but it is essential to understand how file visibility works:

- **Files shared in a public group** are accessible to all employees.

- **Files uploaded in a private group** can only be accessed by group members.

- **Direct message attachments** remain visible only to the participants of the conversation.

Best Practices for Secure File Sharing:

✅ Use Microsoft OneDrive or SharePoint for sensitive documents and link them instead of uploading directly.
✅ Apply access restrictions on files before sharing.
✅ Monitor file downloads and sharing activity for security compliance.

Revoking Access to Files and Attachments

If a user shares a file unintentionally or needs to restrict access later, they can:

- **Modify sharing permissions** in SharePoint or OneDrive (if integrated).

- **Delete the file from the Viva Engage post** to prevent further access.

Admins can also remove files if they pose a security risk.

4. Group and Community Visibility Settings

Viva Engage supports different types of groups, each with its own **visibility and access control** settings.

Types of Groups in Viva Engage

1. **Public Groups** – Open to all employees; anyone can join, post, and view discussions.

2. **Private Groups** – Restricted membership; only invited members can see content.

3. **Secret Groups** – Completely hidden from non-members; only accessible via direct invitation.

Each organization must determine which group type best fits its needs based on **confidentiality requirements** and **collaboration objectives**.

Best Practices for Group Management:

✓ Use private groups for sensitive or project-related discussions.
✓ Regularly audit group membership to ensure only relevant users have access.
✓ Enable approval settings for joining private or restricted groups.

Managing Membership and Access

Group owners and administrators have the ability to:

- **Add or remove members** to control access.

- **Adjust group settings** to change visibility (public ↔ private).

- **Restrict external access** to prevent unauthorized sharing.

5. Privacy Settings for User Profiles and Data

Beyond content visibility, **user profile settings** also play a role in data privacy within Viva Engage.

Controlling Profile Visibility

Users can manage how much of their profile information is visible to others:

- **Public Profile:** Displays full details (name, title, department).

- **Limited Profile:** Restricts certain details (e.g., hiding email address or contact information).

- **Anonymous Posting (if enabled by admins):** Allows users to contribute without revealing identity.

Managing Personal Data and Activity History

Employees can:

- **Download their activity logs** to see what they've shared.

- **Delete old posts** to remove outdated or irrelevant content.

- **Request data deletion** under **GDPR** or company policies.

Best Practices for Profile Privacy:

✅ Review profile settings regularly to ensure only necessary information is visible.
✅ Avoid sharing personal or sensitive data publicly.
✅ Use alias options if anonymity is required for certain discussions.

6. Admin Controls for Data and Content Visibility

Organizational Compliance and Data Retention

Viva Engage allows admins to **set policies** for data retention, ensuring compliance with industry regulations like:

- GDPR (General Data Protection Regulation)

- HIPAA (Health Insurance Portability and Accountability Act)

- ISO 27001 Information Security Standards

Admins can:

- **Define data retention periods** (e.g., automatically delete old posts after X months).

- **Archive inactive groups** to keep data manageable.

- **Monitor user activity logs** for security and compliance audits.

Monitoring and Reporting for Policy Violations

Admins can:

- Monitor flagged posts and inappropriate content.

- Generate reports on data sharing activities.

- Enforce security policies through automated workflows.

7. Conclusion

Managing data and content visibility in Viva Engage is a critical aspect of workplace security and privacy. By leveraging the platform's built-in privacy controls, users and administrators can:

✓☐ Ensure that sensitive data is only accessible to the right people.
✓☐ Maintain compliance with corporate policies and regulations.
✓☐ Foster a collaborative yet secure work environment.

Organizations should continuously review their content visibility settings, educate employees on privacy best practices, and utilize admin governance tools to maintain a safe and productive communication space in Viva Engage.

7.2.3 Reporting and Blocking Users

Maintaining a safe and respectful digital workplace is essential for fostering productive and meaningful communication. Microsoft Viva Engage offers robust privacy and security settings, including **reporting and blocking users**, to ensure that interactions remain professional, appropriate, and aligned with company policies.

This section explores the **importance of reporting and blocking features**, when to use them, and a step-by-step guide on how to manage inappropriate content or disruptive users. Whether you are an employee, manager, or administrator, understanding these tools will help maintain a positive and secure digital environment.

---

1. Why Reporting and Blocking Features Matter

In any digital communication platform, **misuse and inappropriate behavior** can occasionally occur. Whether it's unintentional or deliberate, inappropriate behavior may include:

- **Harassment or Bullying** – Unwanted messages, offensive comments, or repeated targeting of an individual.

- **Spam or Irrelevant Content** – Unnecessary promotional material, excessive self-promotion, or unrelated content.

- **Misinformation or Harmful Content** – Spreading false information, offensive material, or violating corporate policies.

- **Privacy Violations** – Sharing confidential or sensitive company information publicly.

By using **reporting and blocking features**, users can take control of their online experience while also helping **IT teams and administrators** enforce company policies and maintain workplace integrity.

---

2. Reporting a User or Inappropriate Content

Viva Engage allows users to **report inappropriate behavior or content** so that administrators can take necessary action. Reporting ensures that community guidelines and company policies are upheld.

When Should You Report a User or Content?

You should consider reporting a user or content when:
✓☐ The content violates company policies or professional standards.
✓☐ A user is engaging in harassment, discrimination, or offensive behavior.
✓☐ The post includes confidential, misleading, or false information.

✓☐ The content contains spam, promotional material, or phishing attempts.

✓☐ There is hate speech, threats, or inappropriate images shared in a group or conversation.

⚠☐ **Note:** Always ensure that the report is based on genuine concerns and **not personal disagreements** or opinions. False reports can lead to unnecessary disruptions.

How to Report a Post or Comment

If you come across a post, comment, or reply that violates workplace communication guidelines, you can **report it directly in Viva Engage**. Follow these steps:

1. **Locate the Post or Comment**

   o   Find the specific message, post, or comment that you want to report.

2. **Click the "More Options" Button (Three Dots •••)**

   o   On the right side of the post or comment, click the **three-dot menu** for additional options.

3. **Select "Report"**

   o   From the drop-down menu, select the **"Report"** option.

4. **Choose a Reason for Reporting**

   o   Viva Engage will prompt you to select a reason for reporting the post. Common options include:

      ▪   Harassment or Bullying

      ▪   Inappropriate or Offensive Content

      ▪   Spam or Irrelevant Content

      ▪   Privacy Violation

      ▪   Other (Describe the issue in detail)

5. **Submit the Report**

- o Once you've selected the reason, click **"Submit"**. The report will be sent to the designated **moderators or IT administrators** for review.

6. **Monitor the Status of Your Report**

- o Depending on company policy, you may receive a notification when your report has been reviewed and action has been taken.

How Administrators Handle Reported Content

After a report is submitted, the **IT team or platform administrators** review the case and take appropriate action. This may include:

- ♦ **Removing the content** if it violates company policies.
- ♦ **Issuing a warning** to the user who posted the content.
- ♦ **Temporarily or permanently banning** the user if multiple reports are filed.
- ♦ **Escalating serious violations** to HR or legal departments.

Best Practice: If you're a manager or administrator, establish **clear content policies** to ensure employees understand the guidelines and consequences of violating them.

3. Blocking Users in Viva Engage

If you find yourself **receiving unwanted messages, spam, or harassment**, you can block a user to prevent further interactions. Blocking is a useful feature when reporting content alone is not sufficient.

When Should You Block Someone?

Blocking is recommended when:
✓☐ A user repeatedly sends unwanted messages.
✓☐ Someone is harassing or spamming you.
✓☐ You no longer want to see someone's posts or activity in your feed.
✓☐ The user is engaging in disruptive behavior that affects your work environment.

How to Block a User in Viva Engage

Blocking someone prevents them from:

- • Sending you direct messages.

- Tagging you in posts or comments.

- Seeing your activity or profile (depending on organization settings).

To block a user, follow these steps:

1. **Go to the User's Profile**

   o   Click on the person's name or profile picture to open their profile page.

2. **Click the "More Options" Button (Three Dots •••)**

   o   Locate the menu with additional options.

3. **Select "Block User"**

   o   A confirmation message will appear, asking if you're sure about blocking the person.

4. **Confirm the Action**

   o   Click **"Block"** to finalize.

5. **The User is Now Blocked**

   o   They will no longer be able to interact with you directly on Viva Engage.

Managing Blocked Users

To view or unblock users:

- Navigate to **Settings > Privacy & Security**.

- Find the **"Blocked Users"** section.

- Select the user you want to unblock and click **"Unblock"**.

4. Best Practices for Reporting and Blocking Users

To ensure that Viva Engage remains a **safe, professional, and inclusive** platform, follow these best practices:

Encourage Employees to Report Issues

◆ Educate employees on when and how to report inappropriate content.

◆ Create a clear process for reporting and handling violations.

Use Blocking as a Last Resort

◆ Blocking should be used only when necessary, especially for severe or repeated issues.

◆ If workplace issues persist, involve HR or management.

Set Clear Workplace Communication Policies

◆ Define acceptable behavior for posting, commenting, and messaging.

◆ Communicate company policies through onboarding materials and training sessions.

Review Reports Regularly

◆ IT teams and administrators should regularly check reported content to prevent unresolved conflicts.

◆ Consider automated moderation tools to detect inappropriate content early.

5. Conclusion

Microsoft Viva Engage provides a safe and controlled communication environment by offering tools to report inappropriate content and block disruptive users. By understanding and using these features correctly, employees can contribute to a more inclusive, respectful, and productive digital workplace.

By combining reporting mechanisms, blocking features, and clear workplace policies, organizations can prevent misuse, foster professionalism, and ensure that Viva Engage remains an effective communication tool for all employees.

PART VIII
Troubleshooting and Support

8.1 Common Issues and How to Fix Them

8.1.1 Login and Access Problems

Microsoft Viva Engage is a powerful platform for workplace communication, but like any software, users may occasionally encounter login and access issues. These problems can be frustrating and hinder productivity, so understanding how to troubleshoot them effectively is crucial.

In this section, we will explore common login and access issues, their potential causes, and step-by-step solutions to resolve them. Whether you are an individual user trying to access Viva Engage or an IT administrator managing company-wide access, these troubleshooting methods will help you quickly resolve issues and regain access.

1. Common Login and Access Issues

Users may experience various login and access problems when trying to use Microsoft Viva Engage. The most common issues include:

- Incorrect Username or Password Errors
- Account Lockout or Suspension
- Multi-Factor Authentication (MFA) Issues
- Expired or Revoked Permissions
- Browser and Cache Problems
- Network Connectivity Issues

- Microsoft 365 Licensing or Subscription Issues

- Organization-Wide Restrictions or IT Policies

Each of these issues has specific causes and solutions, which we will discuss in detail below.

2. Troubleshooting Steps for Login and Access Problems

Incorrect Username or Password Errors

When users see an error message indicating an incorrect username or password, it is often due to:

- Typing mistakes (case-sensitive passwords, extra spaces, incorrect capitalization)

- Forgotten or recently changed passwords

- Using an incorrect Microsoft account (personal vs. work account)

Solution:

1. **Double-Check Credentials:** Ensure that your username and password are entered correctly. Watch for case sensitivity and accidental spaces.

2. **Use the Password Reset Option:**

   o   Go to the **Microsoft 365 login page** and click **"Forgot Password?"**

   o   Follow the on-screen steps to reset your password via email or phone verification.

3. **Verify You're Using the Correct Account:**

   o   If you have multiple Microsoft accounts, confirm that you're logging in with the right one (work vs. personal).

4. **Contact Your IT Administrator:**

   o   If your credentials still don't work, your account may require a reset by your IT department.

Account Lockout or Suspension

If a user enters the wrong password multiple times, their account may become temporarily locked due to security policies. Additionally, accounts may be suspended by IT for policy violations or inactivity.

Solution:

1. **Wait for Automatic Unlock:**

   o   Microsoft automatically unlocks accounts after a short period (typically 15-30 minutes).

2. **Reset the Password:**

   o   Use the **password reset** option to create a new password.

3. **Check with IT for Suspended Accounts:**

   o   If the account has been suspended, IT administrators will need to restore access.

Multi-Factor Authentication (MFA) Issues

Microsoft Viva Engage may require Multi-Factor Authentication (MFA) for added security. Common issues include:

- Not receiving verification codes

- Authenticator app not working

- Lost access to registered phone/email

Solution:

1. **Check Your Registered Device:**

   o   Ensure your phone/email is accessible and notifications are enabled.

2. **Use Backup Verification Methods:**

   o   Try using an **alternative method** (e.g., email instead of SMS).

3. **Update or Re-register MFA Devices:**

   o   If you changed your phone number, update it in the **Microsoft Security settings**.

4. **Contact IT for MFA Reset:**

   o   If locked out, IT administrators can reset your MFA settings.

Expired or Revoked Permissions

If your company uses role-based access controls, your account permissions may have expired or been revoked.

Solution:

1. **Confirm Your Access Role:**

   o   Check if you still have the correct permissions in your Microsoft 365 settings.

2. **Request a Permission Update from IT:**

   o   If your access has been revoked or downgraded, IT can restore it.

Browser and Cache Problems

Sometimes, login failures are caused by browser issues, such as outdated settings, corrupted cache, or incompatible browser extensions.

Solution:

1. **Clear Browser Cache and Cookies:**

   o   In Google Chrome:

       ▪   Go to **Settings > Privacy and Security > Clear Browsing Data**

   o   In Microsoft Edge:

       ▪   Go to **Settings > Privacy, Search, and Services > Clear Browsing Data**

2. **Try an Incognito or Private Mode Window:**

   o   If login works in incognito mode, a browser extension may be interfering.

3. **Disable Browser Extensions:**

o Turn off extensions (like ad blockers) and try logging in again.

4. **Use a Different Browser:**

o Try switching to another browser like Edge, Chrome, or Firefox.

Network Connectivity Issues

If your internet connection is unstable or blocked by a firewall, Viva Engage may not load correctly.

Solution:

1. **Check Your Internet Connection:**

o Try opening another website to verify if your internet is working.

2. **Disable VPN or Proxy Settings:**

o If connected to a VPN, try disconnecting and accessing Viva Engage directly.

3. **Restart Your Router or Switch Networks:**

o If using a corporate network, try switching to a different Wi-Fi network.

Microsoft 365 Licensing or Subscription Issues

Viva Engage requires a valid Microsoft 365 license. If your company's subscription has expired, you may lose access.

Solution:

1. **Check Your Subscription Status:**

o Go to **Microsoft 365 Admin Center > Billing > Your Products** to verify your license.

2. **Contact IT for License Renewal:**

o If your license has expired, IT can renew or assign a new license.

Organization-Wide Restrictions or IT Policies

Some companies apply strict security policies that limit access to certain platforms, including Viva Engage.

Solution:

1. **Check If Your Company Allows Viva Engage:**

   o   Ask IT if there are any restrictions on the use of Viva Engage.

2. **Request IT to Whitelist the Platform:**

   o   If Viva Engage is blocked, IT can grant exceptions for authorized users.

---

3. Preventing Future Login and Access Issues

To minimize login and access issues in the future, follow these best practices:

Keep Your Credentials Secure

- Use a password manager to store and manage your Microsoft credentials.

- Avoid sharing passwords or using the same password across multiple accounts.

Regularly Update Your Passwords

- Change your password every 90 days to enhance security.

- Use a strong password with a mix of letters, numbers, and special characters.

Enable Backup Authentication Methods

- Register multiple MFA methods (e.g., phone, email, Microsoft Authenticator) to prevent lockouts.

Stay Updated on IT Policies

- Regularly check with IT to ensure your account permissions and licenses are up to date.

Use Approved Browsers and Devices

- Ensure that you log in from company-approved devices to avoid security restrictions.

4. Conclusion

Login and access issues can be frustrating, but with the right troubleshooting steps, they can be quickly resolved. Whether it's a simple password reset, browser issue, or a more complex IT restriction, identifying the root cause is the first step to regaining access. By following best practices, users can prevent many of these issues from occurring in the future.

If you continue experiencing problems, contact **your IT department** or **Microsoft Support** for further assistance.

8.1.2 Notification Issues

Notifications play a crucial role in Microsoft Viva Engage by keeping users informed about important updates, new messages, group activities, and mentions. However, users may occasionally experience issues with notifications, such as not receiving alerts, receiving too many notifications, or delayed notifications. These issues can disrupt workflow and reduce engagement within the platform.

In this section, we will explore common notification issues, their potential causes, and step-by-step solutions to fix them. Additionally, we will discuss best practices for managing notification settings to ensure you receive the most relevant updates without being overwhelmed.

Common Notification Issues and How to Fix Them

Issue 1: Not Receiving Any Notifications

Possible Causes:

- Notifications may be **disabled** in the settings.

- Email notifications could be **filtered into spam or junk folders**.

- Push notifications might be **turned off for the Viva Engage mobile app**.

- IT administrators may have **restricted notifications at the organization level**.

How to Fix It:

✓ Step 1: Check Notification Settings

- Go to **Settings > Notifications** in Viva Engage.

- Ensure that **email, in-app, and push notifications** are enabled for relevant actions (e.g., mentions, replies, group updates).

✓ Step 2: Verify Email Filters

- Check your **email spam/junk folder** to see if Viva Engage notifications are being filtered out.

- If found in spam, mark them as **"Not Spam"** to ensure future notifications arrive in the inbox.

✓ Step 3: Enable Push Notifications (For Mobile Users)

- On your mobile device, go to **Settings > Apps > Viva Engage** and ensure that **notifications are enabled**.

- If using Microsoft Teams for notifications, check **Teams settings** to ensure Viva Engage alerts are turned on.

✓ Step 4: Contact IT Support (If Notifications Are Still Blocked)

- If notifications are still not working, reach out to your IT administrator. **Some organizations disable external email notifications** or enforce security policies that restrict alerts.

Issue 2: Receiving Too Many Notifications

Possible Causes:

- The user is subscribed to **all group notifications**, causing excessive alerts.

- Email preferences are set to **receive updates for every post** instead of **highlights only**.

- Notifications are enabled for inactive or unnecessary groups.

How to Fix It:

✓ Step 1: Adjust Email Notification Frequency

- Go to **Settings > Notifications** and change email updates to **"Daily Digest"** instead of **"Every Post"** to reduce clutter.

✓ Step 2: Unsubscribe from Unnecessary Groups

- Navigate to **My Groups** in Viva Engage.

- For groups you don't actively follow, **turn off notifications** to stop receiving updates.

✓ Step 3: Disable Unnecessary Push Notifications

- On mobile, go to **Settings > Notifications** and disable push alerts for non-essential updates.

✓ Step 4: Use Microsoft Teams for Important Notifications

- Instead of relying on email, **integrate Viva Engage with Teams** and receive only high-priority notifications in your Teams activity feed.

Issue 3: Delayed or Missing Notifications

Possible Causes:

- There may be **server delays** in sending notifications.

- Email or push notifications could be **queued** due to high system load.

- The mobile app may not have **background refresh enabled**, preventing real-time updates.

How to Fix It:

✓ Step 1: Check System Status

- Visit the **Microsoft Service Health Dashboard** to check for any known outages or delays in Viva Engage services.

✓ Step 2: Manually Refresh Notifications

- Open the Viva Engage web app and refresh the notifications tab to ensure updates are loading correctly.

- On mobile, **swipe down** on the notification panel to force a refresh.

✓ Step 3: Enable Background App Refresh (For Mobile Users)

- On iOS: Go to **Settings > Viva Engage > Background App Refresh** and ensure it's enabled.

- On Android: Navigate to **Settings > Battery > Viva Engage** and allow the app to run in the background.

✓ Step 4: Reinstall the Viva Engage Mobile App

- If push notifications are still delayed, uninstall and reinstall the Viva Engage app to reset notification settings.

Issue 4: Notifications Stopped After a Recent Update

Possible Causes:

- A recent **Viva Engage update** may have reset notification settings.

- Mobile device permissions may have changed after an **operating system update**.

How to Fix It:

✓ Step 1: Recheck Notification Settings

- After an update, go to **Settings > Notifications** and verify that your preferred alerts are still enabled.

✓ Step 2: Grant Necessary App Permissions

- On mobile, go to **Settings > Apps > Viva Engage > Permissions** and ensure notifications are allowed.

✓ Step 3: Restart the App and Device

- Sometimes, a simple **app restart or device reboot** can restore notification functionality.

✓ **Step 4: Check for Further Updates**

- If an update introduced a bug, check the **Microsoft Support page** for any new patches or fixes.

3. Best Practices for Managing Viva Engage Notifications

To maintain an optimal balance of notifications without being overwhelmed, follow these best practices:

◆ Customize Notification Preferences Regularly – As your engagement in groups changes, update your settings to receive only the most relevant notifications.

◆ Use "Highlights Only" for Email Notifications – This reduces email clutter while keeping you informed of the most important updates.

◆ Prioritize In-App and Teams Notifications – If your organization uses Microsoft Teams, enable Viva Engage alerts in Teams for a seamless workflow.

◆ Set "Quiet Hours" on Mobile Devices – Prevent notification overload by setting "Do Not Disturb" hours when you don't want to receive work-related alerts.

◆ Encourage Team-Wide Best Practices – Train employees to manage their notification settings efficiently to enhance workplace communication without distractions.

4. Conclusion

Notification issues in Microsoft Viva Engage can disrupt workflow, but most problems can be resolved by adjusting settings, checking permissions, and staying updated on system changes. By following the troubleshooting steps outlined in this guide, users can ensure they receive the right notifications at the right time—improving engagement, responsiveness, and productivity in workplace communication.

By implementing best practices for notification management, employees can stay informed without being overwhelmed, allowing for a smoother and more efficient Viva Engage experience.

8.1.3 Missing or Deleted Posts

Microsoft Viva Engage serves as an essential platform for workplace communication, knowledge sharing, and collaboration. However, like any digital platform, users may occasionally encounter issues such as missing or deleted posts. Whether you accidentally delete an important post, cannot find content you previously saw, or believe a post has been removed due to system errors or administrative actions, this guide will help you troubleshoot and recover missing posts.

In this section, we will explore the common reasons why posts may go missing, methods to recover deleted content, and preventative measures to ensure your important communications remain accessible.

1. Common Reasons for Missing or Deleted Posts in Viva Engage

Before attempting to recover a missing post, it's important to understand the possible reasons why it may no longer be visible. Here are the most common reasons why a post might disappear from Viva Engage:

Accidental Deletion by the User

One of the most common reasons for a missing post is that the user who created it accidentally deleted it. Viva Engage allows users to delete their own posts, but once deleted, they cannot be restored directly by the user.

How to confirm if this happened:

- Check your activity history or notifications to see if you posted something recently.
- If you recall deleting the post, check if you have a saved backup (such as a draft in another application).

Administrative or Moderator Removal

Company administrators, IT teams, or group moderators may delete posts that violate company policies, contain sensitive information, or are flagged as inappropriate.

How to confirm if this happened:

- If your post was removed for compliance reasons, you may receive a notification explaining the deletion.

- If you suspect an administrator removed your post but didn't receive a notification, check with your IT department or group admin.

Content Hidden Due to Privacy Settings

Viva Engage includes various privacy settings that might make a post invisible to some users. If a post appears missing, it may be due to restricted visibility settings.

How to confirm if this happened:

- Try logging into Viva Engage with a different account or device.

- Ask a colleague if they can still see the post.

- Check if the post was originally shared in a private group, which you may no longer have access to.

Archiving of Older Content

Some organizations have automatic retention policies that archive or delete old posts after a set period. This can happen if Viva Engage is configured to limit data storage or comply with organizational policies.

How to confirm if this happened:

- Check your company's retention policy for Viva Engage.

- If the post was older, ask IT if it was archived.

Network or Display Issues

Occasionally, posts may appear missing due to temporary network errors, syncing issues, or a browser cache problem.

How to confirm if this happened:

- Try refreshing the page or clearing your browser cache.

- Open Viva Engage on a different device or network.

- Check if other users can see the post.

Unintentional Filtering or Sorting

Posts may not actually be missing but hidden due to filtering or sorting settings. If you cannot find a post, it might be due to the way your feed is configured.

How to confirm if this happened:

- Check if you have applied a filter (e.g., "Unread" or "Most Recent").

- Try searching for the post using keywords or hashtags.

2. How to Recover a Deleted or Missing Post

Once you've determined the reason your post is missing, you can take the following steps to recover or retrieve it.

Restoring Posts from the Viva Engage Trash Bin (If Available)

Unlike some Microsoft 365 applications, Viva Engage does not have a traditional "Recycle Bin" for deleted posts. However, some organizations enable data retention policies that allow administrators to retrieve deleted content.

Steps to check if your post can be recovered:

1. Contact your Viva Engage administrator and ask if they can restore deleted posts.

2. If your organization has Microsoft Purview or a compliance center enabled, IT may be able to recover deleted posts within a certain timeframe.

Checking Microsoft 365 Compliance Center for Archived Content

If your organization has enabled compliance logging and retention policies, deleted posts may still be accessible through Microsoft 365 Compliance Center.

Steps to check:

1. Ask your IT team if Microsoft Purview (Compliance Center) is used for archiving Viva Engage content.

2. If enabled, request access to logs that might contain the missing post.

Checking Email Notifications or Activity Logs

If you had email notifications enabled for Viva Engage, your missing post may still be visible in email alerts.

Steps to check:

1. Search your email inbox for Viva Engage notifications related to your post.

2. If found, you may be able to recover the post's content and timestamp.

Searching for Cached or Copied Versions

If your post was recently visible but now missing, a cached version might still exist.

Steps to try:

1. Use Google Cache or Bing Cache by searching for a snippet of your post's text.

2. If someone else quoted, shared, or replied to your post, their response might still contain parts of your original message.

3. If the post contained links, images, or files, check if those still exist separately in Microsoft 365 or SharePoint.

Reposting the Content if It Cannot Be Recovered

If none of the above recovery methods work, you may need to rewrite and repost your content.

Best Practices for Reposting:

- If your post was important, consider drafting a summary version.

- Mention that the original post was deleted to avoid confusion.

- Tag users who engaged with the original post to regain their input.

3. Preventative Measures to Avoid Losing Important Posts

To reduce the risk of losing important posts in the future, follow these best practices:

Save Important Posts in a Backup Location

- Copy critical posts into a OneNote notebook or Word document.

- Use email notifications to keep records of all your posts.

Use the "Drafts" Feature

If you're working on a long post, save it as a draft in a text editor before posting.

Enable Retention Policies for Viva Engage (For Admins)

If you are an IT admin, configure Microsoft Purview to retain and archive Viva Engage content.

Check Visibility Settings Before Posting

Ensure posts are shared in the correct group and have the appropriate visibility settings.

Review Company Policies on Post Deletion

Understand how your organization handles content moderation and compliance policies.

4. Conclusion

Missing or deleted posts in Viva Engage can be frustrating, but by understanding the common causes, using recovery techniques, and applying preventative measures, you can minimize disruptions to communication and collaboration. If a post cannot be recovered, using backup strategies, reposting content, and leveraging Microsoft 365 tools can help maintain engagement and continuity in workplace discussions.

8.2 Where to Find Help and Support

8.2.1 Microsoft Support and Documentation

When using Microsoft Viva Engage, you may occasionally encounter issues or have questions about specific features. Fortunately, Microsoft provides comprehensive support resources and detailed documentation to help users troubleshoot problems, learn best practices, and maximize their use of the platform.

In this section, we will explore where to find Microsoft support and documentation for Viva Engage, including:

- The official Microsoft Viva Engage Help Center

- Microsoft Learn and documentation

- Microsoft 365 support channels

- Community forums and user groups

- Microsoft Tech Community and blogs

Understanding these resources will empower users to resolve common issues efficiently, stay updated on new features, and enhance their experience with Viva Engage.

1. Microsoft Viva Engage Help Center

Overview of the Viva Engage Help Center

The Microsoft Viva Engage Help Center serves as the primary destination for official support and troubleshooting guidance. It provides a structured knowledge base, including:

- Step-by-step user guides

- Troubleshooting instructions for common issues

- Best practices for engaging with the platform

- Security and compliance information

The Help Center is continuously updated with the latest information as Microsoft improves Viva Engage and adds new features.

Accessing the Help Center

To access the Viva Engage Help Center, follow these steps:

1. Open Viva Engage in your web browser.

2. Click on your profile icon in the upper-right corner.

3. Select Help & Support from the dropdown menu.

4. You will be redirected to the official Microsoft Viva Engage Help Center.

Alternatively, you can visit the Help Center directly via https://support.microsoft.com and search for "Viva Engage" in the search bar.

How to Use the Help Center Effectively

To make the most of the Help Center, consider these best practices:

- Use the search bar to quickly find relevant topics.

- Browse by category (e.g., "Getting Started," "Security & Privacy," "Collaboration Features").

- Check the "Top Issues" section for frequently reported problems.

- Follow the step-by-step troubleshooting guides before reaching out for further support.

If you cannot find the solution to your issue, you may need to explore additional Microsoft support channels, which we will discuss next.

2. Microsoft Learn and Documentation

What is Microsoft Learn?

Microsoft Learn is a free, online learning platform that provides detailed documentation, tutorials, and courses on Microsoft products, including Viva Engage. It is ideal for users who want to:

- Learn how to use Viva Engage effectively

- Discover advanced features and integrations

- Find in-depth technical documentation

How to Access Microsoft Learn for Viva Engage

You can access Microsoft Learn at https://learn.microsoft.com. To find information on Viva Engage:

1. Visit Microsoft Learn and go to the Microsoft 365 section.

2. Search for "Viva Engage" in the search bar.

3. Explore official documentation, video tutorials, and hands-on training modules.

Benefits of Microsoft Learn for Viva Engage Users

- Structured Learning Paths – Microsoft Learn offers structured courses to help both beginners and advanced users understand Viva Engage.

- Hands-on Exercises – Some courses include interactive exercises to practice using Viva Engage.

- Up-to-Date Information – As Microsoft releases updates, the documentation is refreshed to reflect the latest changes.

By using Microsoft Learn, you can proactively improve your skills in Viva Engage and resolve issues without needing external support.

3. Microsoft 365 Support Channels

Microsoft 365 Admin Center Support

For enterprise users, the Microsoft 365 Admin Center provides dedicated support for IT administrators. If you are part of an organization using Viva Engage through Microsoft 365, your IT team can:

- Open support tickets directly with Microsoft.

- Manage permissions and security settings for Viva Engage.

- Request technical troubleshooting assistance.

To access Admin Center Support:

1. Go to https://admin.microsoft.com.

2. Sign in with admin credentials.

3. Navigate to Support > New Service Request.

If you are not an IT admin, you can request assistance from your internal IT department, who will escalate issues to Microsoft if necessary.

Contacting Microsoft 365 Support

For direct technical support, users can also contact Microsoft 365 Support:

- Visit https://support.microsoft.com.

- Select "Contact Support" and follow the prompts to describe your issue.

- Choose whether to receive support via chat, email, or phone call.

4. Community Forums and User Groups

Microsoft Tech Community

The Microsoft Tech Community is a valuable resource where Viva Engage users can:

- Ask questions and get answers from other users and experts.

- Learn best practices from experienced professionals.

- Stay updated on new features and product announcements.

You can access the Microsoft Tech Community for Viva Engage at: https://techcommunity.microsoft.com

Microsoft Answers Forum

The Microsoft Answers Forum is another helpful platform where users can:

- Search for solutions to previously asked questions.

- Post their own questions and receive crowdsourced answers from other users.

- Get responses from Microsoft employees and MVPs (Most Valuable Professionals).

Visit the Microsoft Answers Forum at: https://answers.microsoft.com

LinkedIn and Social Media Groups

Many Microsoft users also participate in LinkedIn groups, Reddit communities, and Facebook groups dedicated to Microsoft 365 and Viva Engage. Joining these groups allows you to:

- Engage with professionals using Viva Engage in real-world business scenarios.

- Exchange tips, strategies, and troubleshooting advice.

- Stay connected with industry trends and updates.

5. Microsoft Tech Blogs and Updates

Microsoft Viva Blog

Microsoft regularly posts news, updates, and insights about Viva Engage on its official Viva Blog. This is an excellent resource for:

- Learning about new features and improvements.

- Reading case studies on how organizations use Viva Engage.

- Discovering tips and tricks for effective communication.

Check the latest articles at: https://techcommunity.microsoft.com/t5/Microsoft-Viva/bg-p/MicrosoftViva

Conclusion

Microsoft provides a wealth of support resources to help users troubleshoot issues, learn new features, and optimize their experience with Viva Engage. Whether you prefer self-service documentation, online learning, or direct support, there are multiple ways to find help:

- Use the Microsoft Viva Engage Help Center for official guides.

- Explore Microsoft Learn for in-depth training.

- Contact Microsoft 365 Support for technical assistance.

- Engage with the Microsoft Tech Community for peer-to-peer support.

- Follow Microsoft Blogs and social media for the latest updates.

By leveraging these resources, you can efficiently resolve problems, enhance your knowledge of Viva Engage, and ensure seamless workplace communication.

PART IX
Future of Workplace Communication with Viva Engage

9.1 The Evolution of Internal Communication

Internal communication has evolved significantly over the past few decades, shaped by the advancement of technology and changing workplace dynamics. As businesses and organizations continue to adapt to new challenges, methods of communication within teams and departments must evolve to keep pace. One of the most notable shifts in this evolution is the growing reliance on digital platforms to facilitate collaboration, foster engagement, and streamline information sharing. Microsoft Viva Engage, as part of the broader Microsoft Viva suite, is a tool that embodies the future of workplace communication, providing a comprehensive platform for teams and organizations to engage, connect, and collaborate in real-time.

In this section, we will explore the journey of internal communication, the changes in communication methods and tools over the years, and how Viva Engage represents the next step in that evolution.

1. The Early Days of Internal Communication

Historically, internal communication was mostly **face-to-face interactions**, written memos, and telephone calls. These methods, while effective in their time, had limitations. Information could only be exchanged within a limited scope, and messages were often slow to circulate across large organizations. Communication was predominantly **top-down**, with leadership providing updates to staff through meetings, emails, or newsletters. While this approach worked in many traditional industries, it was inefficient, especially in larger, more complex organizations.

For instance, businesses often relied on **physical bulletin boards** to communicate updates or memos across departments. While this was useful for localized communication, it did not allow for quick updates, cross-team collaboration, or real-time discussions. These early methods of internal communication were also limited by geography—employees in different offices or locations had to rely on phone calls, faxes, or mail, which made timely and fluid communication a challenge.

2. The Rise of Digital Communication Tools

As businesses grew more global and the digital age took hold, traditional methods of communication were no longer adequate for the fast-paced and interconnected world. Enter the age of **email**, **instant messaging**, and **internal portals**.

The Emergence of Email

Email revolutionized internal communication by enabling **instant delivery** of messages and documents, regardless of location. This allowed employees to communicate quickly with colleagues across different time zones, making it easier for global teams to collaborate. However, as email became the primary method for communication, inboxes quickly became flooded with messages, making it difficult to track important updates and organize conversations.

Instant Messaging and Collaboration Tools

The next significant leap in internal communication came with the rise of **instant messaging (IM)** platforms. Services like **Microsoft Lync**, later evolved into **Skype for Business**, allowed employees to communicate with one another instantly, making collaboration more fluid and reducing the time spent on emails or phone calls. These tools also allowed for the sharing of files, documents, and links in real time, enabling faster decision-making and more dynamic conversations.

However, the transition to instant messaging introduced new challenges, such as maintaining the **balance between synchronous and asynchronous communication**. While instant messaging helped improve the speed of communication, it also created the potential for constant interruptions. Without clear boundaries, teams could easily experience communication overload, leading to decreased productivity.

3. Social Media and the Advent of Enterprise Social Networks

With the rise of social media platforms like **Facebook**, **Twitter**, and **LinkedIn**, the way people communicate in their personal lives changed drastically. These platforms introduced new ways of interacting with others—quick, informal, and often more visual. The next step in the evolution of internal communication was the creation of **enterprise social networks (ESNs)**, tools that allowed businesses to take the best of social media's informal nature and apply it to the workplace.

The Birth of Enterprise Social Networks

ESNs like **Yammer** (now part of the Microsoft Viva suite) were designed to help employees communicate and collaborate in a way that was more **dynamic** and **engaging** than traditional email. These platforms allowed users to post updates, share content, comment on discussions, and **create communities** based on shared interests or departmental functions.

The key benefit of ESNs was their ability to break down communication silos across an organization. Employees from different departments or even geographical locations could communicate in a more open, transparent manner. This created an environment where ideas could flow more freely, innovation could thrive, and cross-functional collaboration became easier.

However, while ESNs offered more engaging features than email, they also introduced challenges related to content overload, managing multiple channels, and ensuring relevant communication was prioritized.

4. The Role of AI, Data, and Analytics in Modern Communication

As the workplace continued to evolve, so did the tools that facilitated communication. **Artificial intelligence (AI)**, **machine learning**, and **advanced analytics** became more integrated into internal communication platforms, bringing new capabilities to the table.

AI for Personalization and Efficiency

AI-powered features such as **personalized content suggestions**, **automated workflows**, and **intelligent meeting scheduling** began to enhance how communication occurred within organizations. Platforms like **Microsoft Viva Engage** can now analyze user behavior, preferences, and interactions to recommend relevant content, discussions, and resources. This not only saves time for employees but also ensures that they are exposed to the most relevant and valuable information.

Data-Driven Decision Making

Analytics also plays a major role in the evolution of internal communication. With data-driven insights, companies can measure **engagement** and **effectiveness** in real-time. Platforms like Viva Engage provide tools that track key metrics such as **post engagement**, **comments**, and **reactions** to help businesses understand which content resonates with employees and how communication strategies can be optimized. By leveraging data, organizations can continuously improve their communication practices, foster a more engaged workforce, and ensure alignment across teams.

5. The Impact of Remote Work on Internal Communication

The shift to **remote work** brought about one of the most profound changes in internal communication. Before the pandemic, remote work was a perk or an occasional arrangement, but it became the norm for many organizations during the COVID-19 pandemic. This forced companies to adapt quickly to ensure effective communication and collaboration despite employees being physically distanced.

The Need for Unified Communication Platforms

With remote work, internal communication tools became even more critical. **Video conferencing**, **instant messaging**, and **document sharing** became essential for maintaining collaboration and team cohesion. Tools like **Microsoft Teams** and **Viva Engage** provided centralized platforms for chat, video calls, file sharing, and social networking, making it easier for employees to stay connected and informed, no matter where they were working from.

The rise of remote work also highlighted the importance of fostering a strong **company culture** and maintaining employee engagement. With face-to-face interactions limited, organizations needed to find new ways to keep employees engaged, informed, and motivated. This led to a shift toward **more informal, engaging, and personalized communication** that mimicked the dynamics of in-person collaboration.

6. The Future of Workplace Communication with Viva Engage

As organizations continue to embrace digital transformation, the role of tools like **Microsoft Viva Engage** in shaping the future of workplace communication will only grow more critical. Here are some trends and developments that are likely to shape the future of internal communication:

Greater Integration with Microsoft 365

Viva Engage is already integrated with other Microsoft 365 tools, but as the platform evolves, we can expect even deeper integrations with applications like **Word**, **Excel**, **Teams**, and **SharePoint**. This will make it easier for employees to access information, collaborate on documents, and share knowledge directly within the communication platform, reducing the need to toggle between multiple tools.

More Personalized Communication

AI and machine learning will continue to drive more personalized communication experiences. For example, Viva Engage could analyze an individual's communication preferences and habits to tailor the content they see, creating a more **efficient** and **engaging** experience. Additionally, personalized messaging and recommendations could help drive employee participation and ensure that communication is always relevant.

Increased Focus on Well-being and Employee Experience

Internal communication tools like Viva Engage will increasingly play a role in promoting employee well-being and creating a positive employee experience. As organizations become more focused on mental health, well-being, and work-life balance, Viva Engage may introduce features that allow employees to share personal milestones, celebrate achievements, and support each other's well-being.

The Rise of Hybrid Communication Models

With hybrid work becoming the standard in many industries, organizations will need communication tools that support both in-office and remote employees. Viva Engage will be integral in ensuring that teams, regardless of their physical location, are able to collaborate, communicate, and stay connected.

Conclusion

The evolution of internal communication has come a long way, from face-to-face interactions and memos to real-time messaging and enterprise social networks. As we look ahead, tools like **Microsoft Viva Engage** represent the future of workplace communication, where collaboration is not limited by location, time, or technology. By embracing these advancements, organizations can foster a more connected, engaged, and productive workforce, paving the way for a new era of workplace communication. The future is digital, collaborative, and people-centric, and Viva Engage is helping organizations build the foundation for that future.

9.2 How Viva Engage is Shaping the Future of Work

The modern workplace is evolving rapidly, with businesses shifting towards digital-first communication, hybrid work environments, and employee experience-driven engagement strategies. As companies move away from traditional office structures, the need for seamless, interactive, and inclusive communication tools has never been greater.

Microsoft Viva Engage is at the forefront of this transformation, enabling organizations to build stronger employee communities, enhance collaboration, and drive engagement through rich, interactive experiences. By fostering a culture of connectivity and open communication, Viva Engage is shaping the future of work in several critical ways.

This section explores how Viva Engage is revolutionizing workplace communication and collaboration, its impact on employee experience, and how organizations can leverage its capabilities to prepare for the future of work.

1. Breaking Down Silos and Enabling Open Communication

One of the biggest challenges in traditional workplace structures is **communication silos**—when different departments or teams operate in isolation, making it difficult to share information efficiently.

Encouraging Cross-Team Collaboration

Viva Engage breaks down these silos by providing an open and interactive platform where employees across different departments, locations, and job roles can:

- Share ideas and best practices

- Ask questions and get quick responses

- Collaborate on projects and discussions in real-time

With features like groups, communities, and @mentions, employees can easily connect with subject matter experts, ensuring knowledge is shared effectively rather than confined within specific teams.

Example: A marketing team working on a product launch can collaborate with the sales team by using a dedicated Viva Engage group, ensuring alignment on messaging, customer insights, and promotional strategies.

Strengthening Leadership Communication

Leaders play a crucial role in shaping company culture, and Viva Engage empowers executives to communicate more transparently and directly with employees.

- Company-wide announcements ensure important updates reach everyone.

- Leadership Q&A sessions allow employees to engage with executives in real-time.

- Live events and video messages help humanize leadership and foster a culture of trust.

By enabling leaders to interact with employees through Viva Engage, organizations create a more inclusive, transparent, and connected workplace.

2. Supporting Hybrid and Remote Work

As hybrid and remote work continue to be the norm, companies need digital tools that support flexibility, collaboration, and engagement across different work environments.

Creating a Virtual Community

With fewer opportunities for in-person interactions, remote employees often feel disconnected from their workplace culture. Viva Engage helps bridge this gap by providing:

- Digital communities where employees can participate in discussions based on interests, departments, or projects.

- Recognition and appreciation tools, such as shoutouts and employee spotlights, to celebrate achievements and milestones.

- Virtual events and town halls to keep everyone informed and engaged, regardless of location.

Encouraging Asynchronous Communication

In a global workforce, employees work in different time zones, making synchronous meetings challenging. Viva Engage enables asynchronous collaboration by allowing users to:

- Post questions, discussions, and updates that colleagues can respond to at their convenience.

- Use polls and surveys to gather input without needing real-time meetings.

- Share recorded meetings and videos, ensuring no one misses important information.

This flexibility ensures that communication remains inclusive and accessible, accommodating different work schedules and locations.

3. Enhancing Employee Experience and Engagement

Fostering a Sense of Belonging

Employee experience is no longer just about benefits and compensation; it's about creating an inclusive and engaging work culture. Viva Engage enhances the employee experience by:

- Providing a space for recognition and appreciation, where peers and managers can celebrate contributions.

- Supporting diversity and inclusion initiatives through dedicated groups and discussions.

- Empowering employees to have a voice, allowing them to share feedback and insights in an open forum.

Driving Engagement Through Interactive Content

Unlike traditional intranet systems that focus on one-way communication, Viva Engage offers rich, interactive features that keep employees engaged:

- GIFs, emojis, and reactions make conversations more dynamic and expressive.

- Live polls and Q&As encourage active participation.

- Multimedia posts (videos, images, and documents) create more engaging content.

By making workplace communication more interactive and enjoyable, organizations see higher levels of engagement and participation.

4. Leveraging AI and Data for Smarter Communication

AI-Driven Insights and Recommendations

With the power of Microsoft AI, Viva Engage provides personalized recommendations and insights to improve communication efficiency.

- Trending topics and conversations help employees stay updated on important discussions.

- Suggested groups and connections foster networking and collaboration.

- Automated summaries and highlights ensure employees never miss key updates.

Measuring Impact with Analytics

Organizations can leverage Viva Engage's analytics dashboard to track communication effectiveness:

- Engagement metrics (likes, comments, shares) to measure participation.

- Employee sentiment analysis to understand how teams are feeling.

- Content performance insights to identify what type of messaging resonates most.

Using data-driven strategies, companies can continuously refine their communication approach to keep employees engaged and informed.

5. Future-Proofing Workplace Communication with Viva Engage

As technology continues to evolve, organizations must stay ahead of emerging workplace communication trends. Viva Engage is well-positioned to future-proof businesses by adapting to these trends:

Integration with Emerging Technologies

Microsoft is constantly improving Viva Engage with AI, automation, and new collaboration features. Future developments may include:

- AI-powered chatbots for automated responses to common queries.

- Enhanced integration with Microsoft Teams, SharePoint, and Outlook for seamless communication.

- Voice and video messaging to further enrich digital conversations.

Supporting the Future Workforce

With Gen Z and younger professionals entering the workforce, companies must adopt social-media-style workplace tools that align with their communication preferences. Viva Engage's conversational, user-friendly interface makes it a natural fit for the next generation of employees.

Building a Culture of Continuous Learning

As companies emphasize employee development, Viva Engage can play a key role by:

- Facilitating knowledge-sharing communities where employees can learn from one another.

- Hosting virtual training sessions and workshops.

- Encouraging microlearning through bite-sized content and discussions.

This ensures that employees are constantly growing and staying engaged with their organization's goals.

6. Conclusion

Microsoft Viva Engage is more than just a communication tool—it is a driver of the future workplace. By breaking down silos, enabling hybrid work, enhancing engagement, leveraging AI, and adapting to future trends, Viva Engage is shaping how businesses connect, collaborate, and engage employees in an increasingly digital world.

Organizations that embrace Viva Engage today will be better positioned to navigate the evolving work landscape, ensuring that employees remain connected, informed, and engaged—no matter where they work.

Conclusion

1. Recap of Key Learnings

Throughout this book, we have explored Microsoft Viva Engage and its role in revolutionizing workplace communication. As organizations increasingly adopt digital-first communication strategies, Viva Engage has proven to be an essential tool in fostering collaboration, knowledge sharing, and employee engagement.

From understanding the platform's features to customizing group settings, creating engaging posts, leveraging analytics, and integrating with Microsoft 365 applications, we have covered a comprehensive guide on how to effectively use Viva Engage in a professional environment.

Let's briefly summarize the most crucial takeaways:

- Introduction to Microsoft Viva Engage: We explored what Viva Engage is, its key benefits, and how it integrates into Microsoft 365.

- Getting Started: We walked through how to access Viva Engage, navigate its interface, set up profiles, and manage notification settings.

- Engaging with Posts and Conversations: We discussed best practices for creating posts, using media, engaging with content, and leveraging polls, questions, and announcements to drive interaction.

- Collaborating with Teams and Colleagues: We covered how to use Viva Engage for team collaboration, including file sharing, co-editing, and knowledge-sharing strategies.

- Advanced Features and Integrations: We explored how Viva Engage connects with Microsoft Teams, SharePoint, and analytics tools to enhance communication, track engagement, and improve workplace conversations using data.

By now, you should have a solid understanding of how to make the most of Viva Engage to enhance workplace communication, drive engagement, and create a collaborative company culture.

2. The Impact of Viva Engage on Workplace Communication

Breaking Down Silos in Organizations

One of the greatest challenges in large organizations is overcoming communication silos, where teams and departments operate independently, limiting information sharing. Viva Engage bridges these gaps by providing an open space where employees can connect, share ideas, and collaborate regardless of hierarchy or location.

Key Benefits:

- Ensures that **knowledge flows across departments**, increasing transparency.

- Encourages **cross-functional collaboration**, leading to innovative problem-solving.

- Enables leadership teams to **communicate directly with employees**, fostering inclusivity.

Fostering a Culture of Engagement and Knowledge Sharing

Engaged employees are more productive, satisfied, and committed to their organization. Viva Engage empowers employees to participate in discussions, contribute insights, and learn from their peers.

How Viva Engage supports engagement:

- Encouraging discussions: Open communication channels allow employees to ask questions and share insights.

- Recognizing contributions: Features like mentions, reactions, and rewards create a culture of appreciation.

- Knowledge retention: Important discussions are documented, making them searchable and accessible anytime.

Strengthening Leadership Communication

Leadership communication plays a crucial role in shaping company culture and employee trust. Viva Engage allows leaders to connect with employees in an authentic and transparent way.

- Executives can post regular updates to keep employees informed and aligned with company goals.

- Live events and announcements allow leaders to engage with teams in real-time.

- Analytics provide insight into employee sentiment, helping leadership refine their messaging.

By using Viva Engage effectively, organizations can create a leadership culture that is transparent, engaging, and responsive to employee concerns.

3. Challenges and Considerations When Using Viva Engage

Overcoming Resistance to Change

As with any new communication platform, some employees may be hesitant to adopt Viva Engage. Common challenges include:

- Lack of awareness of the platform's benefits.

- Fear of information overload due to excessive notifications.

- Reluctance to engage in open conversations for fear of saying the wrong thing.

Solutions:

- Provide onboarding training to introduce employees to the platform.

- Customize notification settings to reduce distractions.

- Encourage leaders to set the tone by actively engaging in discussions.

Managing Information Overload

With multiple posts, comments, and notifications, users may find it difficult to keep up with conversations.

Best Practices to Avoid Overload:

- Use **groups and tags** to categorize content effectively.

- Encourage **concise and meaningful posts** instead of excessive updates.

- Educate employees on how to **use filters and search tools** to find relevant information.

Ensuring Security and Compliance

As a company-wide communication tool, Viva Engage must align with an organization's data security policies.

- Set up group permissions to control access to sensitive discussions.

- Regularly review and enforce compliance policies.

- Train employees on best practices for sharing confidential information.

4. Future Trends in Workplace Communication and Viva Engage's Role

The Rise of AI-Driven Insights

Artificial intelligence is playing an increasing role in workplace communication. Future AI-driven features in Viva Engage may include:

- Automated content recommendations to help employees discover relevant discussions.

- Sentiment analysis to track workplace morale.

- AI-powered summaries of long conversations to help users catch up quickly.

Deeper Integrations with Microsoft 365

Viva Engage is expected to become even more integrated with tools like:

- Microsoft Teams, making Viva Engage discussions seamlessly accessible.

- Power BI analytics, providing deeper insights into employee engagement.

- Microsoft Loop, allowing more interactive content creation within posts.

The Shift to Hybrid Work and Asynchronous Collaboration

With the continued rise of remote and hybrid work, tools like Viva Engage will become even more critical for keeping employees connected, informed, and engaged regardless of location.

- Asynchronous discussions will help employees across different time zones collaborate effectively.

- Mobile-friendly experiences will ensure users can engage on-the-go.

- Enhanced video and live event features will provide richer communication experiences.

5. Final Thoughts and Call to Action

Microsoft Viva Engage is more than just another communication tool; it is a transformational platform that enhances workplace collaboration, strengthens leadership communication, and fosters an inclusive company culture. By effectively utilizing its features, organizations can:

✔ Break down silos and encourage cross-team collaboration.
✔ Enhance leadership communication through direct employee engagement.
✔ Improve employee engagement by creating interactive discussions.
✔ Leverage analytics to refine communication strategies.
✔ Adapt to the evolving digital workplace with AI-driven insights and integrations.

Call to Action: Get Started Today!

Now that you have a comprehensive understanding of Viva Engage, it's time to put your knowledge into action! Whether you are a team leader, HR professional, or an employee looking to enhance collaboration, start using Viva Engage today by:

📌 Joining and creating groups to build strong communities.
📌 Engaging with posts and conversations to foster workplace connections.
📌 Leveraging analytics to track engagement and improve communication.
📌 Encouraging leadership participation to drive a transparent and open workplace culture.

By integrating Viva Engage into your daily work routine, you can transform the way your organization communicates, collaborates, and connects.

The future of workplace communication is here and now—and with Microsoft Viva Engage, your company is well-equipped to embrace it!

Acknowledgments

First and foremost, I want to express my heartfelt gratitude to you, the reader, for purchasing this book. Whether you are an experienced professional or just starting your journey with Microsoft Viva Engage, I appreciate your time, trust, and willingness to learn. Your investment in this book reflects your commitment to improving workplace communication, collaboration, and engagement—a mission that is more important than ever in today's digital world.

I also want to extend my appreciation to the Microsoft Viva Engage team and the broader Microsoft 365 ecosystem for developing such a powerful platform that enables organizations to connect and thrive. Their continued innovation has transformed the way we work, communicate, and collaborate across teams and locations.

To the professionals who embrace change, drive digital transformation, and champion workplace engagement, your efforts do not go unnoticed. The modern workplace is evolving rapidly, and your dedication to fostering open communication, knowledge sharing, and collaboration plays a vital role in shaping the future of work.

A special thank you to colleagues, mentors, and industry experts who have shared valuable insights and best practices on using Viva Engage effectively. Your expertise and real-world applications have helped make this guide as practical and useful as possible.

Finally, I would like to express my deepest gratitude to my family, friends, and supporters, whose encouragement and belief in this project have been invaluable. Writing this book was a journey, and your support made it all the more rewarding.

Stay Connected and Keep Learning

I hope this book serves as a valuable resource for you as you explore and utilize Microsoft Viva Engage. Technology is always evolving, and so is the way we communicate and collaborate. I encourage you to keep learning, experimenting, and sharing your knowledge with others.

If this book has helped you in any way, I would love to hear from you! Your feedback, experiences, and insights are always welcome. Let's continue the conversation and shape the future of workplace communication together.

Thank you once again for your support, and I wish you success in your journey with Microsoft Viva Engage!

www.ingramcontent.com/pod-product-compliance
Lightning Source LLC
LaVergne TN
LVHW062305060326
832902LV00013B/2057